Women
and
Criminality

WOMEN
AND
CRIMINALITY

THE WOMAN AS VICTIM, OFFENDER, AND PRACTITIONER

Ronald Barri Flowers

CONTRIBUTIONS IN CRIMINOLOGY AND PENOLOGY,
NUMBER 18

Greenwood Press
NEW YORK • WESTPORT, CONNECTICUT • LONDON

Library of Congress Cataloging-in-Publication Data

Flowers, Ronald B.
  Women and criminality.

  (Contributions in criminology and penology,
ISSN 0732-4464 ; no. 18)
    Continues: Children and criminality.
    Continued by: Minorities and criminality.
    Bibliography: p.
    Includes index.
    1. Women—Crimes against.   2. Female offenders.
3. Women correctional personnel.   4. Criminal justice,
Administration of.   I. Title.   II. Series.
HV6250.4.W65F56   1987   364'.088042   86-33646
ISBN 0-313-25365-X (lib. bdg. : alk. paper)

British Library Cataloguing in Publication Data is available.

Library of Congress Catalog Card Number: 86-33646
ISBN: 0-313-25365-X
ISSN: 0732-4464

First published in 1987

Greenwood Press, Inc.
88 Post Road West, Westport, Connecticut 06881

Printed in the United States of America

The paper used in this book complies with the
Permanent Paper Standard issued by the National
Information Standards Organization (Z39.48-1984).

10   9   8   7   6   5   4   3   2

To my two fathers, Johnnie Henry Flowers, Sr., and David James Robertson.

This one's for you, Dad, and those three qualities you instilled in me: perseverance, dedication, and confidence; and for my "second" Dad, who passed the "flaming" torch on to me and filled my life with untold happiness.

Of course, a special dedication must be bestowed upon the moving force behind this volume and, indeed, my life—my wife, Helen (Goldenlocks)!

Contents

Tables

Preface

This book, the second of a four-volume set, breaks new ground in women's studies by presenting a tripartite examination of the woman as both crime victim and offender and as criminal justice practitioner. The set reflects an increasing need to achieve greater knowledge and understanding of the dynamics that contribute to, nurture, and result from crime, criminal justice, and injustice. The major focus of these volumes is criminality and how it relates to children, women, minorities, and demographics.

Although a number of books have been written over the years in the fields of criminology and criminal justice, none have provided such a wide-ranging and comprehensive study of the correlation between these issues and the elements and characteristics of which they are composed. Often, these variables and facets of crime and criminal justice have been hidden, misunderstood, or simply disregarded as insignificant to the study of crime. Our knowledge of this branch of social science will continue to be incomplete as long as certain areas fail to be adequately explored. Hence the aim of this multivolume work is to bridge the gap that exists in the exploration of criminology, criminal justice, and victimology.

The four-volume set has been designed for professional audiences, scholars, and students specializing in criminology, criminal justice, law, victimology, sociology, psychology, and related disciplines. Additionally the volumes were written for a general readership of concerned citizens who, in a world becoming larger and more dangerous, seek to become more informed in areas such as criminality and the system of justice that affect us all.

Volume 2, *Women and Criminality*, is an in-depth analysis of the multifaceted role of women in the areas of criminology and criminal justice.

This unique and thorough examination of women as victims and perpetrators of crime and professionals within the system of criminal justice
discusses these roles of women individually and how they relate to each
other as well as to men's roles. Also explored is the significance of the
historical treatment of women; the women's movement; the rise in wom-
en's crime and victimization; theoretical and statistical approaches;
prominent literature; and social, legal, and future responses to the problems women face in these areas.

Volume 1, *Children and Criminality*, examines children and their relationship to crime. It stands apart from other studies of children and
criminality by focusing on children as both victims and offenders of
crime. This treatise explores the dual phenomenon in historical and
contemporary terms, the literature, and various approaches to understanding inherent problems. The in-depth examination covers the extent
and range of these trends, epidemiological and etiological features,
causal and theoretical models, social and psychological studies, the impact of family violence on children, a statistical analysis, implications of
theory and social action, and the outlook for the future.

Volume 3, *Minorities and Criminality*, explores the relationship between
being a minority in America and being a crime victim or offender. This
volume analyzes the historical implications; theoretical, etiological, and
causal models; and socioeconomic indicators that associate a member of
a minority with crime. Injustice as a factor, critical studies, social action,
and current and future trends are explored as well. The book is unique
in studying the various components of a minority community in relation
to crime rather than in studying the role of a minority merely as part of
criminology in general.

Volume 4, *Demographics and Criminality*, examines the relationship of
demographics to criminality in general. The volume reveals how the
demographic features of employment, marriage and divorce, drug and
alcohol use and addiction, and income correlate with crime in the United
States. Additionally the study analyzes components of the demographics
of crime, theories and implications associated with demographic variables, current trends and approaches, and future prospects.

ACKNOWLEDGMENTS

At Greenwood Press many thanks are directed to James T. Sabin,
Executive Vice President, who recognized the importance of this project.
Gratitude is also extended to Kenneth Brown, my former editor, who,
under somewhat fortuitous circumstances, led me to Greenwood Press
and along the way restored my faith in the notion that some way,
somehow, good things happen to good people.

My acknowledgments would not be complete without once more thanking my partner, fellow researcher, and executive secretary for her role in bringing this multivolume study to fruition—my wife, Helen Loraine Flowers.

Introduction

The role of women in the field of criminality and the profession of criminal justice has become increasingly diverse as we approach the 1990s. Women continue to be the victims of rape, battering, and other crimes perpetrated mostly by men; they also are strongly represented in traditional female crimes such as prostitution and larceny-theft and in criminal justice professions in which they perform clerical duties and work with female prisoners. However, the women's movement, women's assertiveness, legal precedents, and expanding opportunities have contributed to opening doors to women as well as escalating the conflict between men and women. As a result, today women are experiencing the best and the worst of times.

No longer confined to traditional domestic and nurturant roles based on sex-role stereotypes, many women are now adopting nontraditional roles. These include so-called legitimate roles (for example, working mothers, police officers, lawyers) and illegitimate roles (perpetrators of violent or white-color crimes). Men have steadily resisted equal opportunity for the sexes, which has manifested itself in (a) men's continued dominance in positions of authority that have limited women's professional success, (b) women being subjected to sexual harassment, sexual crimes, domestic violence, and other forms of subjugation and victimization.

Unfortunately, because men also control the direction of research, women as victims, offenders, and criminal justice practitioners have been tragically neglected by research criminologists and criminal justice officials. The explanation most commonly given for this neglect is that the relatively small number of women involved in crime makes such research insignificant and therefore unfeasible. Yet a comprehensive understanding of the etiology of crime and the training and recruitment of women as professionals in the criminal justice system can be accomplished only with research that examines women as well as men. When researchers have explored women's role in criminality and criminal justice, their examination has frequently been based only on one aspect (such as the study of the woman victim), further fragmenting the little we know about women in this field of study.

This volume breaks from tradition and establishes a new standard in women's studies and criminology by exploring in a single monograph the issues of female crime victims, female criminals, and female professionals in criminal justice. The purpose of this tripartite study is to present a broad perspective and to create a basis for further research and funding for research projects regarding women involved in crime and criminal justice by critically examining current research and the dynamics involved in these phenomena.

The book has been divided into four parts. Part I, The Victimization of Women, discusses various aspects of crimes committed against women. Chapter 1 explores the victimization survey in assessing women's victimization patterns, and studies on the murder of women, including *Uniform Crime Reports* data. The female victim of spousal violence is examined in depth in chapter 2, along with antecedent approaches and prominent theoretical explanations.

Chapter 3 focuses on the act of rape—its history, dynamics, fallacies, implications, characterization, causal conceptions, and effects on the victim. Chapter 4 addresses the issue of pornography, its definition and effect on women as sex objects, crime victims, and victims of exploitation. Two government studies on pornography are examined critically within this context. The problems of incest, the battered mother, military spouse abuse, and sexual harassment are explored in chapter 5 as important but often ignored contributions to the overall picture of female victims.

Part II, The Criminality of Women, devotes attention to various issues concerning women as criminals. Chapter 6 begins this section by analyzing official and self-report data, the shortcomings of such data, and the patterns and incidence of criminality. Also examined are the issues of chivalry, paternalism, and the "new" female criminal. Theoretical and conceptual approaches to women's criminality are critically discussed in chapter 7. In chapter 8 the family offenses perpetrated most often by women are examined: murder, spouse abuse, child abuse, and incest.

Chapter 9 presents an in-depth exploration of the prostitute as both an offender and a victim. Chapter 10 looks at several unusual areas of women's criminality, such as the female rapist or terrorist, women in gangs, women as con artists, and drug use among women. In chapter 11 the female prisoner is the object of focus. The study examines the nature and incidence of women who are incarcerated, prison and jail conditions, and the paradox of the female offender-turned-victim.

Chapter 12 in part III addresses the changing roles of female practitioners of criminal justice, conflict theory as it applies to these roles, and the general difficulties women have experienced trying to establish themselves in various fields of the criminal justice system.

Chapter 13 (part IV) explores legal and social responses to the female victim and offender of criminality as well as future approaches to the problems encountered by women as victims, criminals, and criminal justice professionals.

I

THE VICTIMIZATION OF WOMEN

1

Major Crimes Against Women: Survey and Official Data

As we begin our examination of the criminal victimization of women, it immediately becomes evident that women are being victimized in this country at an alarming rate. In the National Family Violence survey conducted by Murray Straus and Richard Gelles, it was calculated that in 1985, 1.7 million women were seriously assaulted by spouses or partners.[1] Sociologist Diana Russell estimates that 1½ to 2 million women are the victims of rape or attempted rape every year.[2] The Justice Department reported that violent crime against women rose from 21.8 per thousand in 1973 to 22.5 per thousand in 1983.[3]

Yet the truth is that our assessment of the problem of female victimization is far from complete because data-gathering methods, the lack of reported crimes, and the comparative newness of studies of the victimization of women have combined to seriously undermine composing an accurate statistical picture. Nevertheless, significant strides have been made over the last two decades that have at once increased knowledge and provided a foundation for a perspective on the magnitude and nature of crime perpetrated against women.

THE DEVELOPMENT OF THE VICTIMIZATION SURVEY

As recently as 1965 very little was known concerning the characteristics of the victims of criminality in the United States. Aside from the crimes of murder and rape, the FBI *Uniform Crime Reports* (*UCR*), the preeminent means for tabulating crime in the United States as reported to the police since 1930, do not include precise characteristics of crime victims because their primary interest is in the offenders of crime. Because of this void, a method designed to focus more attention on the victim of crime was

developed by tapping the most practical source of knowledge: the victims themselves. The self-report victimization survey hoped to

• assess hidden criminality;
• establish victim profiles and the likelihood of victimization;
• create a greater understanding of statistics on violent crime;
• determine crime fluctuation; and
• compare analyses of geographical areas with other data.

The first major victimization survey was conducted in 1965–66 by the
National Opinion Research Center (NORC) for the President's Commission on Law Enforcement and Administration of Justice.[4] Drawn
from 10,000 randomly selected households across the United States, the
respondents (aged 18 and over, or young married people) were asked
whether anyone in the household had been criminally victimized within
the past twelve months and, if so, the type of victimization, whether
the crime had been reported, and, if not, why.

The most prominent finding of the NORC survey was that "crimes
against the person" and property crimes as reported by the victims were
twice as prevalent as those reported to law enforcement agencies. This
differential in reporting was even higher for specific crimes such as
forcible rape, in which nearly four times as many self-reports were made
than the official crime statistics rate. Despite NORC's surprising conclusion that crime and victimization rates are significantly higher than UCR
data indicated, it was believed that even the NORC finding was still a
vast underestimate of the actual frequency of victimization and crime.

Other useful findings of the NORC study as they pertain to female
victims were as follows:

• The ratio of female victimization was .34, or one woman victimized for every
  three men.
• The ratio was higher for all serious crimes except burglary.
• Women were most likely to be victimized between the ages of 20–29 and 40–
  49.

A second President's Commission-sponsored study in 1966 of 13,713
cases of assaultive crimes against the person (excluding homicide), taken
from Chicago Police Department files, revealed the following notable
characteristics of female victims of crime:

Black women were almost eight times as likely to be victimized as white
women.

- Female victimization was predominantly an intraracial phenomenon.
- Women were most likely to be the victims of assault in their homes.[5]

The National Commission on the Causes and Prevention of Violence elected to follow up on the Law Enforcement Commissions' analysis of police reports rather than the NORC victimization survey methodology.[6] The 1967 Violence commission-sponsored study was composed of a 10 percent random sample of offense and arrest data from seventeen large U.S. cities. In the sample data the percentage of female victims of major crimes was as follows: rape, 100 percent; homicide, 21 percent; aggravated assault, 34 percent; armed robbery, 11 percent; and unarmed robbery, 29 percent. The vast majority of these crimes were perpetrated on women by men: all the forcible rapes, four of five homicides and aggravated assaults, and nine of ten robberies. Although these findings were informative regarding criminal victimization rate patterns in the highest crime areas in the country, they fell short of establishing nationwide rates.

RECENT TRENDS IN THE VICTIMIZATION OF WOMEN

The most extensive national research on the victimization of women was conducted by the Department of Justice's National Crime Survey Program (NCS) beginning in 1973. Similar to other victimization surveys, the NCS concentrates primarily on crimes with specific victims (for instance, rape or robbery) and victims who understand the nature of their victimization and are willing to report it. Such a victim, aged 12 or over, is defined as "the recipient of a criminal act, usually in relation to personal crimes, but also applicable to households and commercial establishments."[7]

Table 1.1 provides a comparison of national victimization rates for males and females during selected years over the ten-year period 1973–1983. These data are difficult to equate with the earlier statistics examined, but the basic differences between males and females remain: males are victimized considerably more of then than females. However, when compared to the NORC figures, the NCS data suggest that female victimization in the major crimes of rape, robbery, and assault has increased dramatically over the seventeen-year period.[8]

As for the ten-year figures covering 1973–1983, the ratio of female victimization for crimes of violence increased nearly 1 per 1,000 after it had peaked to 25.4 in 1981; whereas for crimes of theft women were victimized 8.6 per 1,000 less in 1983 than in 1973. The ratio of female to male victimization for crimes of violence increased from .49 in 1973 to .56 in 1983. For crimes of theft the ratio increased from .79 to .87. Both

Table 1.1

Victimization Rates for Persons Age 12 and Over, by Type of Crime and Sex of Victims

(Rate per 1,000 population age 12 and over)				
	Victimization Rates			
Sex and Crime	1973	1975	1981	1983
Females				
Crimes of violence[a]	21.6	22.9	25.4	22.5
Rape	1.8	1.7	1.8	1.4
Robbery	3.8	4.0	5.2	4.0
Aggravated assault	5.2	5.4	5.3	4.5
Simple assault	10.9	11.9	13.1	12.6
Crimes of theft	80.3	84.8	80.0	71.7
Personal larceny with contact	3.4	3.3	3.7	3.3
Personal larceny without contact	76.8	81.5	76.3	68.5
Males				
Crimes of violence[a]	44.1	43.5	46.2	40.2
Rape	0.1[b]	0.1	0.1	0.2
Robbery	9.9	9.8	9.8	8.3
Aggravated assault	15.2	14.1	14.4	11.7
Simple assault	19.0	19.5	21.9	20.1
Crimes of theft	102.9	107.9	90.7	82.7
Personal larceny with contact	2.6	2.9	2.7	2.6
Personal larceny without contact	100.2	105.1	88.0	79.9

[a]Since these statistics are based on self-victimization reports, murder is not included.

[b]Estimates based on zero or on about ten or fewer cases is statistically unreliable.

Sources: U.S. Department of Justice, Criminal Victimization in the United States, 1973, 1975, 1981, and 1983, National Crime Survey Reports. All published by the Government Printing Office (Washington, DC).

increases suggest that the extent of female victimization for serious crimes (excluding rape) is drawing closer to the male rate.

Patterns and rates of female victimization established by the NCS are useful in assessing criminality perpetrated against women in this country. As shown in Table 1.2, in 1983 black females overall were the victims of violent crimes and theft more often than were white females. In fact, the only crimes in which white females were victimized more often than blacks were attempted robbery with injury (to an insignificant degree), attempted crimes of theft, and personal larceny.

A slightly different picture emerges when female victimization is broken down by race, age of victims, and type of crime (see table 1.3). Black females in the 16–19 age group were the victims of crimes of violence at a higher rate than any other age category for both black and white

Table 1.2
Personal Crimes, 1983: Victimization Rates for Persons Age 12 and Over, by Type of Crime and Race of Female Victims

(Rate per 1,000 population age 12 and over)		
Type of Crime	White (85,468,660)	Black (11,624,210)
Crimes of Violence	21.3	32.8
-Completed violent crimes	7.9	14.6
-Attempted violent crimes	13.3	18.1
-Rape	1.3	1.7
-Robbery	3.5	7.4
-Completed robbery	2.4	5.4
-With injury	1.1	1.3
-Without injury	1.2	4.2
-Attempted robbery	1.1	2.0
-With injury	0.5	0.4[a]
-Without injury	0.7	1.6
-Assault	16.4	23.6
-Aggravated assault	3.9	9.2
-Completed with injury	1.3	4.1
-Attempted assault with weapon	2.6	5.1
-Simple assault	12.4	14.5
-Completed with injury	3.8	4.4
-Attempted assault without weapon	8.6	10.0
Crimes of Theft	72.0	74.5
-Completed crimes of theft	67.8	70.4
-Attempted crimes of theft	4.2	4.1
-Personal larceny with contact	2.8	6.3
-Personal larceny without contact	69.2	68.2
-Completed larceny without contact	65.5	64.7
-Attempted larceny without contact	3.8	3.4

[a]Estimate, based on about 10 or fewer sample cases, is statistically unreliable.

Note: Detail may not add to total shown because of rounding. Numbers in parentheses refer to population in the group.

Source: U.S. Department of Justice, Criminal Victimization in the United States, 1983, A National Crime Survey Report (Washington, D.C.: Government Printing Office, 1984), p. 17.

females. However, for crimes of theft, white females in the 20–24 age group, followed by the 16–19 age category, were victimized more often than any other white or black female age group. Other than for crimes of theft among white female victims, victimization rates went down as age increased for both white and black females.

Conversely, black females aged 12–15 and white females aged 12–15 tended to have the highest victimization rates of all age and race groups for crimes of violence and crimes of theft respectively. Yet as our concern is the adult female victims of crime (ages 16 and up), this statistic is

Table 1.3
Personal Crimes, 1983: Victimization Rates for Females Age 16 and Over, by Race and Age of Victims and Type of Crime

(Rate per 1,000 population in each age group)		
Race, Sex and Age	Crimes of Violence	Crimes of Theft
WHITE		
Female		
16-19	41.7	114.4
20-24	39.0	120.2
25-34	32.5	84.6
35-49	16.7	71.9
50-64	5.7	40.5
65 and over	4.7	20.5
BLACK		
Female		
16-19	52.6	71.2
20-24	48.7	95.5
25-34	43.2	88.0
35-49	22.5	70.5
50-64	12.2	49.8
65 and over	0.9[a]	19.4

[a]Estimate, based on zero or on about 10 or fewer sample cases, is statistically unreliable.

Source: U.S. Department of Justice, Criminal Victimization in the United States, 1983, A National Crime Survey Report (Washington, D.C.: Government Printing Office, 1984), p. 20.

mentioned mainly for comparative purposes for the overall picture of female victimization.

Table 1.4 offers some insight into robbery and assault victimization in which victims sustained physical injury, by various victim characteristics and type of crime in 1983. Females who were physically injured were victimized more often in all crime categories, with the highest differentiation (10.9 percent) occurring in the crime of robbery. This suggests not only that women are more vulnerable to attack during a robbery but that often robbery may be only part of such victimization when it occurs. The other breakdowns become a little more difficult to interpret from a gender standpoint because they group male and female victims together. However, they are nevertheless informative in studying females as victims. For instance, the figures show that robbery and assault victims on average tend to fall into the 16–24 age category; most victims are black; most crimes are committed by someone the victim knows; and most

Table 1.4
Personal Robbery and Assault, 1983: Percentage of Victimizations in Which Victims Sustained Physical Injury, by Selected Characteristics of Victims and Type of Crime

Characteristic	Robbery and Assault	Robbery	Assault
SEX			
Both sexes	30.2	32.8	29.6
Male	28.3	29.1	28.1
Female	33.6	40.0	32.1
AGE			
16-19	33.2	29.6	34.1
20-24	31.2	32.4	30.9
25-34	29.6	34.6	28.5
35-49	26.8	38.8	23.6
50-64	23.3	27.2	21.5
65 and over	25.2	38.5	14.4[a]
RACE			
White	29.7	34.6	28.6
Black	34.1	28.4	37.1
VICTIM-OFFENDER RELATIONSHIP			
Strangers	25.6	30.7	23.7
Nonstrangers	37.0	40.6	36.6
INCOME			
Less than $7,500	35.8	30.8	37.4
$7,500-$9,999	31.1	33.6	30.2
$10,000-$14,999	32.1	35.5	31.3
$15,000-$24,999	27.4	32.7	26.1
$25,000-$29,999	26.4	25.8	26.5
$30,000-$49,999	27.9	35.2	26.6
$50,000 or more	27.0	35.6	25.2
Not available	35.2	35.3	25.8

[a]Estimate, based on zero or on about 10 or fewer sample cases, is statistically unreliable.

Source: U.S. Department of Justice, Criminal Victimization in the United States, 1983, A National Crime Survey Report (Washington, D.C.: Government Printing Office, 1984), p. 71.

victims are on the lower socioeconomic scale. These statistics, though far from conclusive, have been generally supported by other data on female victims of crime.

A major reason criminal statistics are suspect is that unreported criminal victimization has proved to be substantial. NCS findings indicate that in 1983 only 33 percent of the female victims of personal crimes nationwide reported the crime to the police (table 1.5). For crimes of violence 52.2 percent of the females reported, but for crimes of theft

Table 1.5
Personal Crimes, 1983: Percentage of Victimizations Reported to the Police, by Selected Characteristics of Victims and Type of Crime

Characteristic	All Personal Crimes	Crimes Of Violence	Crimes Of Theft
SEX			
Both sexes	32.4	47.2	26.5
Male	31.9	44.1	25.9
Female	33.1	52.2	27.1
RACE			
White	32.0	46.1	26.5
Black	35.5	53.5	26.2
ETHNICITY			
Hispanic	31.2	44.7	24.3
Non-Hispanic	32.5	47.3	26.6

Source: U.S. Department of Justice, Criminal Victimization in the United States, 1983, A National Crime Survey Report (Washington, D.C.: Government Printing Office, 1984), p. 86.

only 27.1 percent reported. Although the low reporting rate can be attributed to a variety of reasons, one important reason appears to be the lack of faith that law enforcement will satisfactorily respond to the crime.[9]

Other notable results derived through victimization self-reports of women include the following observations:

• The victimization of Hispanic women is disproportionately high.

• Women who are divorced or separated are more likely to be the victims of rape, robbery, and assault.

• The property crime rate of divorced or separated women is surpassed only by women who have never married (mostly young women).

• Women between the ages of 16 and 24 are most at risk to be raped.

• Victimization rates for women vary by size and type of community.

THE SHORTCOMINGS OF VICTIMIZATION SURVEYS

Victimization surveys have proved to be important supplements to official statistics in measuring crime because they tell us more about the victims. However, the limitations of victimization survey methodology hamper their effectiveness as an accurate indicator of victimization trends and dynamics. The obvious drawback for the purpose of our study of female victims is the exclusion of murder in the survey data: the victim is unable to speak on her own behalf. Nevertheless, because murder is a heinous crime and is often associated with other violent crimes perpetrated upon women, the use of secondary victims (spouse, children) as respondents might allow us at least to draw some inferences about the correlation between other crimes against females and murder, as well as the circumstances of the murder. Equally disturbing is that often all victimized females are grouped together (starting at age 12), giving little indication of where adolescent victimization ends and adult victimization begins.

Another limitation of concern is the absence in the surveys of so-called victimless crimes such as prostitution, pornography, and substance abuse. Although these offenses are construed by many to be engaged in by women as opposed to forced upon them, the women involved are more often victims (see chapters 4 and 9). Background, sexual abuse, socioeconomic characteristics, and racial discrimination are just a few of the causative factors associated with these behavior patterns, but victimization studies have failed to respond to them.

In addition to these shortcomings, victimization survey data are deficient because of underreporting, lack of comparability between survey data and methodology and official statistics and methodology, and the interviewing process itself, in which reliability, communication barriers, and biases render the findings suspect.

FEMICIDE: THE END OF THE ROAD

The omission of murder in self-reported data leaves police statistics as the most reliable means for measuring female victims of this crime. Because of the relatively high proportion of homicides reported to the police and the high clearance rate for homicide, these statistics may be a truer representation of offender and victim characteristics and incidence than any other data on crime and victimology.

According to the *UCR*, in 1985, 3,883 females age 18 and over were murder victims in the United States (see Table 1.6). The majority of the female victims were in the age range 20 to 39; women aged 25–29 were the most vulnerable group. Female murder victims age 15 to 19 are reported together so we cannot determine the number of adults (women 16 and over) in this category.

Much evidence has surfaced over the years associating murder and female victimization as largely an interpersonal phenomenon. The FBI estimates that more than 50 percent of all murdered women in the United States are victimized by men with whom they had an intimate relationship.[10] Edwin Sutherland studied cases of femicide in the 1930s and '40s

Table 1.6
Age of Female Murder Victims, 1985

AGE	NUMBER OF VICTIMS
Total [a]	4,511
18 and over [b]	3,883
15 to 19	330
20 to 24	597
25 to 29	701
30 to 34	577
35 to 39	408
40 to 44	298
45 to 49	212
50 to 54	166
55 to 59	140
60 to 64	147
65 to 69	123
70 to 74	105
75 and over	229
Unknown	78

[a] The total number of female murder victims.

[b] Does not include unknown ages.

Source: U.S. Federal Bureau of Investigation, Crime in
          the United States: Uniform Crime Reports, 1985
          (Washington, D.C.: Government Printing Office,
          1986), p. 9.

and found that 102 of 324 murders were perpetrated by the victims' husbands, 37 by fathers and other close relatives, and 49 by lovers or admirers.[11] Analyzing criminal homicide in Philadelphia's police files for the period 1948 to 1952, Marvin Wolfgang reported that a high incidence of female homicide occurred within the family context. Virtually none of the women were murdered by strangers. Fifty-two percent were killed by family members, 21 percent by lovers, and most of the remaining by friends or acquaintances. Per 100,000 population, black women were ten times more likely than white women to be homicide victims.[12]

Studies by J. Boudouris,[13] F. McClintock, [14] and the National Commission on the Causes and Prevention of Violence[15] lend support to the familiarity and nature of the female victim and homicide perpetrator. Other characteristics typical of murdered women include the following:

• Most women are killed by men.
• Most femicide occurs in the home.
• Firearms are used in most marital homicides.
• Victim provocation is a significant factor in femicide.

THE SHORTCOMINGS OF OFFICIAL DATA

Even with the necessity of *Uniform Crime Reports* information on female murder victims and the comprehensiveness of *UCR* statistics, they do have serious drawbacks. These will be discussed in detail later in the book as we draw more on official data in our study of women and criminality. However, given that law enforcement statistics are the basis for most research on homicide, it is necessary that we address briefly how these data and the findings drawn from them might be flawed.

The foremost problem is that official statistics concentrate most heavily on offenders of crime. This means the researchers are less equipped to deal with victimization studies effectively, even for a crime such as murder, which appears to be the easiest to track because statistics about the victim can be obtained.

A further difficulty is the nature of police data. Their accuracy is contingent on the competency of police departments throughout the country in gathering and recording information. Murder cannot be reported by the victim; therefore such data often are derived through interpretation and inconsistent information. Add to this the fact that many murders are unaccounted for, go unreported, or are misdiagnosed. As with all statistics, however, until we find a better way we must make the best of available sources in assessing criminality and victimization.

What emerges in this chapter is that in one way or another a considerable number of women in the United States are being subjected to criminal victimization. Men are victimized even more, but this should not detract from the extent, nature, and conditions of victimized women who already find themselves at a disadvantage in society, in the workplace, and in their male counterparts' perceptions of them.

Women make up a higher proportion of the victims of property crime as opposed to violent crime. However, such violent crimes as rape are occurring with alarming frequency and remain primarily a female victim phenomenon. Black women are more susceptible to criminality in general than are white women. Young women are the most targeted group for victimization. There appears to be no discernible pattern of female victimization geographically. Perhaps the most pressing concern is recent studies that suggest that crimes against women are on the rise. This is a problem society must confront. We need only look around us to realize the future has arrived.

NOTES

1. Judith Levine, "Crimes Against Women Are Growing. So Are Our Fears," *Glamour* 84 (February 1986):210–213.

2. Ibid., p. 210.

3. Ibid.

4. Phillip H. Ennis, *Criminal Victimization in the United States: A Report of a National Survey*, National Opinion Research Center, University of Chicago (Washington, D.C.: Government Printing Office, 1967), p. 1.

5. President's Commission on Law Enforcement and Administration of Justice, *Task Force Report: Crime and Its Impact—An Assessment* (Washington, D.C.: Government Printing Office, 1967), p. 82.

6. Donald J. Mulvihill, Melvin M. Tumin, and Lynn A. Curtis, *Crimes of Violence*, Vol. 11 (Washington, D.C.: Government Printing Office, 1969), pp. 207–215.

7. Calvin J. Larson, *Crime, Justice and Society* (Bayside, N.Y.: General Hall, Inc., 1984), p. 201.

8. Lee H. Bowker, *Women, Crime, and the Criminal Justice System* (Lexington, Mass.: Lexington Books, 1978), p. 105; U.S. Department of Justice, *Criminal Victimization in the United States*, 1981 and 1983, National Crime Survey Reports (Washington, D.C.: Government Printing Office, 1982–1984).

9. In addition to the belief that law enforcement will be ineffective, other reasons attributed to unreported crimes are fear of the perpetrator, the wish to remain uninvolved, protection of friends or relatives, and the feeling that the offense is a private matter.

10. Lenore E. Walker, "Treatment Alternatives for Battered Women," in Jane Roberts Chapman and Margaret Gates, eds., *The Victimization of Women* (Beverly Hills: Sage Publications, 1978), p. 144.

11. Edwin H. Sutherland, "The Sexual Psychopath Laws," *Journal of Criminal Law and Criminology* 40 (1950):545–546.

12. Marvin E. Wolfgang, *Patterns in Criminal Homicide* (Philadelphia: University of Pennsylvania Press, 1958), pp. 32–35, 56.

13. J. Boudouris, "Homicide and the Family," *Journal of Marriage and the Family* 33, no. 4 (1971):667–676.

14. F. McClintock, *Crimes of Violence* (New York: St. Martin's Press, 1963).

15. Mulvihill, *Crimes of Violence*, pp. 210–222, 268–269, 293.

2

The Female Victim of Spousal Violence

One of the most underdiagnosed yet most prevalent forms of crime in which the woman is victimized takes place right under her own roof. A keen observation on family violence was made by M. Freeman, who noted: "The home is a very dangerous place and we have more to fear from close members of our family than from total strangers."[1] The evidence supports this contention: a Justice Department study held that between 1973 and 1981, 4.1 million homes were struck by some form of family violence. Further, it estimated that 450,000 family members are victimized in this way every year.[2]

A significant percentage of violence in the family is directed toward the wife or mother by the husband or father. Because this abusive pattern has been seen by some as the catalyst for other acts of familial violence and is potentially the most damaging for the family collectively, we shall focus on the battered woman in this chapter.

DEFINING THE BATTERED WIFE

The problem of the maltreated wife has been compounded because professionals have had difficulty identifying who shall be labeled a victim of spousal battering. In its broadest sense, wife victimization can be defined as physical beatings with fists or other objects, choking, stabbing, burning, whipping—any form of husband-inflicted physical violence—as well as psychological mistreatment in the form of threats, intimidation, isolation, degradation, mind games, and directing violence toward other family members or household objects (for example, slamming doors). Common terms used interchangeably to describe this type of domestic violence include "spouse abuse," "wife beating," "wife abuse," "conjugal violence," "woman battering," and the "battered woman syndrome," and can refer as well to women victimized by a lover, boyfriend, or former partner.

Many professionals prefer to narrow their definition of battering to that of a physical nature. One study defined battered women as "adult women who were intentionally physically abused in ways that caused pain or injury, or who were forced into involuntary action or restrained by force from voluntary action by adult men with whom they have or had established relationships, usually involving sexual intimacy."[3] Murray Straus supports the physical violence definition of battered women because of the easier method of documentation.[4] In an in-depth study of family violence, Richard Gelles added police contact to his interpretation of woman battering.[5]

Others, however, contend that psychological "battering" can be as devastating to the woman as physical violence, if not more so. As the number of refugees increased in England in the 1970s, "it became obvious that large numbers of women were seeking safety from psychological abuse."[6] In a study of physical and psychological coercion, Lenore Walker found that both forms of violence were present in assaultive couples and "cannot be separated, despite the difficulty in documentation."[7]

For our purposes, "domestically violated women" comprise both physically and psychologically abused women. One should not make the mistake of downplaying either phenomenon, as each often aggravates the other. The incidence of domestic violence involving women is already believed to be highly underreported and the problem has been neglected, so it is essential that in seeking remedies to this problem we address each facet.

ANTECEDENT TRENDS IN WIFE MALTREATMENT

Although spouse abuse in America only began gaining credence as a serious social problem during the 1970s, it is hardly a new phenomenon. Wife battering has existed and flourished as an acceptable practice since ancient times. Historical literature is replete with examples of the cruelties inflicted upon women by their mates, including biblical references.[8] One article recounts the "scalding death of Fausta ordered by her husband, the Emperor Constantine, which was to serve as a precedent for the next fourteen centuries."[9] Around A.D. 1140 Gratian systematized church law in his work, the *Decretum*, which asserted:

Women should be subject to their men. . . . The image of God is in man and it is one. Women were drawn from man, who has God's jurisdiction as if he were God's vicar. . . . Therefore, woman is not made in God's image. . . . Adam was beguiled by Eve, not she by him. It is right that he whom woman led into wrongdoing should have her under his direction, so that he may not fail a second time through female levity.[10]

Novelists Charles Dickens and Mrs. Gaskell repeatedly refer to violence perpetrated on wives by their husbands.[11]

Frederick Engels advanced that wife abuse began "with the emergence of the first monogamous pairing relationships, which replaced group marriage and the extended family of early promiscuous societies."[12] A stronger contention is that historical condoning of the mistreatment of women is rooted in the subjugation and oppression of women through the male partner exercising his authority as head of the family. The notion of the nearly limitless right of the husband and father as undisputed leader of the family, and father-family relationships defined as a proprietary interest, can be traced to the doctrines of such ancient civilizations as Babylonia, Greece, and Rome. These notions had a significant effect on the early English Common Law and the American statutory system.[13]

In western society wife beating has been supported since the middle ages. The rampant violence imposed upon wives in Europe carried over into American culture, aided by legal precedents.[14] During one period a husband was permitted by law to beat his wife so long as his weaponry was not bigger around than his thumb.[15] Such laws remained in force until the end of the nineteenth century.

Today men throughout the world continue to resort to violence through brute strength and force as a means to maintain respect and domination over their wives and lovers. Although society has recently begun to take more than a passing interest in what was commonly accepted as a family problem, violence against wives still occurs in epidemic proportions, with little end in sight.

THE EXTENT OF WIFE ABUSE

Despite the general belief that wife battering accounts for a large portion of domestic violence, researchers have found that the reporting of this crime is a different story altogether. One estimate is that only one of every 270 incidents of wife beating is ever reported to law enforcement officials.[16] Walker indicated that in her study of Denver victims of battering, fewer than 10 percent ever reported serious violence to the police.[17] The gross underreporting is often attributed to

• denial by the victim;
• disavowal techniques to keep it in the family;
• protection of the abuser;

• fear of alternatives (e.g., further abuse, loss of income); and
• shame

This cloak of silence notwithstanding, researchers have used "a wide variety of techniques to obtain data including intensive studies of small samples of marital dyads, the examination of police incident reports, analyzing groups of cases from agency treatment files, and gathering data on families that are in the process of divorcing."[18] Most indicators suggest that the problem of battering has reached epidemic proportions.

Estimates of the number of battered women have soared as high as half the female population. Sociologists approximate that every year as many as two million women in the United States are beaten by their spouses.[19] According to FBI statistics, woman battering is one of the most frequently occurring crimes in the country—a beating takes place ever eighteen seconds.[20] P. Scott reported that 25 percent of the child-abusing fathers in England also abuse their wives.[21] Rebecca and Russell Dobash's analysis of 3,020 reported cases of violence revealed that wife assaults represent the second largest category of assault that police record.[22] A recent random survey by Diana Russell on women's experiences of sexual assault found that 21 percent of women who had ever been married reported being physically abused by a husband at some point in their lives.[23]

Unfortunately, similar studies on the extent of psychological wife abuse simply do not exist. Nevertheless its incidence is believed to be as high as physical wife battering.

PROFILING THE BATTERED WOMAN

It would be rather simplistic and preferable to believe that the battered and abused woman is a product of the lower class, undereducated, a member of a minority group. The truth is, however, that abused women living in poverty account for only about one-fifth of all battered women. Their visibility is greater than that of other social class groups because of their greater dependency on society's institutions for their basic survival needs. The overt and frequent violence that characterizes lower-class living tends to bring its victims to the attention of law enforcement agencies at a differential rate than is the case with every other class.

Recent studies indicate that as many as 80 percent of battering cases have gone unrecognized because of the more privileged environment in which they occur. Women are being victimized by husbands and boyfriends on every social and economic level. Age, income, education, ethnicity, race, class, and occupation offer no protection from this domestic affliction. What these women share is a characteristically low self-esteem, generally the result of repeated victimization. Some victims' feeling of powerlessness is limited only to their relationship with men; others find that this trait applies to all areas of their lives.

PROFILING THE MALE BATTERER

Like their victims, the perpetrators of wife abuse come from all walks of life. No one is above or beneath becoming a batterer under the right (or wrong) circumstances. However, some emerging trends can be found in the character of an abusive mate. The battering man is typically seen as possessing a dual personality. He is regarded as either extremely charming or especially cruel. Selfishness and generosity are parts of his personality and depend upon his mood. Substance abuse, while sometimes present, is not a central feature in the battering pattern itself. On the other hand, jealousy and possessiveness are considered an integral part of mate-inflicted violence. Most batterers' greatest fear is that their women will leave them.

Based on a study conducted over a four-year period at New York's Abused Women's Aid in Crisis, Maria Roy characterized the abusive partner as follows:

- Most are between 26 and 35 years of age, with the next greatest age category 36 to 50.
- Most children of the victim-perpetrator are between 1 and 13 years of age.
- The relationship with the victim likely began during late adolescence or early adulthood.
- The majority of partnerships are supported by joint incomes.
- Most abuse takes place during the first fifteen years of the relationship.
- Ninety percent of the abusers do not have a criminal record, illustrating that most offenders are not deviant outside the domestic environment.
- The battering occurred almost immediately after the partnership began in over 70 percent of the instances.
- Major changes in the life of the family (i.e., death, loss of income) increases the likelihood or level of violence in relationships of long duration.
- Most abuse is physical and done without the use of weapons.
- More than 80 percent of the perpetrators of wife abuse have a history of childhood abuse or came from abusive families.
- Alcohol was a problem with 35 percent of the abusive partners; only 10 percent were in treatment programs.[24]

While enlightening, Roy's analysis fails to account for the many hidden variables and their interactions in the phenomenon of wife battering. A further limitation in characterizing this volatile situation is the difficulty of establishing a profile of psychologically abusive partners. Be-

cause we now know that many men are guilty of psychologically battering their partners, no characterization of abusive males can be complete without some reference to this facet of abusive behavior.
Unfortunately we have yet to reach the stage where a typology of the
psychological abuser can be accomplished with any degree of accuracy.

SEXUAL FACTORS OF WOMAN BATTERING

Conjugal Rape

The sexual relationship has been shown to be one of the most crucial
and significant features in domestic battering. Most conspicuous and
controversial is the issue of sexual coercion and assault by a loved one,
usually the husband. Rape as it affects women will be discussed in detail
in chapter 3. Our concern here is the subject as it relates to the battered
woman.

Rape by a husband or lover has been found to occur more frequently
than previously believed.[25] Assessing the incidence of such assaults have
proved to be difficult because of confusing or virtually nonexistent definitions of conjugal rape. The right to say no to sex in a marriage situation
is unacceptable to many when intercourse is presumed to be implicit in
the marital vows. Supporting this contention is the fact that only eleven
states include marital rape in sexual assault statutes.[26] Thus, forced sex
in the absence of physical violence may not be considered criminal
behavior.

However, the association between marital rape and battering is very
real and is often the motivating factor for women who submit sexually
and against their wishes. Walker reported that 59 percent of the battered
women in her sample said they were forced to have sex with the batterer,
compared to 7 percent of the nonbattered women.[27] Eighty-five percent
of the battered women claimed that sex was unpleasant for the following
reasons (among others): the sex was initiated to prevent abuse; sex took
place immediately after battering to calm the perpetrator; sex occurred
after the male beat a child for fear he would do so again; and refusing
sex meant the battered women would not receive money for groceries
or bills. These suggest that the fear of violence or psychological intimidation is as significant a variable in marital rape as actual violence.

Other studies also indicate the correlation of rape and battering. K.
Ylló contends that forced sex occurs more often as a form of violent
power and control than as the more common assumption that the sexually deprived husband uses force to satisfy himself sexually.[28] Using a
conservative definition of marital rape that included actual forced intercourse with penetration, Russell found that male spouse sexual assaults
were reported to occur more than twice as often as stranger-perpetrated

sexual assaults. Were these data to be generalized over the entire population in the United States, the result is that battered women could be at risk of being sexually assaulted at a rate three to five times greater than nonbattered women.[29]

Sexual Jealousy

Commonly reported as a prominent factor in violent relationships is sexual jealousy.[30] In addition, many battered women cite that sexual problems such as frigidity, impotence, denial, and excessive demands lead to arguments resulting in physical violence. In such cases the abuser usually doubts his own virility and questions his wife's faithfulness, sometimes to the point of questioning the paternity of one or more of the children. This often results in the batterer either forbidding or severely restricting his wife's activities outside the home. Violence can occur when the wife becomes jealous of her husband. She may even be the instigator of domestic violence, but she still bears the brunt of it.

Pregnancy and Battering

Studies have found that pregnancy as a precipitant to wife abuse is often associated with consequent strain on the relationship caused by jealousy of and resentment toward the unborn child, financial problems, sexual problems, and/or other personal troubles. Both Walker[31] and Gelles[32] reported a high degree of battering during first, second and third pregnancies. In Walker's study over 50 percent of the abusers were initially happy about the pregnancy, but this did not prevent their later violence.

Sexual Intimacy

Two schools of thought exist regarding sex and intimacy as they relate to battered women. One is that the victim of violence as a result of sexual problems often withdraws emotionally and physically from the abuser because of the brutality. According to Roy, this situation often begins very early in the relationship.[33] The women in her study expressed feelings of worthlessness and alienation from their husbands. This low self-esteem derived from violence made sexual intimacy difficult for the woman to achieve. Roy cited that accusations of infidelity and adultery from the husband were part of the sexual problems that contributed to much of the battering.

A second perspective of sexual intimacy seen as part of the battered woman syndrome exists in behavioral patterns of abused women and their inability to distinguish between sex and intimacy. Below are listed some of the reasons why abused women have sex with their mates:

• Manipulativeness in order to "keep the peace."
• Seduction as an unrealistic sense of power.
• The intense concentration on survival.
• Dependency upon a violent though occasionally loving man.
• Knowledge of how to decrease the spouse's violent behavior through a loving relationship.
• Joy from an intense intimate relationship.

Walker noted, "it is quite possible that early exposure to sexual abuse, with or without accompanying physical violence, creates a dependency upon the positive aspects of the intense intimacy experienced prior to the beginning of the battering behavior and continuing during the third phase of loving-kindness."[34]

Although studies have postulated a kink between sex and violence, they do not state clearly if it is more commonly attributed to the aggressive male and the passive or sexually dependent female, or to the passive man with an aggressive woman, or other factors. More research is needed to gain a better perspective on domestic violence and sexual behavior.

PERSONALITY ELEMENTS

The Batterer

Among the more prominent personality characteristics associated with wife battering is the batterer's strict adherence to a traditional male role.[35] Enactment of compulsive masculinity, often referred to as "machismo," is an effort to maintain complete dominance over the wife. On the other extreme, many batterers' personalities contain elements of helplessness and dependency. The violent husband has been characterized as a "little boy wanting to be grown up and superior, as he'd been taught he should be, yet was not in fact; requiring those around him to join in his pretense if he were to survive emotionally, and his family survive physically."[36]

Batterers have been described as "intractable" or "treatable," depending upon how they perceive their violent behavior. The intractable abuser finds no fault in his abusive action, whereas the treatable husband experiences guilt and remorse after the violence. In the latter instance it is possible that with counseling the offender can learn nonviolent means of coping.[37] Other precipitating factors linked to assaultive men are inability to communicate verbally, split personality, insecurity, moodiness, and anger.

The Battered

The battered woman typically follows stereotypical attitudes regarding appropriate masculine and feminine behavior. According to Terry Davidson, "the victims may exemplify society's old image of ideal womanhood—submissive, religious, nonassertive, accepting of whatever the husband's life brings. . . . The husband comes first for these women, who perceive themselves as having little control over many areas of their own lives."[38] Battered women often view themselves and all women as inferior to men, have a tendency to cope with anger either by denying it or turning it inward, and suffer from depression, psychosomatic illnesses, and feelings of guilt.

Shortcomings of Personality Theories

Three central criticisms are directed against personality theories as essential in wife abuse. First is that much of the data used in developing these factors have not been adequately tested. Second is the lack of a complete description of how information used in drawing such inferences was obtained. Third, personality elements cannot be viewed as causal because data about individuals, traits, and perceptions were obtained after or during the violence, not prior to it.

SOCIAL ELEMENTS

No specific sociodemographic characteristics have proved to differentiate between violent and nonviolent couples; however, some areas have drawn considerable support. Childhood experiences of both the victim and offender are believed to be a factor in wife abuse, although the exact correlation and circumstances have been inconsistent. Some studies have found that about half of the batterers sampled experienced some form of abuse in their past (child or spouse abuse).[39] More husbands tend to come from violent backgrounds than wives. For instance, Bonnie Carlson's research showed that only one-third of the victims of battering came from families where wife abuse had occurred,[40] and J. Gayford found an even smaller percentage: 23 out of 100 women had experienced violence in the past.[41] However, another study found no correlation between a female who was formerly a victim of child abuse later becoming a battered wife.[42] Hence the relative importance of exposure to domestic violence during childhood has yet to be clearly established.

Other social factors appear to be more closely related to spousal abuse. Unemployment, job dissatisfaction, financial problems, and chronic alcohol abuse are frequently associated with a battering. Even then the relationship is more a contributory than a causal agent.

Social Structural Theory

Gelles postulates that violence is a direct response to particular structural and situational stimuli.[43] For violence to occur, two conditions must be met: structural or situational stress must be present, and the potential abuser must have been socialized to regard violence as an appropriate response to certain situations (for instance, frustration). Within this theory it is assumed that less educated, lower-income, lower occupational status families are more likely to encounter both structural and situational stress; and that individuals in different socioeconomic groups are socialized differently in their acceptance of violence.

Despite the validity of association of stress and exposure to violence in family background with wife abuse, Gelles's theory has a number of drawbacks. One is that it does not account for the fact that wife abuse can and does occur even when there was no violence in the family background of the abuser. Second, the evidence has not been conclusive enough to support the premise that violence is more prevalent among lower-class groups. On the contrary, many studies indicate that the major differences in social class regarding battered women is the higher-class victim's ability to cover up her victimization or "buy" a different disposition. Greater resources for private care, the ability to get away until recovery, shame, humiliation, and protection of status and a prominent husband in the community are the primary reasons for the differential in reported wife abuse among the higher classes. Therefore, Gelles's theory, while functional in some respects, cannot be considered adequate in explaining the incidence of wife battering.

Societal Structure

General societal values in American culture tend to support domestic battering. Straus describes nine "specific ways in which the male-dominant structure of the society and of the family create and maintain a high level of marital violence":[44]

- The defense of male authority
- Compulsive masculinity
- Economic constraints and discrimination
- The difficulties of child care

- The single-parent household myth
- The preeminence for women of the wife role
- The woman's negative self-image
- The conception of women as children
- The male orientation of the criminal justice system

Lee Bowker contends that "these values and norms bind women into a position in which they are easily victimized at the same time that they encourage men to flex their muscles."[45] Robert Whitehurst combines structural and cultural elements in advancing that cultural elements supporting male dominance will continue in the face of an increase in structural factors favoring equality of the sexes; the result is an increase in the level of domestic battering.[46]

CYCLE THEORY OF VIOLENCE

Walker's "cycle theory" analyzes why the battered woman remains in an abusive situation, not the causes of wife abuse.[47] This tension reduction theory contends that three specific phases exist in a recurring battering cycle: (1) tension building, (2) the acute battering incident, and (3) loving contrition.

During the first phase tension gradually escalates through a series of minor incidents (such as name-calling, other intentionally cruel behavior, and physical abuse), causing increased friction. The batterer expresses nonextreme hostility and dissatisfaction. The wife manages to cope with these episodes by minimizing their importance and/or severity and using general anger reduction techniques. She seeks to appease the batterer by doing what she thinks may please him, calm him down, thereby avoiding a confrontation. Often this strategy is successful for a short time, reinforcing her unrealistic belief that she can control her husband, who may perceive her response as acceptance of his behavior. This becomes "part of the unpredictable noncontingency response/outcome pattern which creates the 'learned helplessness.' "[48]

Tension continues to escalate between the partners, and ultimately the woman is unable to control the man's angry response pattern. Once the stress becomes unbearable (and the frequency of incidents increases), the second phase becomes inevitable if no intervention is forthcoming.

The acute battering incident phase is characterized by "the uncontrollable discharge of the tensions that have built up during phase one."[49] Typically the batterer unleashes a barrage of physical and verbal aggression that can leave the woman severely shaken and injured. It is during the second phase that injuries usually occur, as well as police involvement, if at all. Often there are no witnesses present during acute violence. Once the violence ceases (after lasting anywhere from two to twenty-four hours), shock, denial, and disbelief on the part of both parties usually follow, along with a sharp physiological reduction in tension.

The victimization pattern for the woman is completed in phase three, in which an unusual period of calm exists. The batterer becomes consistently charming and loving, apologetic, kind, and remorseful. He may believe at this point that he will never become violent again. The woman prefers to believe this and, at least early in the relationship, may renew her hope in his ability to change. It is this phase that provides the positive reinforcement for the woman remaining in the relationship. However, eventually phase one tensions begin to build again and a new cycle is enacted.

Walker's cycle theory has been supported by other researchers, such as P. Lewinsohn[50] and E. Lewis.[51] However, the theory fails to account for the many women who do leave violent husbands, some of whom do so "without ever having had a chance to 'practice' necessary behaviors such as initiating legal proceedings, organizing finances, and finding a safe place to stay."[52]

The phenomenon of the battered woman as a paradigm of domestic violence is a problem both extensive and often hidden in our society. It is as closely related to social and societal structure as it is to the dynamics of family life. There are no mutually exclusive patterns or etiological approaches to this problem; rather, the battering of women crosses cultural, racial, ethnic, educational, and occupational lines. Whether or not we gain control over spousal violence will depend on how we apply our knowledge and research.

NOTES

1. M. D. A. Freeman, *Violence in the Home* (Farnborough, England: Saxon House, 1979), p. 4.

2. Bill Nichols, "More Families Reporting Violence," *USA Today* (April 23, 1984), p. 3A.

3. Mildred Daley Pagelow, *Woman-Battering: Victims and Their Experiences* (Beverly Hills: Sage Publications, 1981), p. 33.

4. Murray A. Straus, "Sexual inequality, cultural norms and wife-beating," in Jane R. Chapman and Margaret Gates, eds., *Women into Wives: The Legal and Economic Impact of Marriage* (Beverly Hills: Sage Publications, 1976).

5. Richard J. Gelles, *The Violent Home: A Study of the Physical Aggression between Husbands and Wives* (Beverly Hills: Sage Publications, 1972).

6. Lenore E. Walker, "Treatment Alternatives for Battered Women," In Jane R. Chapman and Margaret Gates, eds., *The Victimization of Women* (Beverly Hills: Sage Publications, 1978), p. 144.

7. Ibid.

8. Terry Davidson, *Conjugal Crime: Understanding and Changing the Wife-Beating Pattern* (New York: Hawthorne, 1979); Lenore E. Walker, *The Battered Woman Syndrome* (New York: Springer, 1984), pp. 108–109.

9. Terry Davidson, "Wifebeating: A Recurring Phenomenon Throughout History," as cited in Maria Roy, *The Abusive Partner: An Analysis of Domestic Battering* (New York: Van Nostrand Reinhold, 1982), p. 12.

10. Maria Roy, "The Nature of Abusive Behavior," in Maria Roy, ed., *The Abusive Partner: An Analysis of Domestic Battering* (New York: Van Nostrand Reinhold, 1982), p. 12.

11. *North and South* and *Oliver Twist* are two good examples. Refer also to F. Basch, *Relative Creatures* (London: Allen Lane, 1974).

12. Frederick Engels, *The Origin of Family Private Property and the State* (Moscow: Progress Publishers, 1948), pp. 53–58; Del Martin, "Battered Women: Society's Problem," in Jane R. Chapman and Margaret Gates, eds., *The Victimization of Women* (Beverly Hills: Sage Publications, 1978), p. 112.

13. Brian G. Frazer, "The Child and His Parents: A Delicate Balance of Rights," in Ray E. Helfer and C. Henry Kempe, eds., *Child Abuse and Neglect: The Family and the Community* (Cambridge, Mass.: Ballinger, 1976).

14. Roy, *The Abusive Partner*, p. 13.

15. R. Calvert, "Criminal and Civil Liability in Husband-Wife Assaults," in Suzanne K. Steinmetz and Murray Straus, eds., *Violence in the Family* (New York: Dodd, Mead, 1975), p. 89.

16. Suzanne Steinmetz, *The Cycle of Violence: Assertive, Aggressive, and Abusive Family Interaction* (New York: Praeger Publishers, 1977).

17. Walker, "Treatment Alternatives for Battered Women," p. 144.

18. Lee H. Bowker, *Women, Crime, and the Criminal Justice System* (Lexington, Mass.: Lexington Books, 1978), p. 125.

19. Frances Patai, "Pornography and Woman Battering: Dynamic Similarities," in Maria Roy, ed., *The Abusive Partner: An Analysis of Domestic Battering* (New York: Van Nostrand Reinhold, 1982), p. 92.

20. Ibid.

21. P. D. Scott, "Battered Wives," *British Journal of Psychiatry* 125 (1975):441.

22. Rebecca Emerson Dobash and Russell Dobash, *Violence against Wives* (New York: Free Press, 1979), pp. 19–20.

23. Diana E. H. Russell, *Rape in Marriage* (New York: Macmillan, 1982).

24. Maria Roy, "Four Thousand Partners in Violence: A Trend Analysis," in Maria Roy, ed., *The Abusive Partner: An Analysis of Domestic Battering* (New York: Van Nostrand Reinhold, 1982), pp. 34–35.

25. Russell, *Rape in Marriage*; idem, *The Politics of Rape* (New York: Stein & Day, 1975).

26. Laura X, *Clearinghouse on Marital Rape* (Berkeley, Calif.: Women's History Research Center, 1981).

27. Walker, *The Battered Woman Syndrome*, pp. 48–49.

28. K. Yllö, *Types of Marital Rape: Three Case Studies*, presented at the National Conference for Family Violence Researchers, University of New Hampshire, Durham, July 1981.

29. Russell, *Rape in Marriage*.

30. Roy, "Four Thousand Partners in Violence," pp. 31–32; E. Hilberman and L. Munson, "Sixty Battered Women," *Victimology: An International Journal* 2, nos. 3–4 (1978):460–471.

31. Walker, *The Battered Woman Syndrome*, p. 51.

32. Richard J. Gelles, "Violence and Pregnancy: A Note on the Extent of the Problem and Needed Services," *Family Coordinator* 24 (1975):81–86.

33. Roy, "Four Thousand Partners in Violence," p. 32.

34. Walker, *The Battered Woman Syndrome*, p. 55.

35. Kathleen H. Hofeller, *Social, Psychological and Situational Factors in Wife Abuse* (Palo Alto, Calif.: R & E Research Associates, 1982), p. 39.

36. Davidson, *Conjugal Crime*, p. 29.

37. Ibid., p. 23.

38. Ibid., p. 51.

39. Hofeller, *Social, Psychological and Situational Factors in Wife Abuse*, p. 43.

40. Bonnie E. Carlson, "Battered Women and Their Assailants," *Social Work* 22, no. 6 (1977):456.

41. J. Gayford, "Wife Battering: A Preliminary Survey of 100 Cases," *British Medical Journal* 1 (1975):194–197.

42. E. Parker and D. Schumacher, "The Battered Wife Syndrome and Violence in the Nuclear Family of Origin: A Controlled Pilot Study," *American Journal of Public Health* 67 (1977):760–761.

43. Gelles, *The Violent Home*.

44. Murray A. Straus, "Sexual Inequality, Cultural Norms, and Wife-Beating," *Victimology* 1 (1976):62–66.

45. Bowker, *Women, Crime, and the Criminal Justice System*, p. 128.

46. Robert N. Whitehurst, "Violence in Husband-Wife Interaction," in Suzanne K. Steinmetz and Murray A. Straus, eds., *Violence in the Family* (New York: Dodd, Mead, 1974), pp. 75–82.

47. Lenore E. Walker, *The Battered Woman* (New York: Harper & Row, 1979).

48. Walker, *The Battered Woman Syndrome*, p. 95.

49. Walker, *The Battered Woman*, p. 59.

50. P. M. Lewinsohn, "The Behavioral Study and Treatment of Depression," in M. Hersen, M. Eisler, and P. M. Miller, eds., *Progress in Behavior Modification* (New York: Academic Press, 1975).

51. E. M. Lewis, "An Experimental Analogue of the Spouse Abuse Cycle." Paper presented at the National Conference for Family Violence Researchers, University of New Hampshire, Durham, July 1981.

52. Hofeller, *Social, Psychological and Situational Factors in Wife Abuse*, p. 48.

3

Rape: The Unspeakable Violation of Women

There is no more degrading, humiliating, painful, shocking victimization of women than the act of rape. Yet its very nature draws most of us into a shell when discussing the subject. It is hoped that the following critical analysis of the dynamics of rape will result in greater understanding of this serious crime.

A HISTORY OF RAPE

Rape has been a part of human interaction perhaps for as long as the sexes have coexisted. Rape is the oldest means by which a man could seize or steal a woman to be his wife. It was enforced marriage minus the art of courtship. A man simply took the woman he wanted, raped her, and brought her into his tribe. She represented little more than a trophy; she held no legal, social, or human rights.

Gradually the respectability of forcible rape declined and culpability for certain rapes shifted to the victim. Herodotus, referred to as the "father of history," documented this way of thinking in 500 B.C. when he observed, "Abducting young women is not, indeed, a lawful act; but it is stupid after the event to make a fuss about it. The only sensible thing is to take no notice; for it is obvious that no young woman allows herself to be abducted if she does not want to be."[1] In other words, women who were raped were obviously asking for it—a contention that still gains considerable support today.

Forcible rape became a crime when marriage evolved into a sanctioned tribal institution. Women were viewed as a proprietary interest, bought and sold like cattle. The right of ownership meant that any infringement upon or damage to one person's (usually the father or husband) human property (as in rape) was a crime, often dealt with severely. To rape a virgin was considered the ultimate and irreparable damage of property and often meant death to the perpetrator.[2]

Many believe the institution of marriage and family life historically are based on the subjugation of women both inside and outside the marriage. In a historical review of rape, Susan Brownmiller asserted that rapists are the "shock troops" whose existence convinced women to mate and marry one man in order to protect themselves against the potential violence of other men.[3] Brownmiller further contends that the predatory nature of men and their desire for property are the fundamental causes of rape and sexual inequality, providing countless examples of rapes throughout history.

DEFINING RAPE

A major problem in dealing with the issue of rape today is the lack of a cohesive, uniform definition among professionals, institutions, states, and even individuals. The word "rape" is derived from the Latin "rapere," which means "to steal, seize, or carry away." Current definitions of rape can be divided into two forms, legal and nonlegal.

Legal Definitions

Legal perspectives on rape generally can be traced to traditional common law and statute law. Common law defined rape as the unlawful carnal knowledge of a woman by force and against her will. Sexual penetration, no matter how slight, was sufficient to constitute criminality, assuming the other elements were present. A resistance standard was instituted for the victim in order to distinguish forcible carnal knowledge (rape) from consensual carnal knowledge (fornication and adultery). Common law made both forms of carnal knowledge criminal acts, but if the act was forcible, the victim avoided punishment for adultery or fornication.[4]

Legal theory has long advanced that

a crime exists only when there is concurrence of an unacceptable act and a criminal intent with respect to that act. The unacceptable act is called the actus reus; the criminal intent is called the mens rea. In traditional definition of rape, the actus reus is the unconsented-to sexual intercourse and the mens rea is the intention or knowledge of having the intercourse without the consent of the victim. Lack of consent of the victim is ultimately the characteristic that distinguishes rape. The concurrence of the act and the intent requires both that the victim in fact not consent and that the perpetrator know at the time that the victim did not consent.[5]

Hence in accordance with theory and common law tradition, the definition of rape is contingent upon both the victim's and offender's perception that the intercourse was not consensual. This dual legal requirement raises obvious interpretational problems given that no criminal intent will be present in many cases in which an unacceptable act is committed. The victim's perception of the intercourse as rape may be quite the opposite of the perpetrator's belief.

Many states have adopted a statutory definition of rape as the act of sexual intercourse with a woman other than the perpetrator's wife committed without her lawful consent. As in common law, only the slightest penetration is necessary to complete the crime. Specifically excluded from this definition are anal and oral copulation and homosexual assaults.

Because of the criticisms directed at these rather narrow definitions in common and statutory law, which are replete with important omissions in sexual assaults of unwilling victims, a number of states have redefined rape in an attempt to encompass a broader description of forcible rape. As of this writing at least eight states have eliminated the word "rape" from their statutes and have replaced it with terminology that more closely reflects contemporary sexual behavior and mores—such as "criminal sexual assault" and "sexual battery"—to connote a crime defined by the perpetrator's behavior. Additionally, many states have defined rape in sex-neutral terms, allowing the act to be considered a crime beyond traditional female victim-male offender patterns.[6]

Nonlegal Definitions

Defining rape outside legal perspectives is usually a matter of individual interpretation of what circumstances should constitute rape. Social, psychological, medical, and individual definitions may vary depending upon the criteria used. In general, however, nonlegal definitions of rape tend to be more liberal and inclusive than legal definitions as more information becomes available about sexual violations, relationships, consensual matters, and other factors on which to form opinions. Rape often becomes sexual assault and can also include attempted rape, which may involve virtually every element of the rape act itself, making the experience just as traumatizing for the victim. Sexual assault or forcible rape in nonlegal terms may extend beyond sexual penetration of a nonconsensual woman (or man) outside the context of marriage and include sodomy, oral and anal copulation, penetration by an instrument, and incest.

Perhaps the most useful nonlegal perspective of rape is that defined by the victimized woman herself. Because this is still essentially a crime of man aggressor-woman victim, it is the woman's point of view or actions as a result of victimization that offer us an important perspective on rape. Unfortunately, because so many women who believed that what happened to them was rape refuse to report it, their perspective is hard to examine. Some limited analysis does exist in studying the victimized woman's definition of rape, however.

Studies have attributed women's attitudes of rape in terms of level of responsibility or fault, virtuous compared to deserving victim, victim precipitation, and sociodemographic variables. Susan and David Klemmack's findings supported the following contentions:

- What constitutes rape is consistent with the woman's positions on a variety of related social issues.

- Women who are more tolerant of sex outside marriage subscribe to a definition of human sexuality that includes rape as simply forced nonconsensual intercourse.

- Women with fewer stereotypically traditional perspectives of the woman's role in contemporary society tend to define rape operationally at the level of forced intercourse.

- Women reared with males more often ascribe responsibility for a sexual assault to the victim.[7]

While we can learn from the woman's point of view about situations she believes to be rape, such definitions tend to be more reflective of norms, labeling, myths, the women's movement, and inconsistencies than they are of male aggression and the realities of a male-oriented culture.

Definitional Limitations

Most of the controversy surrounding definitions of rape concerns the legal designation. Primarily it is the narrow scope of official definitions of rape that creates the need for both reform and nonlegal interpretations. K. Svalastoga illustrated the problem by applying current legal definitions of forcible rape in many states to a particular situation:

Rape is commonly defined as enforced coitus. But this very definition suggests that there is more to the offense than the use of force alone. This must be so, since no society has equipped itself with the means of measuring the amount of force applied in an act of coitus. Hence rape, like any other crime, carries a heavy social component. The act itself is not a sufficient [criterion]. The act must be interpreted as rape by the female actee, and her interpretation must be similarly evaluated by a number of officials and agencies before the official designation of "rape" can be legitimately applied.[8]

Another drawback of legal definitions has been noted by many women: what is actually an offense encompassing a wide range of sexual assaults has in practice been applied to only the most extreme and violent incidents. Then there is the fact that most available statistics about rape are based on legal concepts of rape, immediately offering a considerably lower incidence of rape than broader interpretations would show. Finally, many victims of sexual assault fall outside the protection of the law because the offense perpetrated upon them falls outside the scope of state statutes defining rape.

It is clear that states still subscribing to old concepts of rape need to reassess their standing on a serious issue, and all states must broaden the meaning of "sexual assault" to account for the many ways in which women and children can be sexually victimized.

THE PREVALENCE OF RAPE

No methodology currently exists to tell us precisely how many women are raped or sexually assaulted in this country each year. However, we need only look at the number of forcible rape crimes to see that this problem commands serious attention. According to FBI data, with the exception of a few isolated periods, reported rape has increased steadily and often dramatically since the first *Uniform Crime Reports* (*UCR*) came out in 1933.[9] The latest figures show that in 1985 the number of forcible rapes was estimated at 87,340, with rapes in cities and suburban counties up 4 percent form the previous year and up 9 percent in rural counties.[10] In 1984 the female forcible rape rate in metropolitan statistical areas (MSAs) was 79 victims per 100,000 females, 40 per 100,000 females in cities outside metropolitan areas, and 34 per 100,000 females in rural counties.[11]

Victimization or interview data are generally believed to provide a more accurate and detailed portrait of rape than official data. For example, the National Crime Survey (NCS), based on a representative sample of 60,000 respondents, estimated that 154,000 rapes were committed in 1977, a figure far exceeding UCR data for the same year (or any year between 1977 and 1986).[12] Another notable comparison between official and victimization data is the rate of rape victimization per 100,000 females. The NCS rate of 140 per 100,000 females in 1983 was more than double the official rate of 66 female rape victims per 100,000 in 1983.[13] A 1985 report issued by the Bureau of Justice provides a comprehensive portrait of rape in the United States based on more than 2.6 million interviews.[14] According to the study:

• More than 1.5 million incidents of rape (or attempted rape) are estimated to have occurred between 1973 and 1982.

- In 1983, one in every 600 women and girls over 12 years old was a rape victim.
- Eighty-one percent of all rape victims are white.
- Proportionately, black women were significantly more likely to be victimized than white women.
- Fear of a short prison term for the rapist and an insensitive criminal justice system are prominent factors in unreporting.
- More than 70 percent of the victims were unmarried women.
- A woman was twice as likely to be assaulted by a stranger than by someone she knew.
- Two of every three cases involved victims aged 16 to 24.
- About 15 percent of the incidents involved more than one assailant.
- More than 90 percent of the victims reported income below $25,000; half the victims reported family income under $10,000.
- Rape accounts for 3 percent of all violent crime in the United States.

A national estimate of the incidence of rape of adult women (*UCR* data give no information on the age of victims of rape and attempted rape; victimization surveys are based on victims age 12 and up) was formulated by Diana Russell in San Francisco recently and is particularly interesting for our purposes.[15] Based on interviews with females aged 18 and over (the victim had to be at least 17 at the time of the rape), the Russell survey revealed a rape rate of 3,548 per 100,000 females. This rate is seven times higher than that reported by the 1974 NCS in San Francisco of 500 per 100,000 females.[16] The Russell incidence figure for rape of 35 per 1,000 females is twenty-four times higher than the rate of 1.71 per 1,000 females in the city reported in the *UCR* for 1978.[17] If the incidence rate for the Russell study were applied over the entire country during the year of the survey (1978), multiplying the *UCR* estimates of rapes (and attempts) for that year (67,131) by twenty-four one could project that more than 1.5 million rapes and attempted rapes (reported and unreported) occurred in that year.[18] If the actual total were anywhere close to this, it would indicate that the severity of the problem is far greater than assumed by *UCR* data.

Limitations of Rape Data

Despite the scope of rape figures, limitations exist that obviously affect their reliability. *UCR* data are perhaps the most suspect. (See chapters 1 and 6 for more general discussion of official drawbacks.) The FBI itself acknowledges that forcible rape is among the most underreported crimes. How underreported is it? Nancy Gager and Cathleen Schurr contend that "most women working with victims believe that at least 90 percent of actual rapes are never reported."[19] Brownmiller estimated that "only one in five rapes, or possibly one in twenty, may actually be reported."[20] The fact is, considerably more rapes are occurring than indicated by official sources.

Further difficulty in interpreting official rape statistics is the "unfounding" process, which applies specifically to rape. The FBI defines this as "the police established that no forcible rape offense or attempt occurred."[21] Essentially this euphemistic definition describes the process in which reports of rape are dismissed by law enforcement personnel as false. The level of subjectivity and bias in such decisions and the consequent error rate are not known and are thus unmeasurable, yet they undoubtedly influence the accuracy of statistics. Finally, the narrow FBI definition and classification of rape as "carnal knowledge of a female forcibly and against her will" disregards other sex crimes such as sodomy, oral copulation, male victims, and female victims of spousal rape in the compilation of rape figures.

Victimization surveys, while using different, more effective criteria, are limited for our purposes in their failure to provide adequate data that differentiate adult and child rape victims. (Most surveys, such as NCS, group adolescent with adult victims.) Other weaknesses of the interview and questionnaire process are reflected in insensitivity to victims of rape or attempted rape, bias, and the fact that many victims fail to cooperate with this method of research (see chapter 1).

Regarding the Russell survey, the obvious weakness of her projections is the incompatibility of the survey methodology and criteria with NCS and *UCR* data. Russell's interviews with respondents who were 17 or over at the time of the incident are difficult to equate reliably with the *UCR* data, which give no age information on victims, and NCS figures, which are based on residents aged 12 and over. On the whole, however, Russell's findings most successfully measure rape victimization of adult women.

THE MYTHICAL NATURE OF RAPE

A number of rather disturbing yet popular myths, stereotypes, and beliefs regarding rape have taken root in our society over the years as a result of tradition, fear, ignorance, and disbelief. Because of the damage this has inflicted upon victims of rape and their integrity, considerable research has been devoted in recent years to exploding the myths about rape and sexual assault through more accurate assessments. What follows are the more blatant misconceptions and rebuttals to them.

Misconception: Rape Cannot Occur if the Woman Resists

This belief holds that there is actually no such thing as a rape, for it could not occur if the woman did not want it to. Not surprisingly, many professionals (e.g., doctors and defense lawyers) subscribe to this theory. The fallacy of this notion is that it assumes rape and consensual sexual intercourse are essentially the same thing. They are not. Rape is the forced sexual aggression of the perpetrator, regardless of the victim's wishes; normal sexual relations occur by mutual consent. Nonresistance to rape is not a matter of compliance but often fear, the suddenness of the attack, being overpowered, the survival instinct, and the desire to escape. No foolproof method of resisting or deterring an attack exists that would prevent injury or death for the victim.

Misconception: All Women Secretly Desire to Be Raped

The seduction theme is not uncommon in women's sexual fantasies. However, these fantasies are always under the control of the woman's imagination: she selects the time, place, circumstances, and man. Psychologists exploring the nature of such fantasies have concluded that they are representative of the woman's desire to feel guiltless in sexual encounters—not a wish to be raped.

Misconception: The Majority of Rapes Are Triggered by Women Being Out Alone at Night

Studies indicate that from one-third to two-thirds of all rapes take place in the victim's home or another private residence. More than a third of all reported sexual assaults are perpetrated by men who break into the victim's home. Rape occurs at any time of day or night.

Misconception: Rape Is a Victim-Precipitated Crime

This theory assumes that victimized women asked for rape by their mode of dress or behavior. Some studies have described rape as "victim-precipitated" when the victim merely responded politely to a perpetrator's verbal overtures. The National Commission on the Causes and Prevention of Violence reported that only 4 percent of the sexual assaults studied involved a woman's "precipitative behavior."[22] Menachem Amir, criminologist and author of Patterns in Forcible Rape, postulated that the victim's behavior is not as significant as "the offender's interpretation of her actions."[23]

Misconception: Only Young Attractive Women Are Raped

This myth is especially harmful as it implies that anyone not fitting the qualifications of young and "sexy" could not be raped because no one would want to rape her. In truth, rape is an offense that draws no distinctions by age or appearance. It can and does happen to anyone. Reported cases have included infants and women in their nineties. Vulnerability as perceived by the offender is the key to attack. Often the rapist does not even know, remember or care what the victim looked like.

Misconception: Women Scream "Rape" as a Vengeful Measure or to Protect Their Reputations

New York City's sex crimes analysis squad has reported that false claims, in which proof exists that no crime occurred, constitute only about 2 percent of the rape complaints in the city, which is comparable to the percentage of false claims for other major violent crimes.[24] The police often cite unfounded rapes as proof that women falsify rape in order to punish boyfriends or husbands or to protect themselves from gossip or censure. Some cases are classed as unfounded through lack of evidence.

It is the other extreme that fuels this misconception. A few years ago a believable young woman accused a man of rape. He was subsequently convicted and sent to prison. Recently she recanted the story in a highly publicized showcase. Only she and the alleged offender know whether she was telling the truth the second time. Fortunately, this type of situation rarely occurs in rape cases.

Misconception: It Cannot Happen to Me

Chances are that it will not; however, there is a one in ten chance that a female will be sexually assaulted sometime during her life. This constitutes a considerable number of women at risk who currently believe rape always happens to other women.

Misconception: Rape Is Motivated by the Need for Sexual Gratification

Studies show that the primary motivations behind rape are aggression, dominance, and hatred—not pleasure. Many convicted rapists were married when the assault(s) occurred; others who were unmarried report they had access to willing sexual partners. Wives of rapists often report their sexual relations with their husbands as satisfactory.

Misconception: Most Rapes Are Perpetrated by Strangers

Some studies support this contention, but many others have found that in approximately half of the cases, the victim and offender are acquainted (i.e., boyfriend, relative, neighbor). This figure would be even higher if spousal rape were included (in most cases it is not).

Misconception: The Rapist Looks the Part

Many people believe rapists are a certain type: sinister, edgy, criminal-like, unsavory. In reality they appear no different from anyone else. Studies have shown that the vast majority of rapists are close to the norm in their physical and psychological characteristics, except for a tendency to be more likely to display anger and frustration. However, these traits could apply to nonrapists as well.

Misconception: Rape Is an Impulsive Act

Studies with convicted rapists have shown that most rapes are planned, awaiting only an opportune time and likely victim. Many victims are held captive and subjected to repeated assaults. Far from impulsive, these cases are better described as ritualistic.

CHARACTERIZING THE RAPIST AND RAPE VICTIM

A number of researchers have developed typologies of perpetrators and victims of rape in attempting to derive a standard by which to identify patterns associated with forcible rape. Of course, not all rapists and rape victims can be characterized, as rape is a phenomenon with no specific character traits for victim or offender. However, typologies based on clinical research, review of the literature, and reported rape provide an important means to examine groups more prone or predisposed to risk.

One of the prominent characterizations of the offender/victim of rape was established by Amir as follows:

- Rape is predominantly an intraracial crime.
- Rape between blacks occurs more often than between whites.
- Most rapists are young (age 15 to 29).
- Most victims are young (age 10 to 29).
- Offenders tend to occupy the lower end of the occupational scale.
- Sexual assaults are not occupationally bound.
- The offender and victim generally live in the same neighborhood.
- Alcohol is a factor only in violent rapes.
- Most group rapes involve young men, are planned, and are influenced by peer pressure.[25]

Other researchers' findings and profiles have generally been consistent with Amir's. For instance, Sedelle Katz and Mary Ann Mazur undertook a comprehensive review of the literature on rape victimization and concluded, based on reported cases of rape, that "the high-risk ages are adolescents (ages 13 to 17) through young adulthood (ages 18 to 24)."[26] They also presented data to support the contention that "black women were far more vulnerable to rape than white women."[27] However, Katz and Mazur noted that although most researchers established rape as a lower socioeconomic class phenomenon, few presented systematic data to substantiate this claim. Additionally, the association between black women and rape is a reflection of their overrepresentation in lower income groups.

Such variables as intelligence and physical characteristics do not consistently prove to be central factors in rape. Marital status, however, is a factor. Findings from several studies reveal that victims of rape are more often single than married. Russell found that 85 percent of the victims in her survey were single at the time of the rape or attempted rape.[28]

PSYCHOLOGICAL CHARACTER STUDIES OF RAPE OFFENDERS

More than fifty types of rapists have been identified by researchers.[29] Although none of these typologies should be considered mutually exclusive, each offers a perspective of rapists. Four different yet effective typologies of rapists will be addressed here.

Paul Gebhard and associates, of the Institute for Sex Research in Indiana, offered six categories of what they refer to as "heterosexual aggressors" against adults:

- Assaultive rapists. The most common type of rapists, characterized by sadistic and hostile feelings toward women.

- Amoral delinquents. The second most common type of rapist; nonsadistic. They desire to have coitus regardless of the female's wishes.

- The drunken variety. As common as amoral delinquents.

- The explosive variety. Men whose past gives no indication of their potential to rape. Often their behavior contains psychotic elements.

- The double-standard variety. Divides females into good ones, to be treated with respect, and bad ones, who do not deserve such consideration.

- "Other" types. Mixtures of the first five, as well as mental defectives and psychotics.[30]

Psychiatrist Richard Rada classifies five kinds of rapists:

• The psychotic rapist. Men who are acutely psychotic, violent; neither the victim nor the offender is in control of the situation.

• The situational stress rapist. Rarely very violent or dangerous. The rape is a result of situational stress. The rapist usually has no history of violent behavior or sexual deviations.

• The masculine identity conflict rapist. A broad spectrum of rapists whose common ground is an actual or felt deficiency in their masculine roles. Their rape is usually planned, dangerous, and violent.

• The sadistic rapist. A small percentage of rapists. Usually plans the rape, has a history of perversion, and derives pleasure in ritualistic degrading of women.

• The sociopathic rapist. The most common type. He is impulsive; motivated primarily by sex. The rape is merely a manifestation of general deviant behavior.[31]

Nicholas Groth, Ann Burgess, and Lynda Holmstrom studied the phenomenon of rape from the standpoint of both rapist and victim and advanced that three components are present in nearly every case of forcible rape: power, anger, and sexuality.[32] They concluded that rape is the sexual expression of aggression rather than the aggressive expression of sexuality. Although rape is a sexual crime, it is not sexually motivated. Instead, the researchers postulated that sex becomes a method of expressing nonsexual needs in the psychology of the offender, characterizing such needs as power and anger—hence the power rape offender and the anger rape offender.

Sociologists Diana Scully and Joseph Marolla presented an even more general and unique typology of rapists.[33] They refer to them as admitters and deniers. Admitters acknowledge having had sexual contact with the victim and define their action as rape; whereas deniers, even when admitting there was sexual contact and/or violence, deny their behavior as rape. Both admitters and deniers do not regard their victims as human beings but as objects to be used and conquered.

Critiquing Typologies

As noted earlier, characterizing rapists cannot be considered conclusive because of the ease in which rapists can move from one category or typology to another, or perhaps encompass parts of all typologies or none at all. Additionally, different criteria, methodological and disciplinary biases, and social factors can influence the perceptions of rapist types from one typology to the next.

Scully and Marolla note the problems common in categorizing rapist types:

First, dominated by psychiatry and a medical model, the underlying assumption that rapists are sick has pervaded the field. Second, with very few exceptions, the targets of research have been clinical samples of rapists within prisons. Indeed, the situation in rape research would be analogous to assuming that everyone who steals is emotionally ill and proving it by studying only psychotic burglars, or doing research on psychotic burglars to discover why people, in general, steal.[34]

Studying convicted rapists as representative of all rapists fails for a number of reasons, the most persuasive being that low arrest and conviction rates, underreporting, and criminal justice system biases manage to keep some classes of men out of prison. Clearly what is needed before we can make accurate assumptions are more thoroughly tested hypotheses, critical analysis of the validity of existing typologies, and a broader range of subjects (offenders and victims) with which to study character traits.

THEORIZING THE ACT OF RAPE

A number of theories exist that attempt to explain why rape occurs or why one may be predisposed to raping or being sexually assaulted. Let us review four of the most influential.

Interactionist Theories

Symbolic interaction theories postulate that "social interaction is mediated by signs and symbols, by eye contact, gestures and words."[35] People view and interpret one another's actions and respond accordingly. Rape is the product of such a response. Hence interactionists assume that rape is caused by the way men and women communicate their feelings and attitudes toward each other. Victim-precipitation theories are interaction theories. In emphasizing the rapist's reactions to the victim, this theoretical perspective refers to "those cases in which the victim—actually or so it was interpreted by the offender—agreed to sexual relations but retracted before the actual act or did not resist strongly enough."[36]

The major fault with this theory, which regards the victim as a significant causal agent in rape, is that it cannot be considered a general explanation of rape, for even if it applied to some it would not apply to all situations of rape. Additionally, interactionist theories generally fail to question the oppressive sexist norms that regulate women's lives. This fact was best summarized by Julia and Herman Schwendinger, authors of *Rape and Equality*:

Rather than the victim's response, it is actually the rapist's supremacist attitude and behavior that dominate the situation and determine its violent outcome. . . .

Because of the emphasis on parity, the interaction theories tacitly minimize the structural realities of the situation and the power differentials that characterize the overwhelming number of forcible rapes. By maximizing an illusion of equality, these theories mask the degree to which the rapist's chauvinism is still the essential cause, regardless of the "propriety" of the victim's behavior.[37]

Psychoanalytic Theories

Although only a small percentage of rapists are psychotic, psychoanalytic theories regard most rapists as emotionally disturbed. These theories advance that rapists may have developed an intense hatred of women during childhood or may have had experiences "that triggered their latent homosexual tendencies."[38] Thus rape is put into that category of actions perpetrated by men who are obsessively motivated by hatred of women and an overpowering need to assure themselves of their own masculinity.

Psychoanalytic concepts are also crucial to the sociological theory known as "the subculture of violence," which is applied to rapists by prominent researchers such as Amir and Brownmiller.[39] This subculture is allegedly the creation of men who reside in similar areas and who resort to violence as an answer to their sexual ambivalence and disorders.

Both psychoanalytic theories and the subculture of violence theory are flawed because of their systematic failure to prove their theses scientifically. Psychoanalysis tends to overemphasize considerably the number of rapes attributed to personality disorders while offering causal advancements that have become part of conventional wisdom, even in the absence of empirical validity.

Opportunity Structure Theory

Canadian researchers Lorenne Clark and Debra Lewis employ the concept of an "opportunity structure" in their interpretation of sexual relations that lead to rape.[40] They contend that men view women as possessors of saleable sexual properties.

Female sexuality is allegedly bought and sold in an open market. However, the market is dominated by male conceptions of property and therefore the best bargain a woman can achieve is still restrictive. Furthermore, when bargaining for sex, men reportedly use various forms of coercion. They may make promises they cannot or will not really fulfill. They may harass women or threaten them with physical harm.[41]

The authors advance that those men who have money or other resources can easily make bargains in their own interest. However, men who are poor or perhaps unattractive employ force to take sexuality from women because they cannot bargain successfully.

Clark and Lewis further suggest that rapists from lower-class backgrounds frequently choose middle-class women as victims because these men lack the necessary social and economic means to attract these women and desire what they cannot have. In summarizing rape, the researchers theorize: "Within the technical limits of the term, rape will always be an inevitable consequence of the fact that some men do not have the means to achieve sexual relations with women, except through physical violence."[42]

Clark and Lewis's theory has a number of serious deficiencies. First, it ignores the fact that many men of wealth, charm, and/or good looks are rapists. Second, although considerable data support the contention that most habitual rapists are poor men, there is no evidence to substantiate that they frequently prey upon middle-class women. On the contrary, research suggests that not only are most rape offenders from the lower working class, but the women they victimize usually are members of their own class. Third, the idea of sex as a commodity is unwarranted. There are several reasons for this including the following:

1. Commodity markets emerged centuries ago, not because of sexual relations and the will of men but because of the development of capitalism.
2. The theory is based largely on barter relations as opposed to commodities that are sold in a competitive market.
3. Few men choose sexual commodities (only prostitutes and mistresses might apply) because the woman represents the "best bargain" available.
4. Although some men may treat their wives or girlfriends as slaves, they do not regard them as property to be bought and sold.

The Biologically Based Predisposition to Rape

Many feminists have subscribed to a biological theory of rape. This perspective is made clear by Brownmiller in her book, *Against Our Will*:

Man's structural capacity to rape and woman's corresponding structural vulnerability are as basic to the physiology of both our sexes as the primal act of sex itself. Had it not been for this accident of biology, an accommodation requiring the locking together of two separate parts, penis into vagina, there would be neither copulation nor rape as we know it. . . . In terms of human anatomy, the possibility of forcible intercourse incontrovertibly exists. This single factor may have been sufficient to have caused the creation of a male ideology of rape. When men discovered that they could rape, they proceeded to do it.[43]

Brownmiller's theory that rape and sexual inequality arise from biological facts has not been validated scientifically. Neither Cesare Lom-

broso, Sigmund Freud, nor any other prominent professional in criminology has ever established the theory that biological characteristics
determine crime. Furthermore, Brownmiller's theory places too much
emphasis on traditional male stereotypes but rejects the sexist stereotyping of women. Finally, Brownmiller overlooks perhaps the most crucial biological difference between the sexes as it relates to rape: the
superior strength that gives most men a decided advantage over most
women should forcible rape be the objective.

THE EFFECTS OF RAPE

Discussing the dynamics of the crime of rape would not be complete
without addressing the most critical factor, other than the rape itself,
for the woman: the consequences of rape. No one knows how long or
in what manner each victim will be affected by rape; each person is
different, as may be the circumstances of each sexual assault. However,
rarely can a victim escape the aftereffects. Indeed, for some the trauma
leaves them feeling that life is no longer worth living. According to
psychologists Dean Kirkpatrick, Connie Best, and Lois Veronen, nearly
one rape victim in five reports an attempted suicide, a rate that is more
than eight times higher than that of nonrape victims.[44]

Some of the effects generally associated with rape are physical injuries,
altered psychological and emotional states, lowered self-esteem, and
changes in life patterns and relationships. Additionally, an economic
impact may be felt because of medical and legal costs, lost work time
or loss of employment, school withdrawal, and/or a change in residence
or location.

Carol Nadelson and Malkah Notman suggest that there are predictable
outcomes in rape cases: a feeling of helplessness; heightened conflicts
about dependence and independence; self-criticism and guilt, both of
which affect self-esteem; difficulty in handling own aggression and anger; interference in developing trusting relationships with men; and
increased feelings of vulnerability.[45] These researchers have found at
least three responses to rape that appear to occur almost universally
among victims of rape:

- Disruption of normal adaptive patterns, causing such symptoms as lowered
  attention span, appetite and sleep disturbance, and diminished functioning
  level

- Regression to a more dependent, helpless position

- Increased emotional susceptibility

The long-term effects for victims of rape and other violations of self are summarized aptly by the coauthor of *The Crime Victim's Book*, Morton Bard:

Victims never entirely forget the crime. Their suffering lessens, but other effects of the experience remain as part of the self. Their view of themselves and of the world will be permanently altered in some way, depending on the severity of the crime and the degree of its impact. The violation of self can hardly be called a positive experience, but it does present an opportunity for change. One of two things will happen: either victims become reordered, reborn, put back together so that they are stronger than before, or their experiences during the crisis will promote further disorder with long-term negative consequences.

A great deal depends on the kind of help the victim receives. The victim of a personal crime has been violated by another person. If the victim's recovery is supported by other people, their help provides a kind of counterbalance to the violation, reassuring the victim of the essential trustworthiness of most people. The victim who receives appropriate help from family and friends, for example, will come out of the crisis with a heightened appreciation for them and a greater ability to seek their help again. Weathering a crisis can be a strengthening experience for victims and those who love them.[46]

Rape as a contemporary problem affects not only the victimized woman (men and children) and their close ones but all of us, for it is a crime that violates the very essence of humanity. Yet paradoxically it is the nature of human relations that is responsible for the existence of sexual assaults. A long history of oppression, subjugation, proprietary concepts, degradation, and dominance of women has had a significant impact on how men view women and why rape occurs. Although we have perhaps more information at our disposal today than ever before on the dynamics of sexual assault, two questions continue to elude answer: How can we adequately protect victims? And how do we discourage this type of activity from taking place?

NOTES

1. Carol V. Horos, *Rape* (New Canaan, Conn.: Tobey Publishing Co., 1974), p. 3.

2. Ibid., 4.

3. Susan Brownmiller, *Against Our Will: Men, Women and Rape* (New York: Simon & Schuster, 1975).

4. Battelle Law and Justice Study Center Report, *Forcible Rape: An Analysis of Legal Issues* (Washington, D.C.: Government Printing Office, 1977), p. 11.

5. Ibid., p. 34.

6. Ibid., p. 17.

7. Susan H. Klemmack and David L. Klemmack, "The Social Definition of

Rape," in Marcia J. Walker and Stanley L. Brodsky, eds., *Sexual Assault* (Lexington, Mass.: Lexington Books, 1976), pp. 144–145.

8. K. Svalastoga, "Rape and Social Structure," *Pacific Sociological Review* 5 (1962):48–53.

9. U.S. Federal Bureau of Investigation, *Crime in the United States: Uniform Crime Reports, 1930–1985* (Washington, D.C.: Government Printing Office); Donald J. Mulvihill, Melvin M. Tumin, and Lynn A. Curtis, *Crimes of Violence*, Vol. 11 (Washington, D.C.: Government Printing Office, 1969), p. 54.

10. "Sun Belt Feeds Growth in Crime Rate, FBI Finds," *Sacramento Bee* (July 27, 1986), p. AA1.

11. U.S. Federal Bureau of Investigation, *Crime in the United States: Uniform Crime Reports, 1984* (Washington, D.C.: Government Printing Office, 1985), p. 14.

12. Law Enforcement Assistance Administration, *Criminal Victimization in the United States: A Comparison of 1976 and 1977 Findings*, A National Crime Survey Report (Washington, D.C.: Government Printing Office, 1978); see also *Uniform Crime Reports*, 1977–1986.

13. U.S. Department of Justice, *Criminal Victimization in the United States, 1983*, A National Crime Survey Report (Washington, D.C.: Government Printing Office, 1984), p. 14. The rape victimization rate of 140 per 100,000 females is based on the National Crime Survey rate of 1.4 rapes (or attempted) per 1,000 female population; *Uniform Crime Reports, 1983*, p. 14.

14. "U.S. Report on Rape Cases Cites Victims' Frustrations with Law," *New York Times* (March 25, 1985), p. A17.

15. Diana E. H. Russell, *Sexual Exploitation: Rape, Child Abuse, and Workplace Harassment* (Beverly Hills: Sage Publications, 1984), pp. 46–47.

16. Ibid., p. 46.

17. Ibid.

18. Ibid., p. 47.

19. Nancy Gager and Cathleen Schurr, *Sexual Assault: Confronting Rape in America* (New York: Grosset and Dunlap, 1976), p. 91.

20. Brownmiller, *Against Our Will*, p. 190.

21. Russell, *Sexual Exploitation*, p. 29.

22. National Commission on the Causes and Prevention of Violence, *Crimes of Violence: A Staff Report*, Vol. 2 (Washington, D.C.: Government Printing Office, 1969).

23. Menachem Amir, *Patterns in Forcible Rape* (Chicago: University of Chicago Press, 1971), p. 261.

24. Barbara J. Rodabaugh and Melanie Austin, *Sexual Assault: A Guide for Community Action* (New York: Garland STPM Press, 1981), pp. 24–25.

25. Amir, *Patterns in Forcible Rape*.

26. Sedelle Katz and Mary Ann Mazur, *Understanding the Rape Victim: A Synthesis of Research Findings* (New York: John Wiley & Sons, 1979), p. 38.

27. Ibid., p. 39.

28. Russell, *Sexual Exploitation*, p. 88.

29. Stanley L. Brodsky and Susan C. Hobart, "Blame Models and Assailant Research," *Criminal Justice and Behavior* 5 (1978):379–388.

30. Paul H. Gebhard, John H. Gagnon, Wardell B. Pomeroy, and Cornelia V.

Christenson, *Sex Offenders: An Analysis of Types* (New York: Harper & Row, 1965), pp. 198–204.

31. Richard T. Rada, *Clinical Aspects of the Rapist* (New York: Grune and Stratton, 1978), pp. 122–130.

32. A. Nicholas Groth, Ann W. Burgess, and Lynda L. Holmstrom, "Rape: Power, Anger, and Sexuality," *American Journal of Psychiatry* 34 (1977):1239–1243.

33. Diana Scully and Joseph Marolla, "Incarcerated Rapists: Exploring a Sociological Mode," *Final Report for Department of Health and Human Services,* NIMH (Washington, D.C.: Government Printing Office, 1983), p. 63.

34. Ibid., p. 66.

35. Julia R. Schwendinger and Herman Schwendinger, *Rape and Inequality* (Beverly Hills: Sage Publications, 1983), p. 65.

36. Amir, *Patterns in Forcible Rape,* p. 346.

37. Schwendinger and Schwendinger, *Rape and Inequality,* p. 68.

38. Ibid., p. 71.

39. Ibid., p. 72–73.

40. Lorenne M. G. Clark and Debra J. Lewis, *Rape: The Price of Coercive Sexuality* (Toronto: Canadian Women's Educational Press, 1977), pp. 128–131.

41. Schwendinger and Schwendinger, *Rape and Inequality,* p. 78.

42. Clark and Lewis, *Rape: The Price of Coercive Sexuality,* p. 131.

43. Brownmiller, *Against Our Will,* pp. 13–14.

44. "Female Victims: The Crime Goes On," *Science News* 126 (1984):153.

45. Carol C. Nadelson and Malkah T. Notman, "Emotional Repercussions of Rape," *Medical Aspects of Human Sexuality* 11 (1977):16–31.

46. Morton Bard and Dawn Sangrey, *The Crime Victim's Book* (New York: Basic Books, 1979), p. 47.

4

Pornography: Addressing the Exploitation of Women

An issue that has received a great deal of attention over the past two decades is pornography's disputably harmful effects on the women who are exploited and on the female victims of crime and violence. The debate has raged on, and neither side has been willing to change its view (although some individuals have been persuaded to switch sides from time to time). Let us examine the pornography issue as it applies to the exploitation and victimization of women.

THE PROBLEM OF DEFINING PORNOGRAPHY

The task of defining pornography is great, as evidenced by the reluctance of many researchers to do so (the 1970 Commission on Obscenity and Pornography is a good example). Several reasons account for this reluctance. First is the term "pornography" often used interchangeably with "sexual aggression," "obscenity," "explicit sexual materials," and "erotica." Second, the range of materials, shows, and programs one might regard as pornographic is so broad that often the issue comes down to a matter of individual interpretation. Third, the question arises, "Should the definition of pornography be narrowly based, extensive, include regulatory goals or condemnation, or be a reflection of one's experiences?" Another question arises: Whose definition should carry the most weight, and does that mean everyone must follow a view that may not fit his or her perception?"

These definitional dilemmas notwithstanding, it seems necessary that we establish a foundation for the meaning of pornography that is applicable in the content of this chapter. The word *pornography* comes from the Greek *pornographos*, which is derived from *porne*, meaning prostitute or female captive, and *graphein*, meaning to write; hence writings about prostitutes.

Several modern definitions offer useful perspectives of pornography. For instance, the *Random House Dictionary* defines it as "literature, art, or photography of erotic or sexual acts intended to excite prurient feelings." According to philosopher Helen Longino, pornography is "material that explicitly represents or describes degrading and abusive sexual behavior so as to endorse and/or recommend the behavior as described."[1] Several years ago the Williams Committee in Great Britain defined pornography as "a description or depiction of sex involving the dual characteristics of (1) sexual explicitness, and (2) intent to arouse sexually."[2]

Although these definitions are admirable and probably come close to what most people would consider pornography, they are limited either in their failure to differentiate erotica from pornography, as in the Random House definition, or in their lack of establishing clearly if such material should be considered offensive, exploitive, or acceptable. Thus for our purposes pornography shall be defined as any sexually explicit and/or arousing written, photographic, pictorial (including moving pictures), or live depiction of women, men, or children as objects for commercial exploitation, sexual abuse, degradation, repression, or humiliation that is offensive in its sexual content or acts to the population at large and that has a negative affect on certain elements of society.

Granted such a definition might be open to criticism for its broad range and interpretational features, this latitude seems necessary because of the diversity of dynamics associated with pornography, especially as it applies to the subordination and exploitation of women.

Erotica, then, is defined as tasteful, artistic, nonviolent, nondegrading sexually explicit and/or arousing expression involving equals. Another important concept often associated with pornography is obscenity. The problem with this term—which is commonly attributed to something condemnatory, offensive, indecent, disgusting, or lewd to prevailing concepts of decency—is that obscene issues need not be pornographic and vice versa. Therefore it appears that *obscenity* should not be made synonymous with *pornography* in this chapter, except where it applies to judicial or constitutional interpretation.

THE NATURE OF PORNOGRAPHY

Pornography is big business, taking in more than $6 billion a year according to some estimates. By its very nature it is an industry that has fashioned itself through "systematically eroticizing violence against women by producing and marketing images of men humiliating, battering, and murdering women for sexual pleasure. . . . Pornography is about power imbalances using sex as a weapon to subjugate women. In pornography the theme is assailant vs. victim."[3] The messages and myths portrayed through pornography can be seen as follows:

- Pain is glamorous.
- Women are passive, willing collaborators in their own exploitation and victimization.
- Women should not or are incapable of being independent, self-directed people.
- It is appropriate for women's sexuality and behavior to be defined by men.
- Men are entitled to frequent and unconditional access to and use of women's bodies.

Notes Frances Patai, organizer for Women Against Pornography, "Pornography objectifies women by caricaturing and reducing them to a sum of their sexual parts and functions—devoid of sensibilities and intelligence."[4]

How extensive is the pornographic business? This is one question no one can answer definitively because its parts are diverse, elusive, independent, connected, and subjective. Generally speaking, the major contributors to this industry include producers, distributors, actors, models, and others involved in pornography, including movie houses, magazines, live pornographic entertainment, adult bookstores, and organized crime. The cable television industry as well as independent stations and videocassettes bring porn right into the home. If the exploitation of women in and of itself were defined as pornography (it is by many), then network television would be guilty as a contributor as well. It only takes watching daytime or nighttime soap operas to see that women are often portrayed in terms of their bodies, domination by men, and low level of intelligence. The major contributors to the porn business are the customers themselves—pornographic material would not exist otherwise. Hence it is clear that the prevalence of the pornography business has a far-reaching effect in our society.

A TALE OF TWO GOVERNMENT STUDIES

The most significant question regarding pornography centers on the "victimless" aspect of the crime. That is, is pornography a crime that in fact harms no one? Two important government studies sixteen years apart looked into this question and came up with very different answers, each of which received its share of criticism.

Presidential Commission on Obscenity and Pornography

In 1967 the U.S. Congress, concerned about the growing problem of pornography, established a presidential commission to study the "causal

relationship of (obscene and pornographic) materials to anti-social behavior" and to recommend stronger laws to control smut.[5] The conclusions reached by the commission in 1970 ignited a fire that is still
smoldering today. In a surprising turn of events, the chairman and the
majority of the commission expressed the view that "pornography
causes no harm," and actually urged the "decriminalization" of adult
pornography. Twelve of the eighteen commissioners were in agreement
with the finding that

empirical research designed to clarify the question has found no evidence to
date that exposure to explicit sexual materials plays a significant role in the
causation of delinquency or criminal behavior among youth or adults. The Commission cannot conclude that exposure to erotic materials is a factor in the
causation of sex crime or sex delinquency.[6]

The majority reports decision that pornography does not adversely affect
behavior was based on data derived through questionnaires sent to
clinical psychologists and psychiatrists, as well as the indeterminate
results achieved through examining the physical reaction to pornography as viewed by college student volunteers.[7]

The commission's findings came despite the immediate and vigorous
dissent of the commission minority, who did see a connection between
pornography and "harm." Father Morton Hill and Methodist minister
Winfrey Link demonstrated the methodological shortcomings and noted
the lack of cooperation given to those committee members who rejected
the majority's presumptions.[8] Commissioner Charles H. Keating, Jr., an
attorney and founder of Citizens for Decency Through Law, displayed
his objection even more dramatically. In what must have been unprec-
edented under such circumstances, Keating thought it necessary to file
a lawsuit against the commission chairman so that he might gain access
to specific commission documents and gain sufficient time to prepare a
rebuttal to the majority findings.[9]

Criticism of the Presidential Commission on Obscenity and Pornography Report

Before the commission report was even released, the Nixon administration rejected its findings. President Nixon contended that "the conclusions of the Commission's majority were 'morally bankrupt' and
refused to advocate relaxation of the nation's obscenity laws."[10] The
U.S. Senate also rejected the majority report, voting 60–5 against it, in
effect favoring the minority position.[11] On the judicial front the result
was the same. In the 1973 *Miller* v. *California* case in which the Supreme
Court sought to redefine obscenity as its relates to "hard-core pornog-

raphy," the Court spurned the commission's majority findings and supported and minority position that "there is at least an arguable association between exposure to obscene material and crime."[12]

Others were also quick to criticize the commission's "no harm" contention, including some of the commission's own technical researchers and several prominent social scientists.[13] Author William Stanmeyer commented,

How can otherwise intelligent people think that society is unharmed by "entertainments" which glorify the exploitation of women by men, reduce sex to the momentary couplings of barnyard animals in heat, and which operate as how-to-do-it manuals for criminal assault and statutory rape? . . . The Presidential Commission reached naive conclusions largely because it used a suspect methodology to study pornography. . . . The Commission's researchers made so many mistakes that their errors defy easy summary. Suffice it to say that this approach asks the wrong question in the wrong way and thus produces the wrong answer.[14]

It is difficult to conceive how the commission's final report could be so contradictory to what clearly was an unpopular view at the time, and this continues to be the case.

Attorney General's Commission on Pornography

As if to atone for the misjudgments of its predecessor, a new commission on pornography sixteen years later reached almost the opposite conclusion about the effect of pornography on society. In 1985 the Attorney General's Commission on Pornography was established at the request of President Reagan to "determine the nature, extent, and impact on society of pornography in the United States, and to make specific recommendations to the Attorney General concerning more effective ways in which the spread of pornography could be contained, consistent with constitutional guarantees."[15] A year later the majority of Attorney General Edwin Meese's eleven-member commission concluded that there is a causal link between certain kinds of pornography and sexually violent and abusive crimes. The majority added that exposure to even nonviolent sexually explicit material "bears some causal relationship to the level of sexual violence."[16]

The Meese Commission, which criticized "at least some" of the 1970 commission's findings, reported,

When clinical and experimental research has focused particularly on sexually violent material, the conclusions have been nearly unanimous. In both clinical and experimental settings, exposure to sexually violent materials has indicated an increase in the likelihood of aggression. More specifically, the research . . .

shows a causal relationship between exposure to material of this type and aggressive behavior towards women. . . . The assumption that increased aggressive behavior towards women is causally related, for an aggregate population, to increased sexual violence is significantly supported by the clinical evidence, as well as by much of the less scientific evidence.[17]

Commissioners Ellen Levine, editor of *Woman's Day*, and psychologist Judith Becker dissented from the report's main finding, asserting that the examples of pornography presented to the commission were "skewed to the very violent and extremely degrading."[18]

The commission called for a nationwide crackdown on the purveyors of hard-core smut. The 1,960-page report makes ninety-two specific recommendations urging federal, state, and local authorities not to regard pornography as a victimless crime. The key recommendations impel Congress to

- Enact a forfeiture statute to reach the proceeds and instruments of any offense committed under the federal obscenity laws

- Amend the federal obscenity laws to eliminate the necessity of proving transportation to interstate commerce. A statute should be enacted only to require proof that the distribution of the obscene material "affects" interstate commerce

- Enact legislation making it an unfair business practice and an unfair labor practice for any employer to hire individuals to participate in commercial sexual performances

- Amend Title 18 of the United States Code to specifically proscribe obscene cable and satellite television programming

- Enact legislation to prohibit the transmission of obscene material through the telephone or similar common carrier.[19]

Criticism of the Attorney General's Commission on Pornography

As did its predecessor, the Meese Commission's report received its share of criticism. Some critics accused the commission of trying to "remake society in its conservative image and of distorting the scientific evidence."[20] Others questioned the value of the commission, which spent $500,000 in its year-long study. Yet others felt that the overly extensive use of evidence was anecdotal rather than scientific.

American Civil Liberties Union spokesman Barry Lynn scoffed, "This report is little more than prudishness and moralizing masquerading behind social science jargon."[21] Lynn further contended that studies contradictory to those that supported the link between pornography and sexual violence were largely ignored or suppressed.

Equal, and expected, disagreement of the commission's findings existed within the pornography industry. Christie Hefner, president of Playboy Enterprises, denounced the report as "a joke" while claiming that it had hurt freedom of expression and her company's financial health. Said Hefner, "I believe the Meese Commission is not only wrong in its conclusion but at odds with the mandate given by the voters to President Reagan to get the government out of people's lives."[22] She cited a 1973 opinion by Supreme Court Justice William Brennan in which he stated, "I am forced to conclude that the concept of obscenity cannot be defined with sufficient specificity and clarity."[23]

The commission panel did not attempt to expand the definition of obscenity, which the Supreme Court has defined as depending in part on "community standards," although it did implore citizens to take action against the industry. The strength of the commission's report lies not so much in its weighty findings, which are in large part subjective, interpretational, and directional, but in the vast data that clearly justify the conclusion that there is at least some relationship between the pornography industry and the victimization of women.

PORNOGRAPHY AND SEX CRIMES

Much research has surfaced in recent years supporting the contention that there is a significant association between pornography and sex crimes. Neil Malamuth, psychologist and co-editor of *Pornography and Sexual Aggression*, is among a growing number of academic researchers who have linked pornography to sexual assault. Commenting on the message of "disregard for the value of women as human beings" conveyed in pornographic movies and literature, and its affect on societal acceptance of male aggression, Malamuth holds that "in a culture that celebrates rape, the lives of millions of women will be affected."[24] Using multiple regression analysis to study the extent to which mass-circulation sex magazines correlate with the incidence of rape, Larry Baron and Murray Straus found that "rape increases in direct proportion to the readership of sex magazines [by men]."[25] The researchers cautioned, however, that the evidence merely shows "that there is a strong association between sex magazine readership and rape, not that one causes the other."[26]

Sociology professor and feminist Pauline Bart, in a study of rape victims, says, "I didn't start out being against pornography; but if you're a rape researcher, it becomes clear that there is a direct link. Violent pornography is like an advertisement for rape. . . . Men are not born thinking women enjoy rape and torture. . . . They learn from pornography."[27] The feminist view that the proliferation of pornography is linked to rape and other violent crimes against women is also supported through the works of feminist writers such as Laura Lederer[28] and Andrea Dworkin.[29]

The relationship between pornography and sex crimes can also be found in law enforcement data. Michigan authorities recently used a computer to analyze over two decades of sex-related crimes in that state. In a public lecture entitled "Does Pornographic Literature Incite Sexual Assault?" Detective Darrell Pope of the State police cited

numerous cases where the assailants had immersed themselves in pornographic films or pictures and then gone out and committed sex crimes. These crimes included rape, sodomy, and even the bizarre erotic crime of piquerism (piercing with a knife til blood flows, a kind of sexual torture). In some cases the attacker admitted that the urge to rape or torture erotically came over him while reading an obscene picture magazine or attending a movie showing rape and erotic torture.[30]

The Los Angeles Police Department recently found a solid link between the clustering of "adult entertainment" establishments in Hollywood and an increase in rape incidence as well as other serious crimes.[31]

Another association involving a sex crime with pornography that few would dispute is the crime of prostitution. In this instance, unlike those just discussed in which the woman is clearly a victim, prostitutes have the distinction of being both victims and offenders. (See chapter 9 for a detailed analysis of this subject.) A 1976 Task Force on Organized Crime found that prostitution is often linked to pornography and substance abuse. The young actors in pornographic films often perform for drugs rather than for money, then are forced into prostitution.[32]

The LAPD noted the increase in prostitution in the Hollywood adult entertainment district as compared to elsewhere in the city during the period 1969 through 1975. Arrests for prostitution in Hollywood rose at a rate 15 times above the city average. While prostitution arrests in Los Angeles increased 24.5 percent, the increase in Hollywood was a remarkable 372.3 percent. The pandering arrest rate increase of 475.0 percent in Hollywood was three and one half times greater than the 133.3 percent citywide increase.[33]

The pornography-prostitution connection can also be seen in the strong relationship between organized crime and pornography. The underworld uses its vast profits derived from pornography to gain a greater hold on the market, enforce its manner of doing business, and bring more participants into the world of pornography. Its profits also go into other illicit activities, including prostitution and narcotics trafficking.[34]

Although the correlation between pornography and sex crimes is evident, a cause and effect relationship has not been proven conclusively. Nor, however, can such an assumption be dismissed altogether, at least in some instances. What can be stated confidently is that pornography does play a significant role in a variety of sex crimes.

PORNOGRAPHY AND THE BATTERED WOMAN

The association between battered women and pornography has only recently been given the attention it deserves. As with sex crimes, the link between porn and women-battering can be seen in the violence perpetrated against women in pornography, which mirrors real-life battering and is influential to batterers. Lederer argues that "pornography is the ideology of a culture which promotes and condones rape, woman-battering, and other crimes against women."[35] The following examples vividly illustrate the connection between the ideology of pornography and the acceptance of women-battering:

- In the move *Dressed to Kill* women are portrayed as sexual objects in which they are violated through rape, torture and murder. The critics offered high praise of the film, using such terms as "witty," "funny," "erotic," "irresistible."
- In the movie *Swept Away*, an independent woman is systematically verbally and physically violated until she is reduced to a passive sexual subordinate who yearns for more humiliation while loving her perpetrator.
- The cover of an album accentuating the crotch of a woman with the words, "Jump on it!"
- A well-known adult magazine cover displaying a nude woman being put into a meat grinder and becoming hamburger.
- A shoe advertisement in which a partially nude woman is being attacked by a gun-wielding man.[36]

Contends Frances Patai, co-editor of *Rape and Child Abuse,*

Woman battering objectifies women by reducing them to objects of possession. Both pornography and woman battering legitimize the pain inflicted on the woman by objectifying the woman. In addition, many women are raped and verbally assaulted while being battered. . . . Objectifying the sexual anatomy of women renders them inferior and nonhuman, thus providing the psychological foundation for committing violence against them.[37]

Although it has not been proven, violent pornography presented as "chic," "fun," or "trendy" is suspected by many to be highly influential in the abuse of women in real life. A London study of 100 victims of wife battering revealed that 15 percent of the wives reported that their husbands "seemed to experience sexual arousal from the violence—since the demand for sexual intercourse immediately followed the assault."[38]

It would be oversimplifying to suggest that men merely imitate pornographic scenarios. The reasons for wanting to act out porno scripts or writings are usually far more complicated. What is clear is that "pornography (especially as it is legitimized in mainstream TV shows, ads, movies, fashion layouts, etc.) socializes some men into thinking that the maltreatment of women is erotic, sexually desirable, desired by women, and a necessary proof of virility."[39]

PORNOGRAPHY AND EXPLOITATION OF WOMEN

Perhaps the worst form of victimization associated with pornography is the exploitation of the women in the industry. Whether it is on the movie screen, television, magazine pages, in adult nightclubs, or elsewhere, undeniably women are being exploited in the worst way by the pornography industry. Slasher movies are a good example. Not only are young women overrepresented in terms of violent murders, but it is almost routine to throw in gratuitous sex and nude or partially nude scenes using these women, as if no movie would be complete without seeking to satisfy the perceived male fantasy of seeing women scantily clad or naked, desirous of men, and violated in some way. Other examples of exploitation of women are just as conspicuous.

In assessing the exploitation of women, Stanmeyer argues effectively,

Pornography feeds twisted male fantasies about women. Invariably the pornographic film or photo shows a beautiful woman vulnerable and available to be used, roughly, by the male with whom the viewer identifies. . . . The woman is made to appear no more than a function or an organ. The camera's focus and interest is solely genital: it is irrelevant who this person is; any woman would do, as long as her physical attributes are exaggerated. She has no value in herself; her only value and purpose is for the male. She is quite simply an object. She is a thing. This is true even if the pornography is not explicitly violent. Pornography that is not overtly violent is still implicitly violent because it objectifies and degrades women.[40]

The message pornography sends is apparent; what is not apparent is why women allow themselves to be exploited and manipulated. The argument can be raised and supported that at least some of these women may have been the product of child abuse, sexual abuse, substance abuse, or some other form of degradation or violation that influenced their character. However, it can also be argued that many women who participate in pornography are motivated by ambition for money or fame. In the present climate of sexual liberation, these women see their activity as an assertion of equality and independence. This has put the feminist movement into a quandary. On the one hand, feminists argue for freedom from restraint. On the other hand, feminists such as Susan

Brownmiller denounce the sexual degradation and humiliation of women that is the essence of pornography.[41]

Unfortunately, at least as applied to pornography, it may not be possible for women to have it both ways. Because men control the pornography industry and have shown little willingness to change what brought them success, women seem destined to continue to be portrayed in an offensive, subordinated light. And with more women today displaying the sexual liberation and promiscuity that men dominated for so many years, the job of pornography producers has become infinitely easier.[42]

Yet the issue of women exploited by pornography goes beyond the willing victims and the feminist movement.

Pornography hurts all women by portraying them only as sexual objects. And it hurts men and boys as well, especially those who are exposed to pornography at an early age, by giving them a limited, leering view of women. In sum, pornography damages everyone in our society.[43]

Equally at stake are the children who are exploited, degraded, and abused in child porn. Many of them move into adult porn; many others suffer the consequences of the social influence of pornography: child abuse, prostitution, and violent crime. The pornography industry thrives on exploiting those who are the most exploitable: women and children. The negative images pornography transmits to men has been shown to influence how men view women and children in the real world. It may well be that the only way to halt this cycle is for exploited women to say no.

The dissemination of pornography in our culture has in some way influenced all our lives. Much of this influence is reflected in the way we regard others, ourselves, society. Still believed by many to be a victimless crime, pornography has swallowed more victims than most of us could imagine. Women and children especially have been brutalized by an industry that reduces them to objects to be used, tortured, raped, degraded, subjugated—a misguided message that has been clearly associated with sexual crimes, woman battering, child abuse, and other social ills of our society. Yet because we are not in accord about the effects of pornography, it continues to exist. Until we face the fact that pornography causes more bad than good, it will not be eliminated, and those most vulnerable among us will have to pay the price.

NOTES

1. Helen E. Longino, "Pornography, Oppression, and Freedom: A Closer Look," in Laura Lederer, ed., *Take Back the Night: Women on Pornography* (New York: William Morrow, 1980), p. 44.

2. U.S. Department of Justice, *Attorney General's Commission on Pornography: Final Report*, Vol. 1 (Washington, D.C.: Government Printing Office, 1986), pp. 227–228.

3. Frances Patai, Pornography and Woman Battering: Dynamic Similarities," in Maria Roy, ed., *The Abusive Partner: An Analysis of Domestic Battering* (New York: Van Nostrand Reinhold, 1982), pp. 91–92.

4. Ibid., p. 93.

5. Steven Penrod and Daniel Linz, "Using Psychological Research on Violent Pornography to Inform Legal Change," in Neil M. Malamuth and Edward Donnerstein, *Pornography and Sexual Aggression* (New York: Academic Press, 1984), p. 259; Commission on Obscenity and Pornography, *Report of the Presidential Commission on Obscenity and Pornography* (Washington, D.C.: Government Printing Office, 1971).

6. Commission on Obscenity and Pornography, *Technical Report of the Commission on Obscenity and Pornography: Legal Analysis*, Vol. 2 (Washington, D.C.: Government Printing Office, 1971), p. 223.

7. William A. Stanmeyer, *The Seduction of Society* (Ann Arbor, Mich.: Servant Books, 1984), pp. 27–28.

8. Ibid., pp. 105–106.

9. Ibid., p. 106.

10. Penrod and Linz, "Using Psychological Research on Violent Pornography," p. 260.

11. Stanmeyer, *The Seduction of Society*, p. 105.

12. Penrod and Linz, "Using Psychological Research on Violent Pornography," p. 260; *Miller* v. *State of California*, 413 U.S. 15 (1973).

13. Stanmeyer, *The Seduction of Society*, p. 28; Herbert L. Packer, "The Pornography Caper," *Commentary* 51, no. 2 (1971); James Q. Wilson, "Violence, Pornography and Social Science," *The Public Interest* 22 (1971).

14. Stanmeyer, *The Seduction of Society*, p. 105.

15. *Attorney General's Commission on Pornography*, p. 215.

16. Ibid., p. 326; Thomas Ferraro, "Christie Hefner Blasts Porn Study, Says Playboy Hurt," *Sacramento Bee* (August 21, 1986), p. A2.

17. *Attorney General's Commission on Pornography*, pp. 324–325.

18. J. M. Johnson, "U.S. Panel Ties Smut to Violence," *Sacramento Bee* (July 10, 1986), p. A1.

19. *Attorney General's Commission on Pornography*, pp. 465–481, 483–490.

20. Johnson, "U.S. Panel Ties Smut to Violence."

21. Ibid.

22. Ferraro, "Christie Hefner Blasts Porn Study."

23. Ibid.

24. Hillary Johnson, "Violence against Women—Is Porn to Blame?" *Vogue* 175 (September 1985):678.

25. Larry Baron and Murray A. Straus, "Sexual Stratification, Pornography, and Rape in the United States," in Neil M. Malamuth and Edward Donnerstein, eds., *Pornography and Sexual Aggression* (Orlando, Fla.: Academic Press, 1984), p. 206.

26. Ibid.

27. Johnson, "Violence against Women."

28. Laura Lederer, ed., *Take Back the Night: Women on Pornography* (New York: William Morrow, 1980).

29. Andrea Dworkin, "Pornography's Part in Sexual Violence," *Los Angeles Times* (May 26, 1981).

30. Stanmeyer, *The Seduction of Society*, pp. 29–30.

31. Ibid., p. 49.

32. Ibid., p. 42.

33. Ibid., p. 49.

34. Ibid., p. 45.

35. Lederer, *Take Back the Night*, pp. 19–20.

36. Patai, "Pornography and Woman Battering." p. 93.

37. Ibid., pp. 93–94.

38. Kathleen Barry, *Female Sexual Slavery* (Englewood Cliffs, N.J.: Prentice-Hall, 1979), p. 145.

39. Patai, "Pornography and Woman Battering," p. 96.

40. Stanmeyer, *The Seduction of Society*, pp. 67–68.

41. Ibid., p. 77.

42. See also Johnson, "Violence Against Women"; Stanmeyer, *The Seduction of Society*; Martha Kirkpatrick, ed., *Women's Sexual Experiences* (New York: Plenum Press, 1982); Maurice Yaffe and Edward C. Nelson, *The Influence of Pornography on Behavior* (London: Academic Press, 1982).

43. Linda T. Sanford and Mary E. Donovan, "What Women Should Know about Pornography," *Family Circle* (February 1981):12

5

Current Issues in Women's Victimization

In our study of the criminally violated woman, four areas of victimization deserve special consideration: the female incest survivor, the battered parent, military spouse abuse, and sexual harassment.

THE FEMALE INCEST SURVIVOR

Although incest is generally associated with childhood sexual abuse (see Volume 1 of this series, *Children and Criminality*), women who were once victims continue to suffer from the violation often long after its occurrence. Incest is defined both legally and nonlegally; for our purposes we will refer to incest as "incestual violation" and define it as any exhibitionism; fondling; oral, genital, or anal contact; intercourse; or other actual or attempted exploitive sexual contact between an adult family member (biological or nonbiological) and an adolescent (age 17 and under). It does not matter whether the adolescent consented, for a child is incapable of fully understanding the implications of sexuality and thus can not be held responsible for interaction with an adult who presumably knows it is wrong.

The Nature of Incest

Most incest victims are girls. H. Stoenner found the ratio of reported incest to be ten girls to one.[1] According to the American Humane Association, 85 percent of incest victims are females.[2] The active aggressor is usually a male, often the father or father figure. Current research suggests that in 90 to 97 percent of the incest cases the perpetrator is male. Nearly 80 percent of all incest today occurs between fathers and daughters.

No one can be certain of the prevalence of incest because it is perhaps the most closely guarded family secret, as evidenced by the low reporting rate.[3] Remarked one researcher, "The family as a whole supports actively or passively their own incestuous equilibrium."[4] Sociologist David Finkelhor contends that the vast majority of children never tell anyone of their incestuous violation. He estimates that 75 to 90 percent of the incidents are never discovered.[5]

Early studies suggested that the incidence of incest in the United States was relatively low. S. Kirson Weinberg's study, originally published in 1955, estimated that only one case of incest per million occurred annually.[6] Weinberg's work became the statistical basis for incest behavior until the early 1970s. Recent data and estimates indicate that the incidence of incest in both the past and the present may be considerably higher. G. Pirooz Sholevar, a psychiatrist, estimated that between 11 and 33 million Americans are involved in incestuous relationships.[7] A report from the Family Violence Research Program at the University of New Hampshire postulated that 5 to 15 percent of all girls under the age of 17 in this country are victims of familial sexual abuse.[8] This compares with social worker Mary Donaldson's estimate that 5 to 28 percent of all girls in the United States are incest victims, the latter estimate including other forms of sexual abuse.[9] Sociologist Diana Russell's survey revealed that 16 percent of her female respondents had been sexually assaulted by a family member before reaching the age of 18.[10]

Despite such high figures, they remain speculative at best as most victimized females remain close-mouthed about their experiences well into adulthood. Although the women's movement and the increase in women's support groups is creating an atmosphere in which women can state their incestuous violations aloud, "women's socialization and the lack of understanding of (or perhaps refusal to give credence to) the long-term effects of incestuous assaults on women's lives are powerful silencers in themselves."[11] Further reinforcing silence is self-doubt and the internalization of confusion.

Initially the frequently violated female child (particularly when very young) is unable to grasp what is happening to her. Factors such as trust, love, and coercion are usually exploited to gain her cooperation. By the time she is old enough either to understand or at last to perceive that something is wrong, the feelings of guilt, shame, self-blame, humiliation, and fear may be firmly rooted. Even should she succeed in stopping the violations of her body and mind, she is left with scars as permanent reminders of her humiliation and degradation.

The Future For Incest Victims

What are the long-term effects of incestuous violations during childhood? This issue has been debated for some time. Some believe the effects are minimal, but many (particularly victims) hold an entirely different view. "Researchers have found that incestuously assaulted women report feeling 'frightened' or 'upset' years later and state that the experience was 'unpleasant' or 'extremely unpleasant,' in effect overwhelmingly 'negative.' "[12] Hence the most devastating effect of incest could well be merely knowing that it happened, reliving it, and realizing it can never be erased from one's mind.

Elizabeth Stanko, author of *Intimate Intrusions*, notes

Part of these effects is the result of years of smothering terrifying experiences of the most intimate invasion. Perhaps the most insidious, the deepest violation, is the intrusion into a female child's sexual being. As a result of incestuous experiences, research indicates some women develop various forms of "sexual dysfunction," some may fall prey to other forms of sexual or physical violation, still others, with the help and support of friends and lovers, come to terms with the assault.[13]

Some women, as a result of their victimization, "may learn what it means to be a sexual object, some may block out their sexuality altogether, avoiding sexuality, yet still others struggle with both extremes."[14] Additionally, a strong correlation has been found between childhood incest and adult prostitution, pornography, substance abuse, mental problems, and sexual or physical abuse by a former incest victim of her children.[15]

THE BATTERED PARENT

What has gained increased recognition in recent years as a serious familial and social problem is the maltreatment of parents by their children. Often referred to as the "battered parent syndrome," Richard Gelles states, "This is the next layer of family violence to be exposed. And if we were talking about some communicable disease, we'd be talking in terms of an epidemic."[16] Researchers have estimated that 2.5 million parents are struck by their children every year in this country; of these, approximately 900,000 are the victims of severe violence, including the use of weapons.[17]

Often, the recipient of this child-directed violence is the mother or grandmother. (This phenomenon is "granny bashing.") The perpetrators range from adolescent children or grandchildren to adult children. Because of the reverse nature of parent battering, most victims keep quiet through it, making this an even more silent form of family violence than child abuse. The typical perpetrator-victim scenario is described below:

• Most frequently teenage sons are the batterers.
• Mothers are most often the victims.

- Shame, guilt, and embarrassment characterize the victim. To acknowledge the victimization is to admit failure.
- To keep the family intact, victims and perpetrators maintain secrecy.

Carol Warren, who studied fifteen adolescents in a psychiatric hospital, postulates three primary reasons for children's violence against parents: (1) violence in response to the victim's alcohol use, (2) violence in the frustration-theory model (when one's goals are blocked), and (3) violence as a resource (used as status or money might be).[18]

Other researchers view parent abusers as the recipients of poor models of social behavior and highly stressful social situations, causing them to strike out as they have been directed or in the only way they can. The relationship between parental abuse and child abuse has been noted by many. A study by Suzanne Steinmetz and associates indicated that "parents who are not violent toward their children stand only a one in 400 chance of being on the receiving end. But if a parent is violent toward the child, the probability of attack goes up to 200 out of 400."[19]

Other factors believed to play a role in parent battering are disciplinary practices (or lack thereof), role reversal, economic restraints, stress, parent power struggles, and mental problems. Child psychiatrist Rudolf Dreikurs argues that given supporting parenting and encouragement, children will not become involved in violent behavior directed against either parents or other family members.[20]

MILITARY SPOUSE ABUSE

Very little research has been conducted on spouse abuse in the armed forces, even though the nature of military life appears to place women at higher risk for abuse. In general, the incidence and causes of spouse abuse are similar whether in a civilian or a military setting (see chapter 2). However, some recent studies suggest that certain variations of the dynamics of domestic violence are unique to the military. In *Battered Wives*, Del Martin found a correlation between military experience and marital violence.[21] Military social worker Nancy Raiha contends, "Whatever the relationship between rates of abuse in military and civilian communities, it is true that certain factors inherent in military life may well tend to create a climate conducive to domestic violence."[22]

It is not known how much spouse abuse occurs in the military community; however, awareness of the problem has increased to the extent that Armed Forces Commander Robert McCullah recently stated, "family stresses among military personnel can compromise our nation's defense posture."[23] According to the report, *Wife Abuse in the Armed Forces*, there are approximately 2,000,000 active duty personnel in the armed services, with more than 1,100,000 spouses and 1,600,000 children.[24]

Thus the majority of the military community is composed of women and children, a fact that the military establishment must address as a serious factor in military life.

Sociologist Murray Straus asserts that domestic violence occurs most often in younger families, the rate of violence for husbands and wives 30 years of age or under is more than double that of the 31–50 age group. Given the fact that over 55 percent of active military personnel are age 30 or younger, compared to 25 percent of civilian adult males, Straus postulated that "this factor alone makes the military a high risk population for wife abuse."[25]

Other factors believed to make wives of military men particularly susceptible to abuse at one time or another include financial difficulties, job stresses, frequent moves, intercultural marriages, family separation, isolation from peer and family support groups, and strong pressure on the spouse not to put her husband's service career in jeopardy. Although no single factor can be considered causal, any of the factors may be the impetus to trigger wife beating or other domestic violence in the military family.

Counseling, concrete services, drug and alcohol treatment, and child advocacy, among other programs, are now available in the military community to help families deal with stresses and other problems that disrupt the family unit. However, as in civilian life, more effective approaches are needed to combat or prevent spouse and child maltreatment within the military.

SEXUAL HARASSMENT

An important facet of the victimization of women that has been given far too little exposure over the years is the occupational sexual harassment of women. Yet this form of victimization can be just as detrimental to the woman's growth, health, and well-being as sexual assault or domestic abuse. What exactly is sexual harassment? Some consider it harmless workplace fun and games. Others take a far more serious view of what they believe to be another form of sexual intrusion often disguised as normative behavior between men and women. In a broad sense sexual harassment can be defined as various and/or deliberate

forms of unwanted sexual attention that occurs in working situations: visual (leering) or verbal (sexual teasing, jokes, comments or questions) behavior; unwanted touching or pinching; unwanted pressure for sexual favors with implied threats of retaliation for non-cooperation.[26]

The particular form of sexual harassment women face is often not as significant as its effects. Says author Elizabeth Stanko,

Women are as likely to be distressed by persistent "low-level" harassment—leering, for instance—as they are by more blatant touching. . . . Harassed women report becoming nervous and irritable; they feel humiliated; they feel they cannot control the encounters with the harassers(s) and thus feel threatened and helpless. Many develop techniques to protect themselves, through for example, avoidance. . . . These women describe the daily barrage of sexual interplay in the office as psychological rape. The day in and out exposure to what many assume to be "harmless" behavior produces reactions similar to those of sexually assaulted women. In fact, rape crisis centers receive calls from sexually harassed women who report having similar feelings as raped women.[27]

Although forms of harassment may vary greatly, its pattern and effects represent a serious violation to the personal integrity of its victims. Such women are no longer regarded as employees or colleagues but sexual objects.

The Increase in Awareness

Sexual harassment has proved to be a common condition in the workplace for American women (as well as women in countries such as England). Yet only in the last decade has the subject gained serious attention as a problem. A 1975 survey by the Working Women United Institute,[28] followed by a survey conducted in 1976 by *Redbook*[29] magazine, opened the door to greater awareness and understanding of sexual harassment while documenting its prevalence in the workplace. These studies played an important role in dispelling the myths that sexual harassment is fun, that it affects only women in low-status jobs, that it is easy for women to handle, and that it is a trivial issue.

The most comprehensive U.S. survey to date on sexual harassment was conducted in 1981 by the U.S. Merit Systems Protection Board (MSPB).[30] Querying 23,000 federal employees, the MSPB found that 42 percent of all female employees and 15 percent of all male employees reported sexual harassment at work within the twenty-four-month period prior to the survey.[31] According to the MSPB,

every form except actual or attempted rape or sexual assault was experienced by a sizeable percentage of both men and women. The more ambiguous forms of sexual harassment—"sexual comments" and "suggestive looks"—were reported most often. These forms were more likely to be repeated.

However, with the exception of actual or attempted rape or assault, most victims reported experiencing all forms of sexual harassment repeatedly. In addition, many reported experiencing more than one form of sexual harassment. We also found that the incidents of sexual harassment were not just passing events—most lasted more than a week, and many lasted more than six months. Thus, not only did the sexual harassment occur repeatedly, it was of relatively long duration as well.[32]

The following conclusions of sexually harassed women emerged from the survey:

- Victims varied in age, ethnicity, marital status, and occupation.
- Sixty-seven percent of the women aged 16 to 19 reported being harassed compared to 33 percent of those between ages 45 and 54.
- Fifty-three percent of the single women reported experiencing harassment compared to 37 percent of the married women.
- More highly educated women reported more harassment, possibly indicative of their occupying nontraditional jobs or perceiving a broader extent of male behavior to be harassment.

Although no comparable research in the private sector has been conducted, Patricia Mathis of the Office of Merit Systems Review and Studies concluded that the MSPB's finding "that people of all ages, salary levels, education backgrounds, and hometowns are potential victims—leads us to the observation that sexual harassment cannot be uniquely associated with Federal employment."[33]

Fighting Sexual Harassment

Aside from seeking to settle harassment disputes within the work setting, three other options available to harassed women (or men) are the unemployment insurance system (seeking benefits through establishing a good cause for quitting work),[34] the courts (claiming sex discrimination and denial of equal employment conditions via the provisions of the 1964 Civil Rights Act),[35] or simply taking the law into their own hands (an option many women may feel is their last alternative). None of these measures has worked very well. The fact that women have found it difficult to receive a favorable response to harassment complaints is a reflection of the lack of progress we have made in terms of equality and respect.

The issues reviewed in this chapter were meant to shed some light on facets of women's victimization that often go unrecognized or, taken out of context, are minimized as significant parts of the victimized woman in today's society. Only through drawing attention to problems such as incest, battered parents, spouse abuse in the military, and sexual harassment in the workplace can we hope to understand and effectively combat them.

NOTES

1. H. Stoenner, *Child Sexual Abuse Seen Growing in the United States* (Denver: American Humane Association, 1972).

2. Elizabeth Stark, "The Unspeakable Family Secret," *Psychology Today* 18 (May 1984):42–46.

3. Ronald B. Flowers, *Children and Criminality: The Child as Victim and Perpetrator* (Westport, Conn.: Greenwood Press, 1986), pp. 7–8.

4. Marshall D. Schechter and Leo Roberge, "Sexual Exploitation," in Ray E. Helfer and C. Henry Kempe, eds., *Child Abuse and Neglect: The Family and the Community* (Cambridge, Mass.: Ballinger Publishing Co., 1976), p. 129.

5. Jean Renvoize, *Incest: A Family Pattern* (London: Routledge & Kegan Paul, 1982), p. 51.

6. S. Kirson Weinberg, *Incest Behavior* (Secaucus, N.J.: Citadel Press, 1976), p. 34.

7. Carol Lynn Mithers, "Incest: The Crime That's All in the Family," *Mademoiselle* 96 (June 1984):127.

8. Kathy McCoy, "Incest: The Most Painful Family Problem," *Seventeen* 43 (June 1984):18.

9. Anita Manning, "Victims Must Face the Hurt," *USA Today* (January 10, 1984), p. 5D.

10. Diana E. H. Russell, *Sexual Exploitation: Rape, Child Sexual Abuse, and Workplace Harassment* (Beverly Hills: Sage Publications, 1984), p. 183.

11. Elizabeth A. Stanko, *Intimate Intrusions: Women's Experience on Male Violence* (London: Routledge and Kegan Paul, 1985), p. 15.

12. Ibid., pp. 25–26.

13. Ibid., p. 30.

14. Ibid., p. 31.

15. Flowers, *Children and Criminality*; McCoy, *Incest*; Joel Greenberg, "Incest out of Hiding," *Science News* 117, no. 14 (1980):218–220.

16. Richard Gelles, "Parental Abuse," *USA Today* (March 18, 1983), p. 1D.

17. Karen S. Peterson, "The Nightmare of a Battered Parent," *USA Today* (March 18, 1983), p. A6.

18. Carol A. Warren, "Parent Batterers: Adolescent Violence and the Family," *Pacific Sociological Association* (April 1978):3–5.

19. Cliff Yudell, "I'm Afraid of My Own Children," *Reader's Digest* (August 1983), p. 79.

20. Rudolf Dreikurs and Vicki Saltz, *Children: The Challenge* (New York: Hawthorne Books, 1964), p. 201.

21. Del Martin, *Battered Wives* (San Francisco: Glide Publications, 1976).

22. Nancy K. Raiha, "Spouse Abuse in the Military Community: Factors Influencing Incidence and Treatment," in Maria Roy, ed., *The Abusive Partner: An Analysis of Domestic Battering* (New York: Van Nostrand Reinhold, 1982), p. 104.

23. Robert D. McCullah, "Effects of Family Dysfunction on Military Operations: Mental Health Needs," in Edna J. Hunter and Thomas C. Shaylor, eds., *The Military Family and the Military Organization* (Washington, D.C.: The Adjutant General Center, 1978), p. 33.

24. Lois A. West, William M. Turner, and Ellen Dunwoody, *Wife Abuse in the Armed Forces* (Washington, D.C.: Center for Women Policy Studies, 1981), p. 5.

25. West et al., *Wife Abuse in the Armed Forces*, p. 6; Murray A. Straus, Richard J. Gelles, and Suzanne K. Steinmetz, *Behind Closed Doors: Violence in the American Family* (New York: Anchor Press, 1980), pp. 141, 146, 148.

26. Stanko, *Intimate Intrusions*, p. 60.

27. Ibid., pp. 60–61.

28. Laura J. Evans, "Sexual Harassment: Women's Hidden Occupational Hazard," in Jane Roberts Chapman and Margaret Gates, eds., *The Victimization of Women* (Beverly Hills: Sage Publications, 1978), pp. 203–222.

29. "Questionnaire: How Do You Handle Sex on the Job?" *Redbook* (January 1976).

30. U.S. Merit Systems Protection Board, *Sexual Harassment in the Federal Workplace: Is It a Problem?*, Office of Merit Systems Review and Studies (Washington, D.C.: Government Printing Office, 1981).

31. Ibid., p. 3.

32. Ibid., p. 5.

33. Ibid., p. v.

34. Evans, "Sexual Harassment," pp. 211–213.

35. See Title VII of the 1964 Civil Rights Act.

II

THE CRIMINALITY OF WOMEN

6

Exploring Women's Criminality

The woman's role in criminality does not end with her victimization but extends into her becoming the perpetrator of crime. In this section we will examine the female offender as both a criminal and a reflection of her victimization. Our first step is to gain a perspective on the incidence, trends, and nature of female crime.

THE MEASUREMENT OF FEMALE CRIMINALITY

Since 1930, the predominant source of data for assessing and estimating crime committed by women has been the Federal Bureau of Investigation's *Uniform Crime Reports (UCR)*. This annual tabulates crimes reported to the police, as well as the number of people arrested and for what crimes, and their age, sex, racial background, and trends.

Offenses are separated into two categories: Type I and Type II. Type I, referred to as the Crime Index offenses, comprises violent crimes (murder and nonnegligent manslaughter, forcible rape, robbery, aggravated assault) and property crimes (burglary, larceny, motor vehicle theft, arson). Type II, also referred to as non-Index offenses, includes forgery and counterfeiting, embezzlement, prostitution and commercialized vice, sex offenses, and drug violations.

Supporting official statistics in the measurement of crime are self-report studies. These play a crucial role in telling us about crime, but they contain built-in limitations, which we will examine in detail later. (See also victimization surveys in chapter 1.)

THE MAGNITUDE AND NATURE OF FEMALE CRIME

The most recent official arrest statistics in 1985 distributed by sex show that females account for only 17.4 percent of the total arrests (table 6.1).

For Crime Index offenses, females make up 21.4 percent of all arrests but show a large percentage differential between violent and property crime arrests (10.9 to 24.0), indicating that female involvement in serious crime is largely concentrated in property offenses. Female arrestees are also considerably underrepresented in non-Index offenses, with the exception of prostitution and runaways, where they predictably outnumber male arrestees. The crime in which the two sexes are closest in arrests is fraud, with females accounting for nearly 43 percent of the total.

Although these data are useful in assessing how females compare to males in overall arrests, because the figures include all male and female arrestees regardless of age, they are not as meaningful for our purposes. A better analysis of arrest patterns of women (defined as females age 18 and over) can be obtained from tables 6.2 and 6.3.

Table 6.2 provides an age distribution for serious crime arrests of women in 1985. Females age 18 and over account for 71.6 percent of the female arrests for Crime Index offenses (and 78 percent of female arrests for all offenses). The figures demonstrate that the overwhelming majority of women arrested fall into the 18–39 age category. However, the patterns within specified age groups appear to be inconsistent. For instance, women ages 18 to 21 make up the highest percentage of all Crime Index offense arrests. But when Type I crimes are broken down, the 25–29 and 30–39 age groups had higher rates of arrest for violent crimes. Meanwhile, women aged 22 to 24 had a lower percentage of arrests for both violent and property crime than any other age categories. Although these patterns cannot be considered conclusive in women's criminality, particularly with the variable age distribution present and general statistical problems, they nevertheless provide a provocative point for additional study.

A further analysis of the nature of the criminality of women is presented in table 6.3, which lists the ten most frequent and least frequent arrests of women by offense in 1985. This interesting study clearly indicates that the majority of women who participate in crimes are basically nonviolent, or minor crime offenders. In the "most arrests" category only larceny-theft is a Crime Index offense, although it ranks as the second most frequently committed crime in which women are arrested. The highest incidence of arrest is for "all other offenses," or those crimes that are violations of state and local laws and ordinances. Of the remaining most frequent arrests, the bulk fall under so-called victimless crimes such as prostitution, drug abuse, driving while under the influence, drukenness, liquor law violations, and disorderly conduct.

Not surprisingly, forcible rape ranks as the crime in which females were arrested least often in 1985. A scan of the list shows that some of the most serious crimes such as murder, arson, and motor vehicle theft, along with rape, represent the lowest incidence of arrests of women.

Table 6.1
Total Arrests, Distribution by Sex, 1985
(11,249 agencies; 1985 estimated population 203,035,000)

Offense Charged	Total Arrests	Percent Male	Percent Female
TOTAL.............................	10,289,609	82.6	17.4
Murder and nonnegligent manslaughter......	15,777	87.6	12.4
Forcible rape.............................	31,934	98.9	1.1
Robbery...................................	120,501	92.4	7.6
Aggravated assault........................	263,120	86.5	13.5
Burglary..................................	381,875	92.6	7.4
Larceny-theft.............................	1,179,066	69.0	31.0
Motor vehicle theft.......................	115,621	90.7	9.3
Arson.....................................	16,777	86.9	13.1
Violent crime[a]	431,332	89.1	10.9
Property crime[b].........................	1,693,339	76.0	24.0
Crime Index total[c]......................	2,124,671	78.6	21.4
Other assaults............................	550,104	84.6	15.4
Forgery and counterfeiting................	75,281	66.8	33.2
Fraud.....................................	286,941	57.4	42.6
Embezzlement..............................	9,799	64.4	35.6
Stolen property; buying, receiving, possessing.............................	110,415	88.2	11.8
Vandalism.................................	224,046	90.0	10.0
Weapons; carrying, possessing, etc........	157,304	92.4	7.6
Prostitution and commercialized vice......	101,167	30.5	69.5
Sex offenses (except forcible rape and prostitution...........................	86,861	92.6	7.4
Drug abuse violations.....................	702,882	86.2	13.8
Gambling..................................	28,034	85.4	14.6
Offenses against family and children......	48,699	87.3	12.7
Driving under the influence...............	1,503,319	88.4	11.6
Liquor laws...............................	467,149	83.6	16.4
Drunkenness...............................	834,652	91.1	8.9
Disorderly conduct........................	583,532	81.3	18.7
Vagrancy..................................	29,825	88.3	11.7
All other offenses (except traffic).......	2,142,121	84.4	15.6
Suspicion.................................	11,229	85.1	14.9
Curfew and loitering law violations.......	71,608	75.3	24.7
Runaways..................................	139,970	42.7	57.3

[a]Violent crimes are offenses of murder, forcible rape, robbery, and aggravated assault.

[b]Property crimes are offenses of burglary, larceny-theft, motor vehicle theft, and arson.

[c]Includes arson.

Source: U.S. Federal Bureau of Investigation, Crime in the United States: Uniform Crime Reports, 1985 (Washington, D.C.: Government Printing Office, 1986), p. 181.

Table 6.2
Crime Index Arrests of Females, Percent Distribution by Age, 1985

OFFENSE CHARGED	Total All Ages[c]	Ages 18 & Over	18–21	22–24	25–29	30–39	40–49	50 & Over
Violent crime[a]	100.0	83.2	16.6	14.1	19.9	21.3	7.3	4.0
Property crime[b]	100.0	70.2	17.2	10.4	14.2	15.9	6.2	6.5
Crime Index total	100.0	71.6	17.2	10.8	14.8	16.4	6.3	6.1

[a]Violent crimes are offenses of murder, forcible rape, robbery, and aggravated assault.

[b]Property crimes are offenses of burglary, larceny-theft, motor vehicle theft, and arson.

[c]Because of rounding, percentages may not add up to total.

Source: Adapted from U.S. Federal Bureau of Investigation, Crime in the United States: Uniform Crime Reports, 1985 (Washington, D.C.: Government Printing Office, 1986), pp. 178-179.

Interestingly, crimes such as robbery, aggravated assault, and burglary attained neither ranking, suggesting that they fall somewhere in the middle in assessing patterns of women's criminality.

Race and Social Class

Official data do not record race and social class of female criminals, an unfortunate omission when one considers the biases and assumptions so pervasive in official interpretation of criminality. Equally, national statistics do not provide the racial breakdown of women offenders.

However, individual studies have managed to shed some light on these important variables of female crime. Research by Marvin Wolfgang and Charles Winick and Paul Kinsie indicates that the criminality of black women is close to that of black men than white female crime is to white male crime.[1] Another study contended that "the black female's criminality exceeds that of the white female by a much greater margin than black males over white males."[2] *The National Study of Women's Correctional Programs* in fourteen states recently found that although black women made up 10 percent of the adult female population in those states, they accounted for half of those incarcerated.[3]

Victimization studies also support the higher crime rate of black

Table 6.3
Arrest Patterns for Women, 1985

Rank	Most Arrests By Offense	Rank	Least Arrests By Offense
1	All other offenses (except traffic)	1	Forcible rape
2	Larceny-theft	2	Suspicion
3	Driving under the influence	3	Arson
4	Fraud	4	Murder and nonnegligent manslaughter
5	Disorderly conduct	5	Vagrancy
6	Drug abuse violations	6	Embezzlement
7	Drunkenness	7	Gambling
8	Prostitution and commercialized vice	8	Sex offenses (except forcible rape and prostitution)
9	Other assaults	9	Offenses against family and children
10	Liquor laws	10	Motor vehicle theft

Note: Based on 11,249 agencies: 1985 estimated
        population 203,035,000.

Source: Compiled from U.S. Federal Bureau of Investigation,
        Crime in the United States: Uniform Crime Reports,
        1985 (Washington, D.C.: Government Printing Office,
        1986), p. 178.

women. V. Young's analysis of the National Crime Survey reveals that black women were more than twice as likely to be viewed as offenders than were white women.[4]

Although these studies show black women to be offenders more often than their white counterparts, they fail to interpret what this means. For instance, is this crime rate differential the result of differences in criminal activities between black and white females? And to what degree does bias in law enforcement influence such figures? Additionally, data regarding other female minorities are particularly scarce for comparison studies, even though institutional data suggest that Hispanics and Native Americans are also highly represented in proportion to their population and, hence, compared to white female prisoners.

Social class among female criminals can and does vary. Several studies have found that women who are arrested are frequently poor, responsible for supporting themselves and others, and undereducated.[5]

LONG-TERM STUDIES OF FEMALE CRIME

Examining crime trends over a period of time is important in assessing patterns, incidence, and the future of criminality. However, long-term studies can also be misleading because of differences in the number of agencies reporting, procedures, crime fluctuations, and other factors.

Table 6.4 compares male and female Crime Index arrest trends from 1960 to 1985. Although some of the limitations noted exist in this analysis, the study should be useful in establishing the composition of female involvement in serious crime for the last quarter of a century. The data indicate that although males were arrested considerably more often overall, female arrestees increased at a substantially higher percentage. Between 1960 and 1975, female arrests for Crime Index offenses rose by a huge 373.5 percent compared to 119.3 percent for males. However, the bulk of that increase was for property crimes, in which female arrestees soared 432.7 percent by 1975. The rate of increase was virtually the same for males and females arrested for violent crimes.

Male arrests for Crime Index offenses decreased slightly over the 1975–1984 period, whereas female arrests rose 6.6 percent. The biggest increase was for violent crimes, at 10.4 percent, suggesting that females are slowly gaining on their male counterparts in this area. In fact, as the total number of arrests indicates, female arrests for violent offenses over the ten-year period more than doubled compared to the male incidence, creating an even wider margin between the two by the end of 1984. However, the increase in female Crime Index offense arrests was considerably lower from 1975 to 1984 than from 1960–1975, indicating that the differential between the sexes for serious crimes appears to be increasing at a slower rate than previously.

The 1984–1985 arrest trends support this. The overall increase in female arrests remained steady. However, male arrests for Crime Index offenses rose nearly 3 percent after lowering by almost 4 percent in the previous period. Violent crime arrests decreased for both sexes, with females gaining a slight edge in terms of percentages. Female involvement in property crime continued to rise, as it has since 1960; but despite their 3.9 percent gain on males in this category in 1985, males still outnumbered females in the volume of property crime arrests by more than 800,000.

Because most female criminality comprises less serious offenses or Type II crime, long-term trends are particularly valuable in this area. Table 6.5 reflects non-Index female arrest trends from 1960 to 1985. Although no age breakdown is given, because we know that adult females account for nearly 80 percent of all female criminality, the patterns should be fairly representative of female arrests.

As in Crime Index offenses, the percentage change among female

Table 6.4
Crime Index Arrest Trends by Sex, 1960–1985

TOTAL ARRESTS

MALES

OFFENSE CHARGED	1960	1975	Percent Change
Violent crime[a]	84,912	217,797	+156.5
Property crime[b]	336,311	708,207	+110.6
Crime Index total[c]	422,801	927,335	+119.3
	1975	1984	Percent Change
Violent crime	231,065	237,878	+ 2.9
Property crime[d]	867,566	818,742	- 5.6
Crime Index total[e]	1,098,631	1,056,620	- 3.8
	1984	1985	Percent Change
Violent crime	359,172	358,398	- .0.2
Property crime	1,138,847	1,182,346	+ 3.8
Crime Index total[f]	1,498,019	1,540,744	+ 2.9

FEMALES

OFFENSE CHARGED	1960	1975	Percent Change
Violent crime	10,139	25,937	+155.8
Property crime	38,526	205,209	+432.7
Crime Index total	48,852	231,324	+373.5
	1975	1984	Percent Change
Violent crime	25,941	28,651	+ 10.4
Property crime	243,972	259,068	+ 6.2
Crime Index total	269,913	287,719	+ 6.6
	1984	1985	Percent Change
Violent crime	43,832	43,682	- 0.3
Property crime	346,155	372,902	+ 7.7
Crime Index total	389,987	416,585	+ 6.8

[a]Violent crimes are offenses of murder, forcible rape, robbery, and aggravated assault.

[b]Property crimes are offenses of burglary, larceny-theft, and motor vehicle theft.

[c]Based on comparable reports from 2,090 cities representing 82,195,000 population and 636 counties representing 14,234,000 population; 2,726 agencies, 1975 estimated population 96,428,998. Subtotals of data do not always add up.

[d]Arson was added as of 1979 and thus is reflected in the figures.

[e]Based on 5,907 agencies; 1984 estimated population 132,927,000.

[f]Based on 19,596 agencies; 1985 estimated population 183,022,000.

Source: U.S. Federal Bureau of Investigation, Crime in the United States: Uniform Crime Reports, 1960-1984 (Washington, D.C.: Government Printing Office, 1961-1985).

Table 6.5

Non-Index Arrest Trends of Females, 1960–1985: All Ages

OFFENSE CHARGED	PERCENT CHANGE FROM		
	1960 to 1975[a]	1975 to 1984	1984 to 1985
Other assaults................	+ 137.6	+ 43.0	+15.0
Forgery and counterfeiting...	+ 192.3	+ 32.3	+ 1.4
Fraud.........................	+ 488.5	+ 76.5	+12.0
Embezzlement..................	N/A	+ 91.7	+18.3
Stolen property; buying, receiving, possessing.......	+ 727.2	+ 7.0	+ 4.9
Vandalism.....................	N/A	+ 34.3	+ 5.7
Weapons; carrying, possessing, etc.........................	+ 291.1	+ 8.4	+ 5.3
Prostitution and commercial- ized vice...................	+ 74.4	+123.9	+ 3.3
Sex offenses (except forcible rape and prostitution)......	− 70.3	+ 40.7	+12.1
Drug abuse violations........	+1011.9	+ 17.7	+13.0
Gambling......................	− 65.5	+ 25.5	− 0.3
Offenses against family and children....................	− 3.3	− 25.2	+ 7.9
Driving under the influence..	+ 281.7	+117.8	− 5.8
Liquor laws...................	+ 46.2	+ 60.6	+ 7.8
Drunkenness...................	− 52.9	+ 0.2	− 6.5
Disorderly conduct...........	+ 51.0	− 26.5	+14.8
Vagrancy......................	− 60.5	− 42.2	+ 0.4
All other offenses (except traffic)....................	+ 150.1	+ 92.1	+ 6.7
Suspicion (not included in totals).....................	− 79.1	− 36.9	−21.5
Curfew and loitering law violations..................	N/A	− 31.5	+ 2.4
Runaways......................	N/A	− 37.4	+12.0

[a]Embezzlement, vandalism, curfew and loitering law violations, and runaways have not been tabulated all years.

Source: Adapted from U.S. Federal Bureau of Investigation, Crime in the United States: Uniform Crime Reports, 1960-1985 (Washington, D.C.: Government Printing Office, 1961-1985).

non-Index Crime arrestees is most prominent during the years 1960–1975. Arrests for drug violations rose over one thousand percent, a reflection of a period of rebellion when young males and females experimented with drugs. Other significant increases in arrests occurred for offenses related to stolen property, fraud, weapons, and driving under the influence. Female arrests also declined in several categories during this period, including sex offenses, gambling, drunkenness, and vagrancy.

Between 1975 and 1984 arrest increases lowered substantially in all categories, except prostitution (from +74.4 to +123.9 percent) and liquor laws (from +42.6 to +60.6 percent). Drug abuse violation arrests showed the largest differential from the previous percentage change (+1,011.9 to +17.7). Reversing their course and becoming more frequent were female arrests for sex offenses and gambling; but decreasing, after showing a gain in 1975, was disorderly conduct.

Despite an increase in arrests from 1984 to 1985 in most non-Index offenses, female arrestees again showed smaller gains across the board than in the previous period—in fact, the number decreased in some categories. The most notable pattern of percentage differential is in the traditional female crime of prostitution, in which arrests increased only 3.3 percent after a 123.9 percent increase from 1975 to 1984. Granted the 1984–1985 period may be too short to draw inferences, this statistic nevertheless suggests that long-term trends may not be as reliable for predicting future criminality as nonmeasurable variables (such as sexually transmitted diseases, herpes, and AIDS).

What do these trends tell us about female crime and criminals? First, it is clear that important changes have occurred in the composition of female criminality between 1960 and 1985. Women have gained the distinction of accounting for a greater proportion of arrests than was once the case. This is mainly represented in Crime Index offenses, with most of the increase occurring in serious property crimes, especially larceny-theft. Yet the incidence of violent crime by women has barely changed.

For non-Index offenses, prostitution continues to be the one crime that has a distinct female character, at least as far as arrests are concerned; but it may be lowering in incidence as social diseases and community action combine to fight it. Violations related to simple assaults, forgery-counterfeiting, fraud, and substance abuse are the only other Type II offenses in which women have been strongly and constantly represented. However, it should be noted that the criminality of women is still very low compared to that of men and there is little to indicate any significant change in this differential.

STATISTICAL LIMITATIONS

Arrest Data

Although the *Uniform Crime Reports* constitute the most acceptable and comprehensive source of data on female crime in the United States, they are replete with deficiencies. The FBI, as designated by Congress, is the agency responsible for the national collection of crime data; however, no mandate has been issued to state and local governments to report such information. Consequently, for this and other reasons, crime statistics submitted to the FBI and tabulated in the *UCR* do not include all crimes. Hence, only a fraction of criminal behavior comes to the attention of law enforcement.

Edwin Sutherland and Donald Cressey put into perspective the shortcomings of official measurement of criminality:

The statistics about crime and delinquency are probably the most unreliable and most difficult of all statistics. It is impossible to determine with accuracy the amount of crime in any given jurisdiction or any particular time. Some behavior is labeled "delinquent" or "crime" by one observer, but not by another. Obviously a large proportion of all law violations goes undetected. Other crimes are detected but not reported and still others are reported but not officially recorded.[6]

The researchers mention six types of evidence that crime known to law enforcement is an inadequate index of crime:

- For a variety of reasons, many people fail to report crimes.
- Often, for political reasons, law enforcement agencies may underreport or underarrest offenders, or they may inflate arrest figures or overarrest.
- Certain crimes (for example, homicide) receive more attention and are more likely to be discovered than others.
- Improvements in the law enforcement system (such as specialized units, more personnel, better training of police in crime detection and investigating, and concentration on specific crimes) tend to increase the amount of potential arrests.
- All states and the District of Columbia vary in their classifications of crime, affecting the number of crimes known to and reported by the police.
- Crime and arrest rates are computed on the basis of census-enumerated general population figures that do not take into account population changes, with the exception of a census every ten years that consistently undercounts ethnic groups, particularly blacks.[7]

Additionally problematic in official statistics is the differential application of police and citizen discretion in reporting crime. This almost certainly damages historical comparisons of male-female arrest statistics as the number of police departments in the UCR system has increased over the years, making it more likely that error and reporting omissions will occur. Differential discretion also occurs between jurisdictions in the same time period, "an effect which is heightened by differences in legal definitions and court precedents from one jurisdiction to another."[8]

Finally, the accuracy of FBI crime report data is impeded by a tendency among overworked law enforcement officers to avoid the onerous paperwork essential for completing reports, and the propensity of some administrators to regard such statistical reporting as an added responsibility to be avoided.

The Chivalry Perspective

Along with general drawbacks of arrest statistics, they have also been attacked specifically regarding the measurement of female crime. A chivalry notion holds that female offenders benefit from lenient treatment throughout the criminal justice system. The argument is that the public perceives women as less threatening and therefore rarely requests official intervention for female deviant behavior; male offenders are often protective of their female partners; and police officers themselves are less likely to detain or arrest females. The result of all this is the assumption that female arrest statistics are reduced, thus implying that women are involved in crime to a lesser extent than men, an unrealistic view.

Despite the "naturalness" of this perspective, empirical evidence does not support the chivalry theory. Although the data are inconclusive, they suggest that women are often treated much harsher than men.[9] Furthermore, if chivalry exists, it likely would not be distributed equally. Middle-class and white offenders would be its chief beneficiaries.

Dorie Klein observes this candidly:

Chivalry is a racist and classist concept founded on the notion of women as "ladies" which applies to wealthy white women. . . . These "ladies," however, are the least likely ever to come in contact with the criminal justice system in the first place.[10]

People who subscribe to the belief that police tend to be chivalrous with females are likely visualizing an offender who resembles more a white middle-class housewife than a poor black prostitute. Preferential treatment is in fact extended to both sexes; however, social class and ethnicity play prominent rolls in the official disposition of arrestees. Poor black women rarely receive overly chivalrous treatment in the area of criminal justice.

Nevertheless, black females remain underrepresented in crime compared to males. But although few women pass through the criminal justice system and end up behind bars, those who do are "almost all poor, almost all from racial minorities, and almost all accused or convicted of non-violent crimes."[11]

Paternalism. Some observers postulate that paternalism toward women offenders exists in the criminal justice system that successfully operates as a filtering mechanism. Stuart Nagel and Lenore Weitzman contend that women are less likely to be convicted, detained before trial, or punished as harshly as men.[12] They reported that paternalism exists in both assault and larceny cases, although it is less evident with assault, an indication that assault may be more unacceptable for a woman.

Carol Temin disputes this evidence of the existence of paternalism and presents her own data showing that women, particularly young females, receive more punitive treatment than men.[13] Women also tend to lack protection because they are less likely to have a lawyer, a preliminary hearing, or a jury trial. Additionally, women spend more time in correctional facilities that are stricter and less adequate than those for men.[14]

Convictions and sentencing. There are no national comprehensive judicial statistics. However, some studies of individual state data have examined the preferential treatment issue of women at this level of the criminal justice system. In two recent studies of California court statistics, it was found that treatment generally was even for men and women.[15] For violent offenses, the proportion of men convicted tended to be slightly higher, but for property offenses conviction rates were equal.

Both studies did find that some preferential treatment exists. One found that women who pleaded not guilty stood a greater chance than men of being acquitted for robbery, burglary, and larceny.[16] Sentencing also appeared to favor women; the other study showed that convicted men are twice as likely to be sent to prison.[17]

These findings can be misleading. For instance, women are typically less violent criminals and therefore less of a threat to the community should they be released. The violence they do participate in is often unplanned and frequently of a domestic nature; both are factors a judge may take into consideration, especially as they pertain to the impact imprisonment might have on a woman's family.

Other research suggests that the favorable treatment application described here does not exist. Barbara Babcock maintains that women receive indeterminate sentences of potentially longer duration than men convicted of the same crimes.[18]

SELF-REPORT SURVEYS

The problems and biasing variables that exist in official data on women and crime have led to other means of gathering information on crime. The most significant is asking criminals themselves; these are referred to as self-report studies. Not that problems do not exist here as well; however, the need to gain more accurate estimations of the incidence and nature of female crime makes self-reporting important. What follows is a brief analysis of several notable self-report surveys.

In the mid-sixties, Gary Jensen and Raymond Eve administered questionnaires to 4,000 black and white youngsters in the Richmond, California, area. Analysis of the findings and other research found girls to be less delinquent than boys.[19]

Examining self-report data on delinquency among American youths aged 13 to 16 in 1967 and 1972, Martin Gold and David Reimer concluded that offenses among girls increased during this period but primarily for such non-Index offenses as drug and alcohol use. According to the researchers, were these offenses omitted, they would "find no change over the five years in per capita frequency of offenses among girls."[20] Hence they contended that serious offenses among females had not increased.

Steven Cernkovich and Peggy Giordano surveyed 822 Midwestern adolescents in 1977.[21] They found that males are more likely to be involved in delinquency than females, with the exception of a few minor offenses; but they suggested that the gap between male and female delinquency is not as significant as official statistics indicate.

More recently, the inadequacies of official statistics on female crime have been cited by Douglas Smith and Christy Visher.[22] Summarizing the available information (self-report and official data), the researchers reduced the data on sex and deviance/criminality to a single data base. Their findings indicate that the relationship between sex and deviance is smaller among the young and nonwhites than adults and whites.

Smith and Visher further contend that official statistics reveal a greater disparity between males and females than other sources, but point to the kind of crime as being a significant variable. Males tend to outnumber females in participation in serious crime. The researchers hold that although the distance between the sexes is narrowing on the whole, it is more prevalent for delinquent activities (substance abuse, truancy) and petty crime than violent offenses.[23]

Self-report studies suggest that the differential in crime among males and females is declining more rapidly than official studies indicate. However, as Smith and Visher note, although "it appears that women are closing the gap in terms of involvement in minor deviant acts, . . . equal gender representation in the area of serious criminal behavior has not yet occurred."[24]

The Weaknesses of Self-Report Data

The greatest difficulty in using self-report studies for our purposes is the paucity of research on the criminality of adult females. Without such information it is difficult to determine precisely how these studies apply to women. Other biases in self-report data can be seen in the sampling variables, honesty of the respondents, communication difficulties, and problems of measurement. Most self-report studies are local rather than national samples and depend on both official permission (for instance, gaining entry to an institution) and individual cooperation.

Despite such drawbacks, the assumption (as supported by official data) is that the findings on adolescent female criminality (as opposed to delinquency) closely parallel adult female criminality. Hence self-reporting surveys continue to be a key source of knowledge in the study of women's criminality.

THE NEW FEMALE CRIMINAL MYTH

The notion that a "new," more violent and aggressive female criminal has emerged in our society has gained popularity over the last decade. This perspective, incited by the women's liberation movement, holds that an alarming increase in female crime and arrests indicates that equality exists or soon will exist in male and female deviance, even if women continue to receive preferential treatment, thereby masking their criminality.

Two women who are highly influential in this assessment are Freda Adler, author of the 1975 book, *Sisters in Crime*, and Rita Simon, whose book, *Women and Crime*, published in the same year, received less media attention but was widely circulated among professionals interested in women and criminal justice. Both women suggested that

during the period of 1953 to 1972 there was an explosion in (1) the incidence of total crime and (2) the incidence of what might be called "nontraditional crime," parallel to entry of women into nontraditional occupations. The result of these new trends would be movement toward parity with men in the commission of crime in terms of both incidence and type.[25]

Simon advances that were present trends to continue, "approximately equal numbers of men and women will be arrested for larceny and for fraud and embezzlement by the 1990s; and for forgery and counterfeiting the proportions should be equal by the 2010s."[26]

Discussing the changing pattern of female criminality, Adler states,

By every indicator available, female criminals appear to be surpassing males in the rate of increase for almost every major crime. Although males continue to commit the greater number of offenses, it is the women who are committing those same crimes at yearly rates of increase now running as high as six and seven times faster than males.[27]

In fact, everything we have reviewed in this chapter makes it clear that the new female criminal is much closer to myth than to reality. As we have seen, the rise in female crime has occurred primarily in property crimes (as opposed to violent) such as larceny-theft, and even these offenses are usually far less harmful and aggressive than their Crime Index status would designate. Laura Crites endorses this perspective; she contends that female crimes are indicative of women's roles in society. "They are predominantly small-scale property and victimless offenses reflecting both the female status as a minor consumer and her tendency to inflict self-directed rather than outward-directed injury."[28]

The increases in female property crime are likely a matter of greater participation in petty crimes (such as shoplifting), which some studies suggest. For example, a 1977 study using a combination of *UCR*, police, court, and census data of women arrested between 1965 and 1977 reveals that although female arrests increased more than male arrests for Crime Index offenses, the increase was mainly for larceny-theft crimes. Furthermore, "the changes in the category of petty-property crimes are greater than in any of the other categories examined."[29] These findings support the contention that women are not catching up with men in crime but continue to be arrested predominantly for offenses that had been traditionally considered women's offenses and, therefore, not "new."

Additionally, even when a gain in female crime is present, in actual numbers women still lag behind men in virtually every offense category excluding prostitution. It would be foolish to assume that this considerable differential is the result of some notion of chivalry.

Finally, perhaps the most significant reason to cast doubt on the Adler and Simon studies (and hence the new woman myth) is that they were based largely on *Uniform Crime Reports*. We have already examined the difficulties of official statistics. Combine this misinterpretation and analytical problems in attempting to apply these data to long-term trends, and it becomes clear that such evidence and conclusions can be highly misleading.

Female criminals continue to be in the minority. This is true for both serious and nonserious offenses, and especially violent crime. There is little to support the theory of a new female criminal. Women have shown considerable increases in property crime participation over the years, primarily larceny-theft offenses. However, female criminality is basically of a less serious character as far as official interpretation goes (such as prostitution, substance abuse, forgery).

Limitational problems with statistics on women and crime, underreporting, and other factors make it almost impossible to determine the full extent and range of crime among women. These problems notwithstanding, along with the relatively low incidence of female crime, we cannot ignore the fact that it does exist and is something we must deal with as part of a larger societal problem of crime, criminals, and victims.

NOTES

1. Marvin Wolfgang, *Patterns in Criminal Homicide* (Philadelphia: University of Pennsylvania Press, 1964); Charles Winick and Paul Kinsie, *The Lively Commerce: Prostitution in the United States* (Chicago: Quadrangle Books, 1971).

2. Freda Adler, *Sisters in Crime: The Rise of the New Female Criminal* (New York: McGraw-Hill, 1975), p. 139.

3. R. M. Glick and V. V. Neto, *National Study of Women's Correctional Programs* (Washington, D.C.: Government Printing Office, 1977), p. 104.

4. V. D. Young, "Women, Race, and Crime," *Criminology* 18 (1980):26–34.

5. Laura Crites, *The Female Offender* (Lexington, Mass.: Lexington Books, 1976); Rita Simon, *Women and Crime* (Lexington, Mass.: D. C. Heath, 1975).

6. Edwin W. Sutherland and Donald R. Cressey, *Criminology*, 10th ed. (Philadelphia: J. B. Lippincott, 1978), p. 29.

7. Coramae Richey Mann, *Female Crime and Delinquency* (University: University of Alabama Press, 1984), pp. 4–5.

8. Lee H. Bowker, *Women, Crime, and the Criminal Justice System* (Lexington, Mass.: Lexington Books, 1978), p. 3.

9. Leonard, *Women, Crime, and Society*, p. 37.

10. Dorie Klein, "The Etiology of Female Crime: A Review of the Literature," *Issues in Criminology* 8 (1973):3–29.

11. Barbara Allen Babcock, "Introduction: Women and the Criminal Law," *American Criminal Law Review* 11 (1973):291–294.

12. Stuart Nagel and Lenore Weitzman, "Women as Litigants," *Hastings Law Journal* 23 (1971):171–198.

13. Carol Engel Temin, "Discriminatory Sentencing of Women Offenders: The Argument for ERA in a Nutshell," *American Criminal Law Review* 11 (1973):355–372.

14. Linda Singer, "Women and the Correctional Process," *American Criminal Law Review* 11 (1972):295–308.

15. Crites, *The Female Offender*; Simon, *Women and Crime*.

16. Simon, *Women and Crime*.

17. Crites, *The Female Offender*.

18. Babcock, "Introduction: Women and the Criminal Law."

19. Gary Jensen and Raymond Eve, "Sex Differences in Delinquency: An Examination of Popular Sociological Explanations," *Criminology* 13 (1976):427–448.

20. Martin Gold and David J. Reimer, "Changing Patterns of Delinquent Behavior among Americans 13 Through 16 Years Old: 1967–72," *Crime and Delinquency* 7 (1975):483–517.

21. Steven Cernkovich and Peggy Giordano, "A Comparative Analysis of Male and Female Delinquency," *Sociological Quarterly* 20 (1979):131–145.

22. Douglas Smith and Christy A. Visher, "Sex and Involvement in Deviance/Crime: A Quantitative Review of the Empirical Literature," *American Sociological Review* 45 (1980):691–701.

23. Ibid.

24. Ibid., pp. 697–698.

25. Jane Roberts Chapman, *Economic Realities and the Female Offender* (Lexington, Mass.: Lexington Books, 1980), p. 51.

26. Simon, *Women and Crime*, p. 42.

27. Adler, *Sisters in Crime*, p. 15.

28. Crites, *The Female Offender*, p. 38.

29. Darrell J. Steffensmeier, "Sex Differences in Patterns of Adult Crime, 1965–77: A Review and Assessment," *Social Forces* 58 (1980):1080–1108.

7

Theoretical Explanations of Female Crime

Within the various disciplines of study into the causes and nature of criminality, over the years very little attention has been focused on the female criminal, particularly when compared with male criminals. This can be ascribed to, among other reasons, the low (and therefore, to many, insignificant) crime rate among women, the assumption that women are inferior to men and unworthy of researchers' attention, and the dominance of male writers in this field. When female criminality has been studied, much of the research and conclusions have been rooted in age-old stereotypes about the general and genetic nature of women, and reasons why women are less inclined to commit crimes as opposed to specifically why they do.

In this chapter we will explore the most important research to date on the theoretical and causal features of female criminality.

BIOLOGICAL THEORISTS OF FEMALE CRIMINALITY

Cesare Lombroso

Viewed by some as the founding father of the biological-positivistic school of criminology, Cesare Lombroso, an Italian psychiatrist, was among the first to study female criminality scientifically.[1] In 1894 he collaborated with his son-in-law, William Ferrero, to write *The Female Offender*. Combining quantitative and qualitative data to understand the female criminal, Lombroso and Ferrero applied the hypothesis that crime was " 'biologically predisposed' and recognizable by physical stigmata to female criminality."[2]

Continuing with his research to identify the inherent characteristics of criminals he had developed in *The Criminal Man*, Lombroso examined the skeletal remains of female offenders (particularly the jawbones, face, brain, and craniums), and studied female prisoners for signs of atavism. He postulated that female criminals possessed certain physical traits that were absent in normal women and thus they could be categorized by the type of anomalies they exhibited. For example, a prostitute "was likely to have very heavy lower jaws, large nasal spines, simple cranial sutures, deep frontal sinuses, and wormian bones. A 'fallen woman' usually possessed occipital irregularities, a narrow forehead, prominent cheekbones, and a 'virile' type of face."[3]

Lombroso applied to women the typology of the "born criminal" he had developed for male criminals, describing it as the biological criminal and the woman as the type who possessed a large number of degenerative physical characteristics. He found fewer instances of born female criminals than males, and attributed this to a number of reasons, including these: women are biologically more primitive and evolved less than men; women have more conservative tendencies regarding questions of the social order; women are less exposed to society as homemakers and child rearers; and women intrinsically have less inclination toward crime.

However, Lombroso regarded those women he did find to be born criminals as even more immoral and menacing than male criminals. He explained that women often are less compassionate and sensitive to pain, while possessing jealousy and capable of vengeful behavior. These "ladylike" characteristics tend to be mitigated by common female attributes such as weakness, piety, maternity, and insufficiently developed intelligence. According to the criminologist, women are simply overgrown adolescents who when bad, are far more frightful than men. These women generally lack maternal affection, illustrating their degeneracy and masculinity. He believed the deficiencies found in normal women are extreme, untempered in lawless women.

Lombroso found prostitutes to possess more atavistic qualities than other types of female criminals. This arose logically from the notion that prostitutes were more primitive than either criminal or normal women. Lombroso believed that primitive women were rarely criminal but nearly always prostitutes.[4]

Lombroso also studied the "occasional" criminal, whom he found to account for most of the female offenders. These women generally had none or few degenerative qualities and possessed "moral equipment" near that of a normal woman. The occasional criminal committed a crime for reasons including male persuasion, higher education (preventing marriage and inducing want), and excessive temptation (for example, shoplifting because of the overwhelming display of goods in stores). These female criminals lacked the respect for property that men had, and found good clothing to be essential in terms of attracting men.

Lombroso's work has retained historical significance for his contribution to the field of criminology; however, his propositions have largely been dismissed as inaccurate assessments of female criminals and criminality. Much of the criticism focuses on two things: the inadequacies of his methodology, and his theoretical propositions themselves. Lombroso's data were derived from prisoner and deceased offender samples. The problem here is that imprisoned criminals, then and now, represent only a small proportion of both criminals who are convicted and the total number of people who commit crimes but manage to avoid the law. Hence even if there was any validity in his atavistic theories, they would have been representative of a very small minority of society and thus statistically insignificant.

Probably the most limiting aspect of Lombroso's study was his small sample size. Initially his work was based on data from seventy-two criminals and forty-seven prostitutes. Although later his use of other studies lifted the total closer to one thousand, the data were derived from different sources in different areas, making it difficult (if not impossible) to standardize measurements used in the various studies, particularly when attempting to judge anomalies. Other criticisms of Lombroso's findings include his attributing biological bases to subcultural traits, and his confusion of sex and gender.

Sigmund Freud

Many believe that the most pervasive theoretical perspective pertaining to female criminality is rooted in the psychoanalytic writings of Sigmund Freud.[5] Like Lombroso, Freud regarded women as somewhat biologically deficient. Describing them as passive, narcissistic, and masochistic, he attributed these defective qualities to their lack of a penis. Because of this "physical deficiency" women are unable to resolve the Oedipal conflict. Hence they become morally inferior and are less able to control their impulses, which in turn affects other areas of the female's life such as the intellectual sphere. The end result was a person characterized by jealousy, emotionalism, immorality, and poor judgment.

While Freud does not directly associate superego weakness to female criminality, he believed that "women are inclined toward amorality because of their anatomical 'deficiency.' "[6] His general view of women's antisocial or deviant behavior is that it derives from the "masculinity complex," or penis envy.

Despite the support Freud's theories continue to receive within professional disciplines, some have been quick to criticize his theoretical perspectives, including some of his own psychoanalytic "disciples." Alfred Adler challenged Freud's concept of penis envy when he postulated that a "sense of inferiority was created in women not because they felt less

well endowed physically than men, but because an unnatural relationship of male dominance exists between the sexes."[7] Regrettably, Adler
substituted the notion of masculine protest for that of Freudian penis
envy.

Karen Horney, author of *Feminine Psychology*, totally discredited the
penis envy proposition and the castration complex in the normal development of women.[8] She acknowledged that although both sexes were
mutually envious, girls tended to envy boys' ease in urinating and mas-
turbating. Horney further postulated that male envy of the female, or
men's femininity complex, was more severe than women's masculine
complex.

Contemporary feminist writers have been critical of Freud's theory
because they believe that he exhibited a masculine bias. Their major
objection is that Freud "used men as the normative standard by which
he assessed women, who are seen as inferior 'little men.' "[9] Additionally,
criticism stems from the fact that because Freud's theory of female criminality is based upon psychological variables, other factors such as social,
political, and economic realities of women's crime have been ignored.
In sum, despite the amount of study on the female Oedipus complex,
there is very little evidence of its existence, and modern psychiatry has
generally moved away from this approach.

SOCIOLOGICAL THEORISTS OF FEMALE CRIMINALITY

W. I. Thomas

Sociologist William Isaac Thomas made a significant contribution to
the study of female criminality with two books.[10] In *Sex and Society*,
published in 1907, Thomas criticized anthropologists for their "assumption of the inferiority of women and their subsequent failure to distinguish between congenital and acquired characteristics."[11] He contended
that any differences in intellectual functioning between the sexes were
not a result of brain size or other biological differentials, as Lombroso
had inferred, but are socially influenced.

Despite Thomas's criticism of his contemporaries, he made certain
advances that were parallel to Lombroso's thinking when he divided
the sexes into katabolic and anabolic dimensions.

Men were katabolic, or more rapid consumers (destroyers) of energy, as demonstrated in their feats of strength and bursts of energy. . . . Contrarily, women
represent the more constructive part of the metabolic process, anabolism, in that
they conserve and store energy as the plants store nutrients. Characteristics such
as stability, endurance, and passion are thus associated with the anabolic female
in contrast to the destructiveness of the katabolic male.[12]

Thomas decided that the psychological differences between katabolism and anabolism are indicative of social behavioral differences between the sexes.

However, it was in *The Unadjusted Girl*, published in 1923, that Thomas "established his eminence by fusing sociology and social psychology into the analysis of social organization and personality."[13] This study of female delinquency establishes a clear break from the Lombroso-influenced, biological emphasis present in Thomas's first book: he explores the influences of the social environment on deviant behavior, which he believed contribute, in conjunction with innate instincts, to total behavior.

Thomas proposed a dyadic goals-means conflict theory. He advanced that every human has four basic desires: the desire for security, recognition, new experience, and response. The two that influenced criminality or altruism most were the desire for new experience and the desire for response. "A woman entered prostitution to satisfy a desire for excitement and response; as a woman, prostitution in one form or another was the most likely avenue to satisfy those needs."[14]

A large portion of Thomas's book was devoted to criticism of the community, which he felt was inadequate as a socializing agent. He believed that schools should identify maladaptive, predelinquent children early and treat them before they progress further into deviant behavior. He implored the community to assume its duties in providing legitimate means for attainment of needs, so that criminals and potential criminals would fit into the roles society wanted them to.

Thomas has been criticized by contemporary writers for his liberal paternalism. As one critic expresses it,

He believed in manipulating people's lives "for their own good" to conform to social norms that were not necessarily universal. His theories were sexist in that females were identified as offenders through sexual behavior. The sexual standards of society were rigid, and female deviators were castigated more harshly than male deviators. The significance of this in sociology was that a man's sexual behavior was only one facet of his total character, whereas a woman was actually defined by her sexuality.[15]

Further, Thomas made assumptions, such as the maternal instinct and the female's greater desire for response, that had not been proved and remain to be proved. Although he made several important observations about female criminality, his theory was essentially a "pseudopsychological justification for continuing the rehabilitation methods that were presently being employed."[16]

Sheldon and Eleanor Glueck

The Gluecks' most prominent contribution to the field of female criminality was the 1934 publication, *Five Hundred Delinquent Women*, which
was based on a detailed study the criminologists made of 500 Massa-
chusetts delinquent girls from their childhood through parole.[17] In addition to tracing the backgrounds and social histories of the girls, the
Gluecks also compared their physical and psychological traits.

The object of the Gluecks' work was to determine what factors led to
female deviance. They concluded that female criminality results in large
part from biological and economic factors. Furthermore, they found that
an extremely high percentage of delinquent girls came from abnormally
large families, were mentally defective, and had been arrested mainly for
illicit sexual behavior, and that criminality was likely to be intergenerational.

A host of other findings emerged from the Gluecks' work; unfortunately, much of it either useless or uninformative, such as the connection
between delinquency and a poor socioeconomic background. This was
not exactly a pathbreaking conclusion, given that the link had already
been established between poverty and criminality.

Sheldon and Eleanor Glueck's research, although comprehensive at
the time, was influenced by biases and sexist attitudes. For instance,
they examined the sexual histories of their subjects routinely. This may
have been necessary for the large number of incarcerated prostitutes;
however, in the case of other crimes the sexual life of the offender was
important only because she was female.

Another bias was their approach to the generation-to-generation theory of criminal tendencies. The Gluecks' answer to a proposition that
has never been proved conclusively was to institute a widespread ster-
ilization program to "contain" an incurable problem. The other alternative to preventing procreation was to isolate those women judged as
"defective delinquents." Hence they advocated locking up women for
long periods for the sole purpose of keeping them from getting pregnant.
Aside from the legal and ethical implications the Gluecks' apparently
decided to ignore, to say that their recommendations are faulty would
be an understatement. Fortunately, their supporters were few.

Otto Pollak

The 1950 book, *The Criminality of Women*, by Otto Pollak is considered
the definitive work on women and crime during the postwar years.[18]
Pollak, a sociology professor, integrated data from a comprehensive
survey of American, British, French, and German literature. After ana-

lyzing the conflicting findings and theories, he came to his own conclusions about the causes and nature of female criminality.

Pollak, who was influenced by Lombroso and Freud, nevertheless broke away from most treatments of the subject by posing several new propositions regarding women's criminality. The first was that women's crimes are primarily sexually motivated, whereas men's are mainly economically motivated, with the exception of crimes of passion. This theory was based upon Freudian teachings that the basic problem of a neurotic and deviant woman was her desire to be a man.

Second, according to Pollak, the crime rate among women is probably equal to that of men but that women's crime has a "masked" or hidden character. He postulated that women's crimes are inadequately reflected in the statistics, giving examples of crimes frequently committed by women including shoplifting, illegal abortions, thefts of customers' possessions committed by prostitutes, domestic thefts, perjury, and disturbance of the peace. Pollak subscribed to Lombroso's notion that women are particularly "addicted" to crimes that are easily concealed and rarely reported; he used exhibitionism as an example of a crime that occurs frequently among females but is not prosecuted.

Pollak asserted that the traditional social roles assigned to women by our culture and society (for instance, homemakers, caretakers of children or the sick, domestic workers) are ideal for hiding crimes such as sexual offenses against children, which leaves no physical evidence and even less suspicion given that women are expected to take responsibility for children. Furthermore, he believed women are more deceitful than men in their commission of crimes and teach deceit through physiological tactics. He alleged that women disguise sexual response, fake orgasms, conceal their menstruation, and withhold sexual information from young children; thus women are trained in deception and adopt a different attitude toward candor.

The last significant argument Pollak made in support of his theory of hidden female crime was that women are given preferential treatment throughout the criminal justice system by police officers, judges, prosecutors, and juries who would prefer not to assist in convicting them. He described this as arising partly from men's chivalrous and paternalistic regard for women.

Pollak has been roundly criticized for the statistical conclusions and biases in his propositions. The most serious criticism is that he offers no substantiation for his arguments. This is conveyed decisively by one writer:

It is difficult to argue the existence of undetected crime since its very nature implies that it is unknown. Such a theory cannot be based on evidence, a weakness compounded by assertions that simply defy plausibility. . . . His claims of sex offenses against children and female exhibitionism are boldly stated without evidence or even reasonable explanations. Such arguments could easily be leveled against men, thereby recreating the disparity in crime rates.[19]

Feminist Carol Smart is another who blasted Pollak's conclusions.[20] As summarized adroitly by writer Joy Pollock, Smart rejects

Pollak's prison statistics as indicative of the greater aggressiveness of female crime. The leniency that Pollak had already said existed in the courts would make it natural that those women in prison would likely be there for a violent offense. . . . Pollak felt confident in projecting a large amount of hidden female crime and denied the existence of a similar amount of crime for males. . . . Both are mere speculations on Pollak's part, and in fact, it was likely a large amount of hidden male crime existed in the form of wife beating and child abuse. . . . Pollak's theories on causation were heavily influenced by Freudian analysis and therefore are subject to the same criticism that has been raised against Freudian theory. The assumptions of penis envy and a sexual passivity in the female have no proof and were poorly chosen for use in a causal theory.[21]

Other criticisms of Pollak's findings are just as enlightening. For instance, his contention of lenient treatment of women throughout the criminal justice system ignores the possibility that women may actually be victimized or punished more severely for their failure to meet traditional expectations. Additionally, his assertion that women are deceitful, which is supposedly based on biological and sociological arguments, appears to be contradicted by his descriptions of the character traits of women, which implies sexism.

Despite the weaknesses in Pollak's theories, his work continues to be significant in the field of women and crime. The problems with official statistics are quite evident, and there is evidence that some degree of differential treatment for women exists. However, his most important contribution may be the recognition that the involvement of women in crime is related to their social positions and roles. The relationship of women to society is essential to understanding and interpreting their patterns of criminality.

CONTEMPORARY THEORISTS OF FEMALE CRIMINALITY

During the 1970s and 1980s, the literature on female criminality reflected some significant changes from earlier works, with an emphasis on dismissing long-standing theoretical perspectives of women's crime, exploring economic explanations, and studying the criminality of women in relation to the women's movement.

Economic Factors

Attention has been newly focused on the female's economic position in the social structure given the increase in the proportion of women arrested for crime in this country. The nature of women's crime suggests that, more than any other factor, the motivating force behind most of their criminality is economics.

Property crimes (primarily larceny-theft), which have long represented the offense for which females are most frequently arrested, generally are committed for one reason: monetary return (or goods redeemable for money). Yet as Dorie Klein concluded in her review of the literature on the etiology of female crime, virtually all theories disregarded the economic and social reality of female crime. She contends that poor and Third World females "negate the notions of sexually motivated crime" and "engage in illegal activities as a viable economic alternative."[22]

Past researchers, who seemed more concerned with individual physiological or psychological traits of female criminals, largely excluded sexism, racism, and social class in their studies of female deviance. However, most female offenders tend to be poor, undereducated, racial minority, mothers, self-supporting, and often have others to support. Estimates indicate that 50 to 80 percent of imprisoned female offenders are mothers. Hence, as one researcher suggests logically, "The commission of crimes may be necessary [for women] to provide for themselves and their families, a factor which makes it conceivable to view their larcenies, burglaries, and robberies in simple economic terms."[23]

Empirical evidence suggests that professional shoplifting is a property crime most female participants engage in predominantly for profit. And although no studies have corroborated this, it makes sense to assume that female participation in crimes such as robbery, purse snatching, and burglary is intrinsically tied to financial need.

The economic factor exists in other forms of female criminality as well. The best example is prostitution, which many still attribute as a product of sexual motivation. Contemporary studies based on identified prostitutes have clearly established economics as the primary reason women enter the world of prostitution and remain there. In a study of prostitutes, Jennifer James found that 84.9 percent of her subjects considered the first advantage of being a prostitute "easy money—material goods."[24] (See chapter 9 for an in-depth look into prostitution.)

Economic Pressures

Many researchers believe that the increased economic pressure on women in our society has forced them to turn to crime as a means of survival and to support their families. Laurel Rans finds that "although the number of women in the labor force doubled from 1950 to 1974, their median full-time income was only 57 percent that of their male peers.[25] Rita Simon also addresses this issue: "Even though women's overall representation in the labor force from 1945 to 1971 has increased by 40 percent, their participation in positions of authority, prestige, and higher monetary reward has not kept pace with that increase."[26] Thus because of such economic pressures and inequities, female crime emerges.

Two other researchers, George Noblit and Janie Burcart, believe this perspective would account for the preponderance of minority female crime:

Coupling this increasing economic marginality of lower class women with Konopka's argument that the working class woman perceives the lack of equality and privilege in comparison to men and responds to it through individual acts of vengeance, it may be possible to explain increases in female criminality and increases in arrest rates.[27]

Role/Opportunity Theory

A number of researchers, aware of the weaknesses of earlier studies, have analyzed female deviance not in terms of biological or psychological variables but in terms of sex roles.[28] Instead of treating women's criminality as the masculinization of female behavior, these theorists regard it as the "illegitimate expression" of role expectations. According to Richard Cloward and Lloyd Ohlin, "a person is most likely to become delinquent when legitimate means of reaching social goals are closed but illegitimate means are open."[29] Supporters of this school of thought explore female socialization—opportunities and lack of opportunities—and hold that female criminality is an extension of women's sex roles. Further, the narrowing differentiation between male and female cultural roles contributes to increasing rates of female arrest.

Critics of sex role and opportunity theories in relation to women and crime point out that such theories offer "little understanding of actual women criminals and can easily slide into discussions of inadequate female socialization, implying that individual difficulties rather than structural problems are at issue."[30] Furthermore, the theory fails "to discuss the structural origins of sex-role inequality or to deal with the inferior status of women in historical or cultural terms."[31] This unfortunate omission allows such proposals to be interpreted as further proof of intrinsic differences between women and men.

Female Criminality and the Women's Liberation Movement

Two areas are most prominent when discussing the possible influences the women's movement has had on the increase in female crime: "the increased opportunities for women to participate in the labor force with concomitant increased opportunities to commit certain kinds of crime; and the changing self-concept and identity of women and girls as a result of the consciousness-raising of the movement."[32]

Freda Adler

Freda Adler was one of the first criminology writers to suggest that as the social status of women reaches parity with men, their crime patterns and frequency will more closely resemble those of their male counterparts.[33] She discusses the startling rise in women's crime and women's assertiveness and the possible association between these and the women's liberation movement. Although Adler notes that since most incarcerated women are a product of the lower social classes of this country and therefore are not influenced by the 1960s and 1970s women's movement, she does refer to a "new liberation movement," which she describes as a "new feminism" that affects all levels of women. It is in the "consciousness-raising" movement that she predicts that as women draw closer to men socially, they will become more equal on all counts in criminality as well.

Rita Simon

Rita Simon's treatise on women and crime provides a detailed summary of the contemporary women's movement.[34] In addition to analyzing the social and political implications of the movement, Simon explores the potential relationship of demographic and labor force variables to female criminality and the impact the women's movement has had in altering the treatment of women within the criminal justice system.

In putting particular emphasis on those women employed in the financial world and white-collar positions, Simon contends:

The more parsimonious explanation is that as women increase their participation in the labor force, their opportunity to commit certain types of crimes also increases. This explanation assumes that women have no greater store of morality than do men. Their propensities to commit crimes do not differ, but, in the past, their opportunities have been much more limited. As women's opportunities to commit crimes increase, so will their deviant behavior and the types of crimes they commit will much more closely resemble those committed by men.[35]

Criticism of the Liberation Movement and Women's Crime Theory

Several writers have rejected the proposition that the women's movement has contributed to women's criminality. Crites found little statistical support for an association between the increase in female crime and the women's liberation movement.[36] In a recent study of sex differences in patterns of adult crime, Darrell Steffensmeir found that little change had occurred in female arrest patterns in the twelve-year period reviewed; thus he concluded that the women's movement could not have had an impact on either the type or level of female criminality.[37]

Further criticism of the correlation between liberation and women's crime link has been leveled by Smart, who examined official arrest data for the United States, England, and Wales and argues that dramatic increases in female crime is nothing new.[38] She admonishes researchers who "fail to examine such rates over all periods of time and instead restrict their analyses to one or two decades." And she is critical of "the tendency to fixate on monocausal explanations of female criminality such as the women's movement, when studies of male deviance indicate several possible etiological perspectives."[39] Smart contends that two fallacies exist in the women's emancipation argument: (1) the notion that female crime is changing in a manner different from male crime, and (2) the assumption that an increase for women in legitimate opportunities necessarily means an increase in illegitimate opportunities.

Other critics have challenged Simon's or Adler's assessments singularly. For instance, Noblit and Burcart argue that Simon failed to examine the data by age categories, to use consistent *Uniform Crime Reports* data, or to control for changes in population, although she did make use of proportions of all arrests in support of her analysis.[40] Although the researchers concur with Simon that the greatest increases in rates of female arrest are seen in property offenses, particularly larceny, they found this pattern to be indicative of only female offenders. Furthermore, Noblit and Burcart point out a contradiction in Simon's findings given that women's tendency toward property crime relates to all property crimes as opposed to only larceny. Hence they dismiss the women's movement as a causative variable and postulate that the differential tendency in women's criminality concerns poor minority women, given that typically they are those arrested, rather than white middle-class women who are most commonly associated with the movement.[41]

Another critic takes exception to Adler's discussion of equality and the liberated woman:

First, [Adler's] assumption of rapidly increasing equality among men and women is highly debatable. . . . Women are far from equal to men in terms of occupation, income, social expectations, and so on. . . . My second criticism regards her naive idea of liberation. Obviously, women's liberation is something more than women equaling men in crime, and while Adler might well agree, she does not state this explicitly. Her enthusiasm for women using "guns, knives, and wit," for women who are fully capable of violence, is unmistakable. This view embodies an unreflective notion that women give evidence of liberation by undertaking any typically "male" behavior be it violent or nonviolent. This conception of liberation is a shortsighted one, of women simply becoming more like men. It implies liberation from the female sex role, but not liberation in any large sense.[42]

There is little doubt that the debate over the role of the women's liberation movement on types and incidence of female criminality will continue for some time. Although there does appear to be at least an indirect association between the two phenomena, the fact remains that a direct correlation has not been empirically established; thus no solid conclusions can be drawn one way or the other.

Despite the scarcity of high-quality, useful literature on women and crime, some research does exist which continues to be an important part of our study into the criminality of women. However, the contribution of biological, sociological, and contemporary propositions is limited because at worst their individual drawbacks and biases influence, if not altogether dismiss, their reliability; and at best they can only be considered factors or variables in criminality causation, as no singular explanation can account for all variations and conditions that make a person deviant. Obviously further research is needed to bridge the gap between theoretical perspectives of women's crime as well as the shortcomings that reflect them all.

NOTES

1. Cesare Lombroso and William Ferrero, *The Female Offender* (New York: Appleton, 1900).

2. Joy Pollock, "Early Theories of Female Criminality," in Lee H. Bowker, *Women, Crime, and the Criminal Justice System* (Lexington, Mass.: Lexington Books, 1978), p. 28.

3. Ibid., p. 29; Lombroso and Ferrero, *The Female Offender*.

4. Lombroso and Ferrero, *The Female Offender*.

5. Sigmund Freud, *New Introductory Lectures on Psychoanalysis* (New York: W. W. Norton, 1933).

6. Elissa P. Benedek, "Women and Homicide," in Bruce L. Danto, John Bruhns, and Austin H. Kutscher, eds., *The Human Side of Homicide* (New York: Columbia University Press, 1982), p. 154.

7. Julia A. Sherman, *On the Psychology of Women* (Springfield, Ill.: Charles C. Thomas, 1971), p. 48.

8. Coramae R. Mann, *Female Crime and Delinquency* (University: University of Alabama Press, 1984), p. 91.

9. Ibid., p. 92.

10. William I. Thomas, *Sex and Society: Studies in the Social Psychology of Sex* (Boston: Little, Brown, 1907); William I. Thomas, *The Unadjusted Girl: With Cases and Standpoint for Behavior Analysis* (New York: Harper & Row, 1923).

11. Mann, *Female Crime and Delinquency*, p. 57.

12. Ibid., pp. 57–58.

13. Morris Janowitz, *W. I. Thomas* (Chicago: University of Chicago Press, 1966), p. xxvii.

14. Pollock, "Early Theories of Female Criminality," p. 45.

15. Ibid.

16. Ibid.

17. Sheldon Glueck and Eleanor Glueck, *Five Hundred Delinquent Women* (New York: Alfred A. Knopf, 1934).

18. Otto Pollak, *The Criminality of Women* (Philadelphia: University of Philadelphia Press, 1950).

19. Leonard, *Women, Crime, and Society*, p. 5.

20. Carol Smart, *Women, Crime and Criminology, A Feminist Critique* (London: Routledge & Kegan Paul, 1977).

21. Pollock, "Early Theories of Female Criminality," p. 50.

22. Dorie Klein, "The Etiology of Female Crime: A Review of the Literature," *Issues in Criminology* 8 (1973):6.

23. Mann, *Female Crime and Delinquency*, p. 96.

24. Jennifer James, "Motivations for Entrance into Prostitution," in Laura Crites, ed., *The Female Offender* (Lexington, Mass.: Lexington Books, 1976), p. 202.

25. Laurel Rans, "Women's Crime: Much Ado About . . . ?" *Federal Probation* 42 (1978):5.

26. Rita Simon, "Women and Crime Revisited," *Social Science Quarterly* 56 (1976):663.

27. George W. Noblit and Janie M. Burcart, "Women and Crime: 1960–1970," *Social Science Quarterly* 56 (1976):656–657.

28. Ruth Morris, "Female Delinquency and Relational Problems," *Social Forces* 43 (1964):82–88; Frances Heidensohn, "The Deviance of Women: A Critique and An Injury," *British Journal of Sociology* 19 (1968):160–175.

29. Richard A. Cloward and Lloyd Ohlin, *Delinquency and Opportunity* (New York: Free Press, 1960).

30. Leonard, *Women, Crime and Society*, p. 11.

31. Ibid.

32. Mann, *Female Crime and Delinquency*, pp. 107–108.

33. Freda Adler, *Sisters in Crime: The Rise of the New Female Criminal* (New York: McGraw-Hill, 1975).

34. Rita Simon, *The Contemporary Woman and Crime* (Washington, D.C.: Government Printing Office, 1975).

35. Ibid., p. 48.

36. Laura Crites, ed., *The Female Offender* (Lexington, Mass.: Lexington Books, 1976), pp. 36–37.

37. Darrell J. Steffensmeir, "Sex Differences in Patterns of Adult Crime, 1965–77: A Review and Assessment," *Social Forces* 58 (1980):1098–1099.

38. Carol Smart, "The New Female Criminal: Reality or Myth," *British Journal of Criminology* 19 (1979):50–59.

39. Mann, *Female Crime and Delinquency*, p. 110.

40. Noblit and Burcart, "Women and Crime: 1960–1970."

41. Mann, *Female Crime and Delinquency*, p. 109.

42. Leonard, *Women, Crime and Society*, pp. 10–11.

8

Intrafamilial Offenses Perpetrated by Women

Arguably the crime of which women are most frequently guilty is the one least reported to law enforcement: offenses against family members. According to official 1985 figures, 5,327 females age 18 and over were arrested for offenses against family and children.[1] This is believed to represent only a fraction of such incidences nationwide.[2] Like wife and parent battering and incest, discussed earlier, this form of familial mistreatment often remains a family secret. However, this should not detract from its seriousness as not only a domestic problem but a social problem. Hence we devote this chapter to an exploration of maltreatment perpetrated by women in the family.

WOMEN AND FAMILIAL HOMICIDE

Unlike other family crimes, homicide has a fairly high rate of reported incidence. However, among women homicide ranks as one of the lowest crimes for which they are arrested. Yet official data likely are underrepresentative of either the prevalence or circumstances of homicide committed by women in the United States. One reason is that because *UCR* classification of murder and nonnegligent manslaughter is based entirely on police investigation rather than the additional or other determination by agencies such as the medical examiner's office or court, many murders committed by women may go unrecorded. Other murders are simply undetected or the female murderer remains unidentified or is not investigated. Even when investigated, some offenders are diverted from the criminal justice system or acquitted. Excluded from official murder counts are deaths attributed to suicide, negligence, accident, or justifiable homicide.

The shortcomings of official statistics aside (see chapter 6 for an in-depth analysis of *UCR* data), the female killer is relatively rare, especially when compared to her male counterpart. When women do kill, it is often in the context of the family. In a comprehensive study of homicides and attempted homicides by female offenders in Hungary, G. Rasko found that of the 125 female murderers studied, 40 percent of their 140 victims were their husbands, common-law husbands, or lovers and 20 percent were their children.[3] Similar figures emerged from J. Totman's U.S.-based study of 120 murderers, which revealed that husbands, common-law husbands, or lovers made up 40 percent of the women's victims; children (excluding infanticide), 21 percent; and other relatives, 29 percent.[4]

A recent study of violent female criminals by D. Ward and colleagues supports the contention that women's role in murders and their chosen victims are closely associated with the female sex role.[5] This study of women incarcerated in state prisons for crimes of violence showed that women involved in murders were the sole perpetrator in 77 percent of the incidents, and in more than half a family member or lover was the victim.

The Woman as Spouse Murderer

The woman who kills her husband does so for a number of reasons, including jealousy, mental illness, substance abuse impairment, monetary gain, or desire to be with another. However, the motive most often associated with this form of familial homicide is self-defense or desperation culminating a period of abuse from a husband or father. In recent years much attention has been focused on this battered-wife-turned-killer scenario including a television movie, *The Burning Bed*, based on a real-life episode of the horrors that lead up to spouse killing.

Citing studies by Martin[6] and Hilberman and Munson,[7] Elissa Benedek offers the following description of the classic battered wife who ultimately murders her husband:

Such a woman often comes from a home where she has observed and experienced parental violence and sees violence as a norm in social interaction and as a solution for conflict. Marriage is frequently seen as an escape route, but her choice of husband is not intelligently determined. Thus, the potential offender often chooses a mate with a high penchant for violence. She has been beaten repeatedly and brutally for a period of years by a spouse or lover who may be drunk, sober, tired, depressed, elated, mentally ill, or just angry. Lacking educational and financial resources, she describes a feeling of being "trapped." This feeling increases proportionately with the number of young children she has. Community resources are disinterested, ineffective, or unavailable.... The battered wife has turned to social agencies, police prosecutors, friends, ministers, and family, but they have not offered meaningful support or advice.... Abused women who have murdered their spouses reveal that they feel that homicide was the only alternative left to them.[8]

A further perspective on the battered-woman-turned killer is given by psychologist Lenore Walker:

Most women who killed their batterers have little memory of any cognitive processes other than an intense focus on their own survival. Although, retrospectively, it can be seen where her defenses against denial of her anger at being an abuse victim are unraveling, the women do not have any conscious awareness of those feelings. Their description of the final incident indicates that they separate those angry feelings by the psychological process of a dissociative state and thus, do not perceive them. This desperate attempt at remaining unaware of their own unacceptable feelings is a measure of just how dangerous they perceive their situation. They fear showing anger will cause their own death, and indeed it could as batterers cannot tolerate the woman's expression of anger.[9]

Like the suicide victim, the (physically or psychologically) battered woman who kills her mate is so consumed with helplessness, hopelessness, despair, low self-esteem, and a distorted conception of reality that she fails to think logically, to look beyond a horrible situation for which there seems to be no reasonable solution, and thus she seeks an unreasonable one. Substance abuse or other variables may act as facilitation, but ultimately for most of these women their explosion of violence and escape occurs as a result of an inability to express aggressive or hostile feelings after a long bout of aggressive, often violent victimization.

Justifiable or Criminal Homicide? The battered woman who retaliates by murdering her spouse now finds herself faced with an entirely new and equally dangerous problem as she shifts from a victim to an offender. All too often the killing is the result not so much of a clear case of self-defense as an accumulation of suffering. Thus many of these women must go through at least some part of the criminal justice system. The charges against them and subsequent pleas vary. Some plead temporary insanity or impaired mental state; others simply admit their guilt; yet others opt for a self-defense plea that many lawyers now use as a defense in this sort of case, assuming a jury can be convinced that the wife had a reasonable apprehension or perception of the imminence of danger.

In any event, the woman still loses. Often faced with an unsympathetic public, jury, and certainly prosecutor, she may have to serve time in prison or in a psychiatric facility. If acquitted, she must still make a life for herself and in many cases her children, who also suffered in one way or another. She must come to terms with the fact that for whatever reason, she took another person's life—something that few can ever overcome. The most unfortunate aspect of women's solution to this problem is that it is never the only answer, although to many women it appears to be.

Infanticide

Infanticide is believed to be responsible for more child deaths than any single cause in history, with the exception of bubonic plague.[10] Defined as the willful act of killing children, usually infants, infanticide has traditionally been regarded as a sex-specific crime, or one that "actually excludes the members of one sex by legal definition."[11] In describing the English legal system, Carol Smart notes that infanticide does not apply to the British principle of equal applicability because it is an offense in which only women are considered the perpetrators.[12]

Until the nineteenth century, dead or abandoned infants were almost commonplace on city streets in America; and in 1892, 100 dead infants and 200 foundlings were found on the streets of New York City alone.[13] It is not currently known how many children die at the hands of their mothers each year; not only are statistics absent, varied, or unreliable, but many infant murders are attributed to crib death or some other natural or accidental cause. However, the incidence of infanticide is thought to be high.

The impetus for infanticide has included shame, birth control, illegitimacy, religious appeasement, money, superstition, mental illness, and cannibalism. Although this phenomenon has typically been associated most often with desperate unmarried mothers, in recent years many married women have resorted to "disposing" of an unwanted burden. The methods of infanticide most often recorded are drowning, suffocation, strangulation, and the infliction of wounds or fractures to the skull.

D. Lunde describes the typical mother who kills her child(ren) as follows:

Women who kill their infants or young children usually are severely disturbed, suffer from extreme bouts of depression and may experience delusions. Before a woman kills her offspring, she is likely to go through a preliminary period when she thinks about how to commit the crime, visualizes the dead child, and considers suicide.[14]

In *Infanticide* Maria Piers provides a good example of a common frightening scenario of infanticide:

A doctoral candidate in the social sciences at one of the large midwestern universities, who was teaching courses in the social sciences to employees of a large city sewer system, learned from these employees that during the previous year, four corpses of newborns had been found on the sewer screen. The newborns had been thrown directly after birth into the sewers, a preferred place for children's corpses for millennia. No identification or investigation was attempted in these cases of infant death.[15]

It should be noted that although it is rare, women also kill their older children and men kill babies, and the motivational and characteristic factors often vary or combine. In short, many children die each year at the hands of parents, and the reasons and justifications are often complex.

REVERSE SPOUSE ABUSE

Generally, the typical offender-victim pattern of spousal violence is that of the male aggressor and the female victim. However, recent studies suggest that reverse spouse abuse, or the wife as the perpetrator of spousal maltreatment, may actually occur with more frequency and severity. Steinmetz and Fields and Kirchner have studied this debate in-depth.[16]

Reverse spouse abuse is believed to be the least reported form of family violence. Social scientists contend that millions of husbands are being bruised and beaten but abstain from reporting such maltreatment for fear of humiliation. Robert Langley and Richard Levy estimate that 12 million men are physically abused by their wives at some point in their marriage.[17] Marital characteristics common to reverse spouse abuse include a large woman and a small man; a younger, physically stronger woman married to an older man; and an ill or physically handicapped man who has a healthy wife. Although size and strength variables may be significant in husband abuse, many couples enacting this scenario possess no such extreme differentials in their characteristics, or the male victim may possess the greater size or strength.

Steinmetz estimates that each year 280,000 men are battered but do not defend themselves from their spouses, often because they fear they might badly injure her, or they believe that to counterattack would make them a bully.[18] An analysis of spouse abuse findings from 2,143 American families reveals that, if the results were projected over the entire United States and its 47 million couples, 2 million husbands as compared to 1.8 million wives would be estimated to have experienced at least one of the most severe forms of violence.[19]

Some husband abusers may be reacting to a perceived attack by their husbands in which the women strike first to protect themselves. This is a classic example in which fear, intimidation, or previous abuse by the male partner perpetuates aggression from the female victim-turned-defensive perpetrator.

Another perspective of reverse spouse abuse involves the perception of an incident of abuse by the husband. For instance, in Emily Adler's study of marital violence, although the incidence of violence was similar for husbands and wives, the husband's definitions of the wife-perpetrated violence differed in six of sixteen cases.[20] The husband defined it as amusing, nonthreatening, ineffective, or annoying. None of the victimized wives defined the incident this way. Thus for many men, even if the degree of violence is the same as what a woman experiences, the men are affected by it differently and do not regard it as a problem.

A primary reason wife abuse is more likely to be defined as threatening than husband abuse is that generally men are physically stronger and larger than women, although, as we noted earlier, it certainly is not always the case. Another is men's socialization. Men are supposed to be tough, so they usually try to live up to that role, at least outwardly.

Although it would be difficult to prove that battered men have as tough a go of it as battered women, what is becoming evident among many professionals is that a substantial number of women today are dishing out as much punishment as they receive.

CHILD ABUSE AND NEGLECT

Adult violence directed toward children is certainly the most destructive form of familial violence and the most widespread. For our purposes, in this section *child abuse and neglect* is defined as any physical or emotional abuse or neglect of a child age 17 and under, perpetrated by a parent or guardian, which compromises in any way the child's developmental well-being or right to a childhood absent of parental maltreatment as defined by law.

Incidence figures vary so widely, along with the believed vast amount of unreported child abuse and neglect, that it is not possible to determine its magnitude with any degree of accuracy. However, if the various figures currently being circulated are any indication, the amount of child maltreatment in the United States is indeed staggering.

The National Council of Organizations for Children and Youth estimated that nationwide 580,000 cases of child abuse occur annually.[21] The National Center of Child Abuse and Neglect placed the figure at about one million children a year, of which between 100,000 and 200,000 are the victims of physical abuse; 60,000 to 100,000, sexual abuse; and the balance, neglect.[22] Levine estimated that each year two million cases of child neglect occur.[23] Other experts contend that as many as six million children each year are the victims of beatings or neglect.[24]

Although both parents are equally capable of abusing or neglecting their children, several studies point to the mother as the likely perpetrator. According to recent American Humane Association data, the female parent accounted for 47.7 percent of reported child neglect and the male parent, 30.9 percent.[25] David Gil's epidemiological study of abusing parents showed that mother or mother substitutes inflicted abuse in 47.6 percent of the cases compared to 39.2 percent of the fathers.[26] The remaining abusers were either other relatives or unknown. In Richard Gelles's survey of violence toward children in the United States, 68 percent of the mothers were found to be the perpetrator of at least one violent act of child abuse during the survey years, as opposed to 58 percent of the fathers.[27] These findings were supported by Steele and Pollock's psychiatric study in which the mother proved to be the abuser in 50 of 57 cases.[28]

In a comprehensive analysis of child abuse by Flowers, the following general characteristics of child-abusing mothers emerged:

- The abusers range in age from 20 to 40.
- Most abuse occurs in lower socioeconomic homes and those with a low educational level.
- The average age of the child victim is under 4 years.
- Mothers are the most serious child abusers.
- Black mothers are overrepresented in maltreatment figures.
- Middle- and upper-income abusers are underrepresented statistically.
- Single mothers are most often the perpetrators of neglect.
- Most child abusers married at a young age.
- Abuse often occurs as the result of unwanted or illegitimate pregnancies, or forced marriages.
- Many child abusers were abused themselves as children.
- Many child-abusing mothers are battered by their husbands.
- Substance abuse is associated with child abuse.[29]

Mothers of abused children are often characterized as impulsive, immature, dependent, self-centered, rigid, and rejecting. They generally lack nurturing and coping skills, possess a poor self-image, and have a low tolerance level. Abusive mothers tend to be socially isolated, distrustful of neighbors, highly stressed, and exhibiting a general pattern of social impoverishment. They often find it difficult to be self-sufficient or reliable.

SEXUAL ABUSE OF CHILDREN

Child sexual abuse is herein defined as any form of incestuous child sexual misuse or exploitation (such as fondling, oral or anal sex, intercourse, or molestation) by the mother/mother substitute that is considered illegal or detrimental to the child's optimal well-being. This represents the rarest form of mother-perpetrated child abuse. Reported mother-child incest accounts for under 2 percent of all reported cases of incest; however, the actual incidence is believed to represent a greater percentage, although father-daughter and sibling-sibling incest continues to make up the majority of incestuous liaisons.

Adele Mayer profiles the more typical patterns of mother-child incest.[30]

Type of Incest	Motivations (Individual Psychopathology)
Mother-Son	Substitute gratification for absent father
Mother-Daughter	Psychosis/infantilism

Mother-Son Incest

In mother-son incest, the mother is often severely disturbed, and as Weinberg found in his study, the son usually is as well.[31] In this incestuous relationship the father is often missing or away from the home and the mother seeks substitute sexual gratification with her son. It has been suggested sexual relationships between mothers and their school-age sons are more accepted socially than are incestuous relationships between father-daughter. Apparently only the most disturbed mother-son incest warrants societal condemnation, which indicates an unusual and dangerous double standard.

Mother-Daughter Incest

Mother-daughter incest is less prevalent than mother-son incest, and little is known about its contributing factors.[32] The offender is also usually extremely disturbed and manifests infantile and/or psychotic behavior. By turning to her daughter for emotional nurturance, the mother may effect a complete role reversal in their relationship.

Medlicott cited a case of mother-daughter incest in which the mother slept with the daughter to avoid the father; she then initiated sexual activity with the daughter.[33] Lidz and Lidz studied the adverse influences of a mother's homosexual tendencies toward her daughter.[34] In three cases the erotic relationship involved such matters as physical intimacy while the daughter was asleep, skin contact, and anal preoccupations. This closeness was combined with aloofness, which increased the child's insecurities. All three daughters became schizophrenic once they reached adulthood.

Our study of the woman perpetrator of family offenses clearly illustrates that as a paradigm of the troubled family it can no longer be ignored or downplayed. The somewhat low reported and estimated incidence of female-perpetrated offenses against the family is often misleading, as is the crimes' severity. Of equal concern are the effects of this form of familial dysfunction. A well-established association has been made between the aggressor woman of family violations and wife battering, parent battering, sibling violence, intergenerational abuse, juvenile and adult criminality, and a host of physical and psychological problems common to both victim and offender. Hence in our drive toward resolving the family in crisis, it might behoove us to recognize that the wife/mother is often at its hub.

NOTES

1. U. S. Federal Bureau of Investigation, *Crime in the United States: Uniform Crime Reports, 1985* (Washington, D.C.: Government Printing Office, 1986), p. 178.

2. It is estimated that about two-thirds of the crime committed in the United States is not reported to law enforcement. Additionally, many other crimes that are committed against family members are either ignored by police, known but not compiled, unrecognized because of definitional and jurisdictional perspectives on family offenses and child abuse, or simply put into another category of crime such as sex offenses or murder.

3. G. Rasko, "The Victim of the Female Killer," *Victimology: An International Journal* 1 (1976):396–402.

4. J. Totman, *The Murderess: A Psychosocial Study of the Process* (Ann Arbor: University Microfilms, 1971).

5. D. Ward, M. Jackson, and R. Ward, "Crimes of Violence by Women," in D. Mulvihill, M. M. Tumin, and L. A. Curtis, eds., *Crimes of Violence* (Washington, D.C.: Government Printing Office, 1969).

6. D. Martin, *Battered Wives* (San Francisco: Glide, 1976).

7. E. Hilberman and M. Munson, "Sixty Battered Women," *Victimology: An International Journal* 2 (1978):460–471.

8. Elissa P. Benedek, "Women and Homicide," in Bruce L. Danto, John Bruhns, and Austin H. Kutscher, eds., *The Human Side of Homicide* (New York: Columbia University Press, 1982), p. 155.

9. Lenore E. Walker, *The Battered Woman Syndrome* (New York: Springer, 1984), p. 40.

10. Theo Solomon, "History and Demography of Child Abuse," *Pediatrics* 51, no. 4 (1973):773–776.

11. Carol Smart, *Women, Crime, and Criminology: A Feminist Critique* (Boston: Routledge & Kegan Paul, 1976), p. 6.

12. Coramae R. Mann, *Female Crime and Delinquency* (University: University of Alabama Press, 1984), p. 22.

13. W. Sage, "Violence in the Children's Room," *Human Behavior* 4 (1975):42.

14. D. T. Lunde, "Hot Blood's Record Month: Our Murder Boom," *Psychology Today* 9 (1975):35–42.

15. Maria W. Piers, *Infanticide* (New York: W. W. Norton, 1978), p. 14.

16. M. Fields and R. Kirchner, "Battered Women Are Still in Need: A Reply to Steinmetz," *Victimology: An International Journal* 3, nos. 1–2 (1978):216–226.

17. Roger Langley and Richard C. Levy, *Wife Beating: The Silent Crisis* (New York: E. P. Dutton, 1977).

18. Suzanne K. Steinmetz, "The Battered Husband Syndrome," *Victimology* 2 (1978):507.

19. Richard J. Gelles, "The Myth of Battered Husbands," *MS* (October 1979):65–66, 71–72.

20. Emily S. Adler, "Perceived Marital Power, Influence Techniques and Marital Violence," in Lee H. Bowker, ed., *Women and Crime in America* (New York: Macmillan, 1981).

21. National Council of Organizations for Children and Youth, America's Children (Washington, D.C.), 1976.

22. D. J. Besharov, "U.S. National Center on Child Abuse and Neglect: Three Years of Experience," *Child Abuse and Neglect* 1 (1977):173–177.

23. A. Levine, "Child Abuse: Reaching the Parent," *Social Rehabilitation Record* 1 (1974):26–27.

24. Ronald B. Flowers, *Children and Criminality: The Child as Victim and Offender* (Westport, Conn.: Greenwood Press, 1986).

25. Alene B. Russell and Cynthia M. Trainor, *Trends in Child Abuse and Neglect: A National Perspective* (Denver, Colo.: American Humane Association, 1984), p. 98.

26. David G. Gil, *Violence against children: Physical Child Abuse in the United States* (Cambridge: Harvard University Press, 1970).

27. Richard J. Gelles, "Violence Toward Children in the United States," *American Journal of Orthopsychiatry* 48, no. 4 (1978):580–592.

28. Brandt F. Steele and C. B. Pollock, "A Psychiatric Study of Parents Who Abuse Infants and Small Children," in Ray E. Helfer and C. Henry Kempe, eds., *The Battered Child* (Chicago: University of Chicago Press, 1968), pp. 89–133.

29. Flowers, *Children and Criminality*, pp. 63–67, 72.

30. Adele Mayer, *Incest: A Treatment Manual for Therapy with Victims, Spouses, and Offenders* (Holmes Beach, Fla.: Learning Publications, Inc., 1983), p. 22.

31. S. Kirson Weinberg, *Incest Behavior* (New York: Citadel Press, 1955).

32. J. Goodwin and P. DiVasto, "Mother-Daughter Incest," *Child Abuse and Neglect* 3 (1979):953.

33. R. Medlicott, "Parent-Child Incest," *Australian Journal of Psychiatry* 1 (1967):180.

34. R. Lidz and T. Lidz, "Homosexual Tendencies in Mothers of Schizophrenic Women," *Journal of Nervous Mental Disorders* 149 (1969):229.

9

Prostitution: Women as Offenders and Victims

Whether thought of as sexual deviance, sexually motivated social deviance, immorality, criminality, victim, or victimless, prostitution has long been characterized as almost singularly a woman's offense. This of course is far from true, as men play important roles in prostitution as both customers and as gay or straight prostitutes. There is also a vast child prostitution market that may overshadow adult prostitution in extent and certainly in implications. However, our topic in this chapter will be limited to the dynamics of the female prostitute.

In 1985, 68,579 females aged 18 and over were arrested in this country for prostitution and commercialized vice.[1] This ranked eighth for the offenses in which women were arrested that year. Yet most likely this does not even begin to reflect the real extent of women's prostitution in this country; its range, discreetness (in many cases), and nature dictates that many prostitutes be adept at avoiding the law. Furthermore, police discretion in making arrests as well as official statistics that count each arrest rather than each individual arrested (arrest figures measure every separate occasion on which a person is taken into custody) indicate that arrest totals are not an accurate assessment of the incidence of prostitution, which some experts suggest runs into the hundreds of thousands.[2]

The real question we must address concerns whether women who engage in this activity are offenders or victims of crime. Many would say neither—that prostitution is in fact a "victimless crime" or a "crime without a complainant," or not really even a crime at all. These perspectives are no doubt interpretational. However, from this author's research on the subject, considerable evidence suggests that in most instances prostitution could not be termed totally victimless; whereas prostitutes seem paradoxically to be both offenders *and* victims.

DEFINING PROSTITUTION

Unlike female criminality in general, a great deal has been written about prostitution and the multifaceted perspectives on it as a social phenomenon. Hence many definitions of prostitution exist as well. Some view it explicitly within social or legal boundaries; others regard prostitution as "at most only a marginal type of vice."[3] Yet there are those ensconced in the world of prostitution who supply their own basic definition: "A man is a natural pimp and a woman is a natural whore."[4]

Basically, prostitution, as reflected in the literature, is defined in two ways: social or nonlegal, and legal.

Social Definitions

Social scientists and other professionals commonly define prostitution in terms of sexual relations characterized by barter, promiscuity, and/or emotional indifference. Many regard prostitution as "sexual intercourse on a promiscuous and mercenary basis, with emotional indifference."[5] Edwin Lemert adds barter as a variable of the interaction preceding sexual relations.[6] Charles Winick and Paul Kinsie define prostitution as "the granting of nonmaterial sexual access, established by mutual agreement of the woman, her client, and/or her employer, for remuneration which provides part or all of her livelihood."[7] A somewhat simpler, broader definition is offered by Paul Goldstein: "nonmarital sexual service for material gain."[8]

The definition that perhaps best captures the essence of this tripartite view of prostitution was established in 1914 by Abraham Flexner in his work, *Prostitution in Europe*:

Prostitution is characterized . . . by three elements variously combined: barter, promiscuity and emotional indifference. The barter need not involve the passage of money. . . . Nor need promiscuity be utterly choiceless: a woman is not the less a prostitute because she is more or less selective in her associations. Emotional indifference may be fairly inferred from barter and promiscuity. In this sense any person is a prostitute who habitually or intermittently has sexual relations more or less promiscuously for money or other mercenary consideration. Neither notoriety, arrest or lack of other occupation is an essential criterion.[9]

Flexner advanced the necessity of a broad definition because of the harm society suffers as a result of prostitution, naming four social costs in particular: personal demoralization, economic waste, spread of venereal disease, and the relationship of prostitution to social disorder and crime.

Flexner's definitional conceptualization can be attacked at several turns. One is the view shared by many (virtually all male) early researchers that prostitution is largely a product of female crime, ignoring male prostitutes and customers. Second, the correlation between prostitution and societal suffering has not been generally accepted, much less proved. Other social phenomena seem to have a greater impact on societal ills (for instance, organized crime, which is often behind prostitution). Third, he does not address the role society plays in condoning, creating, and supporting prostitution. Nevertheless, the basic premise of Flexner's assessment of prostitution continues to be supported.

Legal Definitions

The legal definition of prostitution tends to emphasize aspects of both morality and barter, as well as the bias toward the female prostitute. Notes one writer, "Prostitution is really the only crime in the penal law where two people are doing a thing mutually agreed upon and yet only one, the female partner, is subject to arrest."[10]

Early legal perspectives illustrate both inconsistency and sexism in viewing prostitution. Near the turn of the century the United States Supreme Court defined prostitution as relating "to women who for hire or without hire offer their bodies to indiscriminate intercourse with men."[11]

In *Prostitution in the United States*, Howard Woolston advanced that prior to 1918 the only statutory definition of prostitution in the country was Section 2372 of the Indiana Law, which read:

Any female who frequents or lives in a house of ill-fame or associates with women of bad character for chastity, either in public or at a house which men of bad character frequent or visit, or who commits adultery or fornication for hire shall be deemed a prostitute.[12]

A study of court decisions prior to 1918 reflected on the definitional dilemma of prostitution:

In some cases, the element of gain was considered an essential ingredient of prostitution, and in others it was not the case. Dictionary definitions whether those of Webster or of the Law Dictionaries are equally confusing. In Webster the definition varies according to the edition.[13]

As recently as 1968, the Oregon Supreme Court sought to clarify who should be termed a prostitute when it ruled, "The feature which distinguishes a prostitute from other women who engage in illicit intercourse is the indiscrimination with which she offers herself to men for hire."[14]

Hence it becomes apparent that past legal definitions of prostitution are a reflection of not only the legality of the incident but morality and perceptions of what a woman's role in society should be, while putting considerably less emphasis on the male role in prostitution.

Today the law recognizes the existence of heterosexual and homosexual male prostitutes. However, men are rarely charged with prostitution or solicitation. This fundamental reality therefore makes prostitution a sex-specific crime, particularly when one considers that more women are arrested for solicitation than for the act of coitus.[15]

Prostitution is currently a crime in every jurisdiction in the country, with the exception of Nevada, where it is legal in most counties. Thirty-eight states expressly prohibit payment for sexual acts; solicitation laws exist in forty-four states and the District of Columbia; and other states check prostitution through vagrancy and loitering statutes. Legally, prostitution is viewed as a misdemeanor, or an offense that normally consists of a fine and/or thirty days in jail. Consequently, 30 percent of the population in the majority of women's jails consists of prostitutes. Furthermore, 70 percent of all women incarcerated for felonies were originally arrested for prostitution.[16] At present some states are attempting to enact legislation to increase penalties for prostitution, which could only hurt the primary person most laws are geared towards: the female prostitute.

A Definition of the Female Prostitute

Because most nonlegal and legal definitions of prostitution (both past and present) appear to be bound to age-old concepts and stereotypes that seem to define the prostitute as a woman rather than the woman as a prostitute, it seems appropriate that we establish a working definition of the adult female prostitute only for the purposes of this chapter. This position advances that on the whole, prostitution is an act comprising many components and characters, and a definition of prostitution should reflect this nature. However, as our interest is only on the woman and crime, it makes sense to stay within that narrow range.

Thus women as prostitutes will be defined as any females aged 18 and over who engage in any sexual relations (such as intercourse, fellatio, exhibitionism), primarily for material gain, with persons other than their married partners. Such areas as promiscuity and emotional indifference were left out of this definition because many women engage in prostitution without necessarily being promiscuous or emotionally indifferent.

THE ETIOLOGY OF PROSTITUTION

Most theories that explore the causes of prostitution generally can be grouped in one of the following areas: psychological, sociological, social-psychological, economic, or contemporary.

Early Theories

Early psychological approaches to prostitution have been largely rejected. For instance, Cesare Lombroso's "born criminal" or atavism theory, which he attributed particularly to prostitutes, was faulty mainly because of his outlandish proposals themselves and the small size of his sample of female prisoners.[17] Another early theorist, W. I. Thomas, advanced a "dyadic goals-means conflict theory."[18] He postulated that women became prostitutes to satisfy a need for excitement and response. This notion was dismissed by most, principally because it has never been proved a causal factor in prostitution.

Perhaps the theory that influenced much of the early thinking on prostitution causation was the Freudian psychiatric mode, which inferred some type of inherent pathology among women who prostituted themselves.[19] The folk tales resulting from these early notions contended that prostitutes were immoral, psychopathic, and/or feebleminded, as no "normal" woman would engage in such conduct. The literature is replete with psychoanalytic interpretations of prostitution, as well as refutations by other psychoanalytically based researchers.

Although many Freudian disciples viewed prostitutes as frigid with "immature psychosexual development and severely deficient object relationships, case studies of sex delinquents and prostitutes failed to indicate any general state of abnormality."[20] Moreover, Jennifer James's data revealed that prostitutes experienced a higher rate of orgasm than the general female population, which contradicts the idea that prostitutes are frigid.[21]

Sociological View

A number of sociological and social-psychological approaches to prostitution examine the phenomenon in terms of social structure, social pathology and culture. In Winick and Kinsie's sociological perspective, they seek to explain society's hostility toward prostitution by suggesting that the social structure is threatened by prostitution because "people tend to equate sexual activity with stable relationships, typified by the family."[22]

Kingsley Davis proposed a functionalist theory of prostitution.[23] He contended that the function served by prostitution is the protection of the family unit, maintenance of the chastity and purity of the "respectable" citizenry. Davis explores why most women do not choose an occupation in prostitution. He suggests that morality is more potent than the financial benefits of prostitution, and that this societal system of morality creates prostitution by defining the sex drive in terms of a meaningful social relationship and denouncing prostitution as a meaningless sexual relationship.

A social pathology point of view was forwarded by Lemert, who described prostitution as "a formal extension of more generalized sexual pathology in our culture, of which sexual promiscuity and thinly disguised commercial exploitation of sex in informal contexts plays a large and important part."[24] In this perspective the context of prostitution is situational and the act of prostitution is a reflection of the strains and conflicts in our society.

Cultural transmission theories claim that prostitution results from a "weakening of family and neighborhood control and the persistence and transmission from person to person of traditional delinquent activities."[25] Although some evidence exists that the most important source of a prostitute's initial information about prostitution comes from girlfriends, relatives, and the neighborhood, other researchers find that prostitution is not a product of ecological factors and is present at all income and occupational levels because of "urban anonymity and the weakening of traditional and moral values."[26]

Economic Perspective

Many believe basic economics to be the primary factor in prostitution causation. Lemert addresses the inferior status women have in regard to power and control over material gains as an indication of our society and prostitution as the method for balancing this differential in status.[27] According to Winick and Kinsie, the career sequence involved in deciding to become a prostitute is based upon few work opportunities, the recognition of the money to be made, and an inclination toward sexual promiscuity.[28]

Perhaps the most in-depth exploration of motivations for entrance into a life of prostitution was done by Jennifer James. She completed a comprehensive study of prostitutes in the mid–1970s and described five aspects of our economic-social structure that make prostitution alluring or a viable alternative to many women.

- There are virtually no other occupations available to unskilled or low-skilled women with an income (real or potential) comparable to prostitution.
- There are virtually no other occupations available to unskilled or low-skilled women that provide the adventure or allow the independence of the prostitution life-style.
- The traditional "woman's role" is almost synonymous with the culturally defined female sex role, which emphasizes service, physical appearance, and sexuality.
- The discrepancy between accepted male and female sex roles creates the "Ma-

donna-whore" concept of female sexuality, such that women who are sexually active outside the limits of their "normal" sex-role expectations are labeled deviant and lose social status.

- The cultural importance of wealth and material goods leads some women to desire "advantages to which [they are] not entitled by [their] position" in the socioeconomic stratification.[29]

Contemporary Trends

Much of the contemporary research on the etiology of prostitution drifts away from psychological applications and serious pathology and focuses more on the notion of a poor self-concept. Studies on the correlation between negative childhood experiences (such as incest, rape, molestation) and, later, prostitution indicate that such factors potentially contribute to a negative self-image, which may in turn lead to a deviant self-image and prostitutional behavior. Additionally, "negative sexual experiences may also undermine the development of self-respect and enhance the appeal of and identification with alternative feminine roles."[30] One such role is prostitution.

Contemporary, economic, and sociological perspectives of prostitution generally provide us with more reasonable propositions of why prostitution occurs. However, even these approaches must be viewed with caution, because there are always women who fit the model described but fail to enter a life of prostitution, as well as others who do not seem to possess the slightest incentive or motivation yet find their way into this life-style.

TYPOLOGY OF PROSTITUTES

Categorizing prostitutes is not simple because of the different variables that function in prostitution, overlapping qualities of prostitutes, and the different types of women involved in this life-style. For instance, does one categorize them by social class, race, or the area in which prostitution occurs?

Thus it would be virtually impossible to establish a type to account for every person who becomes a prostitute, especially when adult male and child prostitutes are considered as well. However, some general patterns of female prostitutes have been established that would seem to account for the more common types.

Harry Benjamin and R. E. L. Masters, in their book, *Prostitution and Morality*, grouped prostitutes into two general categories: voluntary and compulsive.[31] Voluntary prostitutes are acting rationally and freely choose prostitution. Compulsive prostitutes are to some degree acting under compulsion by "psychoneurotic needs." The researchers ac-

knowledge that in most cases prostitutes cannot be accurately categorized by either type exclusively.

Goldstein "typecasts" prostitutes in terms of occupational commitment and occupational milieu.[32] Occupational commitment focuses on
the frequency of a woman's participation in prostitution and is subdi-
vided into three types: temporary (a discrete act of prostitution not more
than six months in duration in a specific occupational milieu), occasional
(two or more discrete incidents of prostitution in a particular occupational milieu; each episode not more than six months long); and continual
(more than six months long in a specific occupational milieu on a steady
basis).

Occupational milieu refers to the particular type of prostitution in
which the woman is involved. Goldstein divides these into seven types.

- Streetwalker. A woman who overtly solicits males on the street and offers her
  sexual favors for payment.
- Massage parlor Prostitute. A woman who offers sexual services in a massage
  parlor, whose activities may or may not be limited to fondling of the genitals.
- House Prostitute. A woman who works in an establishment set up specifically
  for prostitution where male clients are given sexual services.
- Call Girl. A woman who works in a residence soliciting clients or is solicited
  over the telephone.
- Madam. A woman who supplies other prostitutes with customers for a percentage of the fee.
- Mistress. A woman who is primarily supported by one man at a time, or who
  sees only one man at a time for cash.
- Barterer. A woman who exchanges sexual favors for professional or other
  services, or for material goods such as drugs or clothes.[33]

Three other prostitute types should be noted as well:

- Bar Girl. A woman who works in a bar, lounge, or other entertainment establishment not specifically set up for prostitution, where male clients are
  solicited or the woman is willingly solicited by males for sexual services.
- Referral Prostitute. This type of prostitute is referred to clients by others (often
  prostitutes themselves). This differs from a madam, as the referrer may have
  no financial stake in the referral.
- Sex Ring-Escort Prostitute. These women generally are part of a large-scale
  phone referral operation. The prostitutes, who are set up with clients through
  escort services, are women of all types.

Many of these types cross from one occupational milieu to another or
engage in two or more types at the same time. For instance, the bar
prostitute may roam the streets and barter her services for drugs.

For our purposes, the prostitutional types that appear to exemplify prostitution best in our society are streetwalkers and call girls. Because these two divisions can easily be classified as the lower and upper classes, respectively, of prostitution, we should examine them further.

Streetwalkers

James's extensive data on Seattle streetwalkers provides a provocative study of this type of prostitute and related dynamics, such as the role of the pimp, geographical mobility, and motivational patterns of both prostitutes and customers.[34]

The anthropologist identifies thirteen roles played by prostitutes. These roles include those under the label "true prostitutes": "outlaw," "rip-off artist," "hype," "old-timer," "thoroughbred," and "lady"; and roles affixed to part-timers, women "who had no style," or amateurs, "ho." The "hype" refers to a prostitute who works to support her addiction to ritalin or heroin. A "lady" is identified by her carriage, finesse, class, and professionalism. "Outlaws" are prostitutes independent of pimps. "Rip-off artists" are thieves disguised as prostitutes; prostituting is not their major income source. "Old-timers" are seasoned professionals who lack the class of the "lady"; and "thoroughbreds" refers to young, professional prostitutes. None of these roles can be termed mutually exclusive, "since they describe different dimensions of streetwalker behavior rather than complete behavioral sets, each containing elements from all relevant streetwalker behavioral dimensions."[35]

James refuted a number of misconceptions about the pimp-prostitute relationship. From her research she concluded that

it is not true that pimps force women to work against their will, seduce young girls, turn women into drug addicts for the purpose of control, give no sexual satisfaction to their women, keep them from ever leaving their stable, and are never married to prostitutes who work for them.[36]

Other than the advantages and disadvantages of attaching oneself to a pimp, it seems that the "severe social isolation that preprostitutes feel predisposes them to join up with someone who 'plugs' them into the world, giving them a set of social relations, a place to call their own, and an ideology to make the world intelligible."[37] Although there is something rather oppressive about pimping, it is not as much "the actions of the pimp himself (unless he . . . subjects his prostitutes to severe violence) as it is the structure of the social environment from which these women come."[38]

James identifies three groups of motivations for streetwalkers:

- Conscious: economics, working conditions, adventure, a persuasive pimp.
- Situational: early experiences in life, parental abuse and/or neglect, occupation.
- Psychoanalytic: general factors, oedipal fixation, latent homosexuality, retardation.[39]

James's findings can be criticized because they cannot be considered representative of all streetwalkers. For instance, many prostitutes are victimized by violence, drug abuse, seduction, and fear (which itself is enough to keep them in a pimp's stable even in the absence of physical abuse). Nevertheless, this research is significant in promoting understanding of some of the dynamics common to many prostitutes on the street.

Call Girls

If streetwalkers represent the lowest and most noticeable class of prostitutes, call girls constitute the highest and least noticeable class of prostitutes. Because their visibility is low, their number is not as easily estimated. However, there is some indication that call girls, with participants ranging from part-time college students to housewives to fulltime working women, may represent the largest group of prostitutes.

Unlike their streetwalker counterparts, call girls often lead a life of glamour and prosperity. Many make the amount of money that anyone—man or woman—would envy, sometimes well into six figures annually. Literature and the show business world are infamous for their portrayal of the two classes of prostitution. Black women are typically associated with the unsavory streetwalker's life; a different picture emerges altogether with the attractive white call girl whose problems (such as an unsuspecting boyfriend) seem fairly insignificant by comparison.

Even call girls are capitalizing on the image conveyed of their lifestyle. Two recent books, *Confessions of a Part-Time Call Girl* and *Mayflower Madam*, do everything possible to promote this form of prostitution—the fun, excitement, high profits—while for the most part ignoring some of the realities inherent in prostitution, such as its illicit and immoral nature, the risk of disease or attack by customers, and a risk particular to call girls whose discretion is partly responsible for their success: exposure, arrest, and humiliation.[40] Recently a call girl ring of 150 housewives, nurses, secretaries, and other women was broken up by police in San Francisco.[41] Ironically, the entire operation was run by a former streetwalker-turned-multimillionaire, which illustrates the interchangeability in the world of prostitution. Many call girls spent years on the streets before their circumstances improved.

Research indicates that the association between some form of pathology and prostitution may be influenced by class level:

At the upper level, among the full-time call girls and part-time housewives who appear to lead economically secure, stable, arrest-free lives, there is no evidence of special pathology. At the lower levels, inhabited by streetwalkers, drug addicts, juvenile runaways, and deviants of many different stripes, the population is so prone to psychological pathology that it is difficult to know what part, if any, prostitution contributes to their many difficulties.[42]

A study of white-collar prostitutes found no existence of pathology or even hostility toward males. The women interviewed indicated that the primary factors in their sexual encounters were money or something else of value (such as luxury items, rent, groceries, money for doctor bills).[43]

A number of psychologically oriented studies of call girls have been made, aided by reports by their psychotherapists; this would tend to dismiss the notion that call girls lead lives free of problems. One of the most useful studies was conducted by Harold Greenwald, who wrote *The Elegant Prostitute*.[44] His etiology of prostitution included differential association and economic and other environmental factors.

Greenwald was unsure whether the severe personality problems in his patients had encouraged the original choice of prostitution as an occupation or had come about as a result of years in the profession. He contended that prostitution was "not necessarily more degrading than working at a job one hated or being married to a man one found physically repulsive."[45] According to the author, although prostitution has a complex etiology, there is an easy means of prevention, for "he has never known a call girl who had strong bonds of love and affection with her family."[46] Karen Rosenblum's approach to call girls is intermediate; she found that the etiology of their prostitution "includes strong components of the need to be independent of men and to gain as much money as possible."[47]

James Bryan's sociological study of call girls examined how they learn their trade.[48] Bryan found that the women generally learned their occupation by serving as apprentice to an established call girl, an arrangement that ceased once the apprentice had developed her own "book" of clients or found herself at odds with her trainer. The training comprised two broad areas: verbal behavior and attitude. "The verbal behavior was difficult for many apprentices to master because it was more contrary to traditional sex roles than the overt sexual activity that was sold. Call girls had to learn to be verbally aggressive on the phone and to ask directly for dates."[49] In a later study Bryan found that in terms of attitude, call girls viewed themselves as social workers, counselors, and sexual therapists whose services were badly needed in American society.[50]

THE WOMAN AS A VICTIM OF PROSTITUTION

The female offender of the act of prostitution has been clearly established. Throughout most of the United States, this is a criminal offense, and as the majority of prostitutes appear to be acting of their own free will, few regard them as victims unless they are viewed as deserving victims. But should they be any more negatively labeled than the men who seek their services? Let us explore the other side of the female prostitute offender.

The Harsh Reality

Degradation, condemnation, hatred, and alienation are only a few of the realities in the life of a prostitute. Beatings, psychological abuse, rape, mugging, murder and drugs often come with the territory. Serial killers seem to be particularly taken with the idea of ridding the streets of "ladies of the night," whom they feel the world would be better without. Substance abuse is a serious problem among prostitutes. Psychologically, few can escape without any permanent mental or emotional scars from their experience.

Another major problem is the spread of sexually transmitted diseases. Aside from the usual venereal diseases, prostitutes risk contracting herpes and the far more serious Acquired Immune Deficiency Syndrome (AIDS). A recent government study found that many female prostitutes are carrying the AIDS virus and warned men to avoid prostitutes.[51] It is interesting to note, aside from the danger disease poses to women who engage in prostitution, that the government appears more concerned about protecting the men who use prostitutes than trying to curb prostitution and create greater awareness among preprostitutes and prostitutes about these risks. This is a clear example of how the labeling mechanisms of our male-dominated society arbitrarily pass judgment upon its members, deciding who is deemed deviant and who is not.

Circumstantial Victimization

Although no indirect variables have proven to be causal in prostitution, evidence indicates that many women who enter prostitution have been the victims of child abuse or neglect, sexual abuse, child prostitution/pornography, impoverishment, battering, substance abuse, subjugation, and other social and personal problems that are believed to influence the woman's perception of herself, the world, and her place in it.

Discriminatory Enforcement of the Law

In addition to the many forms of victimization prostitutes face in their daily lives or perhaps en route to prostituting themselves, they are also victims of the laws on prostitution and the enforcement of those laws. For instance, it is clear that illicit sexual behavior is frowned upon more when the offender is a woman as opposed to a man. It has been estimated that 20 percent of the male population has some association with prostitutes, indicating that male customers considerably outnumber available prostitutes. Yet the weight of legal reprisal appears to sit almost solely on the woman's shoulders.[52] Recent official figures show that only two customers are arrested for every eight prostitutes arrested.[53] Further evidence of this disparity can be seen in a report on female offenders in the District of Columbia in 1966, which found that although 1,110 women were arrested for prostitution that year, only four men were charged with procuring.[54]

In theory, prostitution laws are designed to protect the traditional family. Yet by and large only the woman is punished for her role in prostitution. A number of rationalizations seek to explain why prostitutes are penalized and their customers are not; however, as Leo Kanowitz put it candidly, female prostitutes would not exist without male customers.[55] Society must confront this fact when affixing blame and guilt.

Racism

Not only do women face disadvantages because of social and legal discrimination, there is also a differential in societal attitudes and law enforcement along race and social class lines within the female prostitution population. Although the typical customers of prostitutes are middle-class men between the ages of 30 and 60, those most penalized by the law are poor black women who are "forced onto the streets and into blatant solicitation where the risk of arrest is highest."[56] Black women are seven times more likely to be arrested for prostitution than women of other races or ethnic groups.[57] It is no surprise that the largest proportion of black prostitute arrests occurs in the inner cities, where "living standards are low, the level of desperation high, and police prejudice endemic."[58]

Economic Discrimination

Perhaps the most significant area of victimization that pushes women into prostitution is the sex-based inequality in our economic structure. Several studies have addressed prostitution from this perspective and found that money-making potential and the opportunity for a better quality of life that prostitution offers (or so it is perceived by many women)—especially for unskilled, low skilled, undereducated, and financially struggling women—is the primary motivation associated with this occupational choice.[59] Economic discrimination and few money-making options for women in our society continue to pressure women in their struggle to survive, keep pace, and effectively compete in the workplace, making such illegal activities as prostitution a viable and, to some, necessary alternative.

Prostitution continues to be associated almost exclusively with women. Although in reality women comprise only a portion of the components of prostitution, they receive the worst treatment from both society and the criminal justice system. The dynamics of female prostitution are complex and varied. She has the most visible role in women's criminality. Prostitution is a product of a male-supported market that shows little sign of vanishing. Further research is needed to understand better the making of the prostitute and what can be done to alter a course that is a danger to all women and a serious problem to society at large.

NOTES

1. U.S. Federal Bureau of Investigation, *Crime in the United States: Uniform Crime Reports, 1985* (Washington, D.C.: Government Printing Office, 1986), p. 178.

2. Charles Winick and Paul M. Kinsie, *The Lively Commerce* (Chicago: Quadrangle Books, 1971), p. 5.

3. Robert E. L. Faris, *Social Disorganization* (New York: Ronald Press, 1955), p. 269.

4. Nathan C. Heard, *Howard Street* (New York: Dial Press, 1970), p. 86.

5. Marshall B. Clinard, *Sociology of Deviant Behavior* (New York: Holt, Rinehart & Winston, 1957), p. 249.

6. Edwin M. Lemert, *Social Pathology* (New York: McGraw-Hill, 1951).

7. Winick and Kinsie, *The Lively Commerce*, p. 3.

8. Paul J. Goldstein, *Prostitution and Drugs* (Lexington, Mass.: Lexington Books, 1979), p. 33.

9. Abraham Flexner, *Prostitution in Europe* (New York: Century Co., 1914), p. 11.

10. Kate Millett, "Prostitution: A Quartet for Female Voices," in Vivian Gor-

nick and Barbara K. Moran, eds., *Women in a Sexist Society* (New York: New American Library, 1971), p. 79.

11. *U.S.* v. *Bitty*, 208 U.S. 393, 401 (1908); Charles Rosenbleet and Barbara J. Pariente, "The Prostitution of the Criminal Law," *American Criminal Law Review* 11 (1973):373.

12. Howard B. Woolston, *Prostitution in the United States* (New York: Century Co., 1921), p. 35.

13. Ibid.; Isabel Drummond, *The Sex Paradox* (New York: Putnam, 1953), p. 208.

14. *State* v. *Perry*, 249 Oregon 76, 81, 436 p. 2d 252, 255 (1968); Rosenbleet and Pariente, "The Prostitution of the Criminal Law," p. 381.

15. Carol Smart, *Women, Crime, and Criminology: A Feminist Critique* (Boston: Routledge & Kegan Paul, 1976); Marilyn G. Haft, "Hustling for Rights," in Laura Crites, ed., *The Female Offender* (Lexington, Mass.: Lexington Books, 1976).

16. Haft, "Hustling for Rights," pp. 212–213.

17. Cesare Lombroso and William Ferraro, *The Female Offender* (New York: Appleton, 1900).

18. William I. Thomas, *The Unadjusted Girl: With Cases and Standpoint for Behavior Analysis* (New York: Harper & Row, 1923).

19. Sigmund Freud, *New Introductory Lectures on Psychoanalysis* (New York: W. W. Norton, 1933).

20. Ibid.

21. Jennifer James, "Motivations for Entrance into Prostitution," in Laura Crites, ed., *The Female Offender* (Lexington, Mass.: Lexington Books, 1976), p. 190.

22. Winick and Kinsie, *The Lively Commerce*.

23. Kingsley Davis, "The Sociology of Prostitution," *American Sociological Review* 2 (1937):744–755.

24. Lemert, *Social Pathology*, p. 237.

25. Faris, *Social Disorganization*, p. 271.

26. James, "Motivations for Entrance into Prostitution," p. 186; Norman Jackson, Richard O'Toole, and Gilbert Geis, "The Self-Image of the Prostitute," in John H. Gagnon and William Simon, eds., *Sexual Deviance* (New York: Harper & Row, 1967), p. 46.

27. Lemert, *Social Pathology*.

28. Winick and Kinsie, *The Lively Commerce*.

29. James, "Motivations for Entrance into Prostitution," p. 194; Davis, "The Sociology of Prostitution."

30. Jennifer James and Peter P. Vitaliano, "Factors in the Drift Towards Female Sex Role Deviance" (unpublished paper, 1979).

31. Harry Benjamin and R. E. L. Masters, *Prostitution and Morality* (New York: Julian Press, 1964).

32. Goldstein, *Prostitution and Drugs*, p. 34.

33. Ibid., pp. 35–37.

34. Jennifer James, "Two Domains of Streetwalker Argot," *Anthropological Linguistics* 14 (1972):174–175.

35. Ibid.; Lee H. Bowker, *Women, Crime, and the Criminal Justice System* (Lexington, Mass.: Lexington Books, 1978), p. 154.

36. Bowker, *Women, Crime, and the Criminal Justice System*, p. 155; Jennifer James, "Prostitute-Pimp Relationships," *Medical Aspects of Human Sexuality* 7 (1973):147–163.

37. Bowker, *Women, Crime, and the Criminal Justice System*, p. 155.

38. Ibid.

39. Jennifer James, "Prostitutes and Prostitution," in Edward Sagarin and Fred Montanino, eds., *Deviants: Voluntary Actors in a Hostile World* (Morrison, N.J.: General Learning Press, 1977), pp. 390–391.

40. Barbara Ignoto, *Confessions of a Part-Time Call Girl* (New York: Dell, 1986); Sydney Barrows and William Novak, *Mayflower Madam: The Secret Life of Sydney Biddle Barrows* (New York: Arbor House, 1986).

41. "Ring of 150 Call Girls Broken Up, SF Cops Say," *Sacramento Bee* (August 24, 1983), p. A5.

42. Freda Adler, *Sisters in Crime: The Rise of the New Female Criminal* (New York: McGraw-Hill, 1975), p. 73.

43. Coramae R. Mann, "White Collar Prostitution" (unpublished paper, 1974).

44. Harold Greenwald, *The Elegant Prostitute: A Social and Psychoanalytic Study* (New York: Walker and Co., 1970).

45. Ibid., p. xx.

46. Ibid., p. 242; Bowker, *Women, Crime, and the Criminal Justice System*, pp. 151–152.

47. Bowker, *Women, Crime, and the Criminal Justice System*, p. 152; Karen E. Rosenblum, "Female Deviance and the Female Sex Role: A Preliminary Investigation," *British Journal of Sociology* 26 (1975):173–178.

48. James H. Bryan, "Apprenticeships in Prostitution," *Social Problems* 12 (1965):287–297.

49. Ibid.; Bowker, *Women, Crime, and the Criminal Justice System*, p. 152.

50. James H. Bryan, "Occupational Ideologies and Individual Attitudes of Call Girls," *Social Problems* 13 (1966):441–450.

51. Margaret Engel, "Many Prostitutes Found to Be AIDS Carriers," *Washington Post* (September 20, 1985), p. A1.

52. Jennifer James, "The Prostitute as Victim," in Jane R. Chapman and Margaret Gates, eds., *The Victimization of Women* (Beverly Hills: Sage Publications, 1978), p. 176.

53. U.S. Federal Bureau of Investigation, *Crime in the United States: Uniform Crime Reports, 1976* (Washington, D.C.: Government Printing Office, 1977).

54. "Offenders in the District of Columbia," *Report of the D. C. Commission on the Status of Women* (Washington, D.C.: Government Printing Office, 1972), p. 18.

55. Leo Kanowitz, *Women and the Law: The Unfinished Revolution* (Albuquerque: University of New Mexico Press, 1969).

56. Haft, "Hustling for Rights," p. 212.

57. Ibid.

58. Ibid.

59. James, "Motivations for Entrance into Prostitution"; W. Pomeroy, "Some Aspects of Prostitution," *Journal of Sex Research* 11 (1965):177–187; K. Davis, "The Sociology of Prostitution," *American Sociological Review* 2 (1937):744–755.

10

The Heterogeneous Nature of the Female Criminal

Although women's criminality remains fairly low in general and is associated most often with crimes of property, prostitution, and offenses against the family, recent years have nevertheless seen an increase in both the incidence and range of crimes that women commit. Because our aim in this section is to explore the female offender, it seemed appropriate that we take an informative look at a few of the emerging or hidden aspects of the female offender that until recently have received little attention in the criminology literature.

THE FEMALE RAPIST

When women are thought of as violent criminals, few equate this with the crime of rape. Official figures bear this out. In 1985 only 252 females aged 18 and over were arrested for forcible rape.[1] Even this number tells us little about the nature of the rape. For example, did these women actually commit an act of rape? Can there even be such a female rapist? Were these women simply the accomplice of a male rapist and therefore charged with the same offense? Was the victim male or female?

Unfortunately, *Uniform Crime Reports* arrest data provide no answers to these questions. However, some studies have managed to shed light on the female rapist. Not only are women capable of rape, but it may occur much more frequently than figures indicate. Traditionally rape has been defined as penile-vaginal penetration by force or threat of force, or penetration of a woman not married to the offender that was non-consensual because the victim was unconscious or in some other way physically helpless. Only in recent years have a number of states begun to recognize the existence of male rape.

Yet the idea of a woman committing rape or attempting rape continues to defy believability. But it does occur, either by force or threat of force or physical violence, and it is not a new phenomenon. For instance, during a certain time in our country's history, a white woman in the South could force a black man to have sexual intercourse with her by threatening to scream "rape." Since the mere accusation could cost the black man his life, this incident would certainly qualify as rape by the very real threat of bodily harm.

Researchers William Masters and Philip Sarrel refuted the widespread myth that it would be nearly impossible for a man to achieve or maintain sexual arousal if he was assaulted by a woman:

Like most other sexual myths . . . its general acceptance has exerted an unfortunate influence on medicine, psychology and the law. Consequently, men who have been sexually assaulted by women have been extremely loath to admit this experience to anyone. They have feared that either they would be disbelieved or that they would be degraded socially and made the object of lewd jokes, not only by their peers but by representatives of the law and the health care professions.[2]

Although Masters and Sarrel acknowledged that rapes of males by women are rare, they theorized that many probably go unreported by the victims unless they seek help. They further concluded that the cases of males raped by females have a lower rate of reporting than the cases of females raped by males.

Few men who are sexually assaulted by women talk to therapists about their experience. In many cases even the law offers no protection. In seven states women are excluded from the rape statutes; hence "even those few men with the courage to report rape may find that they have no legal recourse against their attackers."[3] Even in states in which male rape laws exist, the chance that a female offender will be prosecuted is very limited. As rape expert Nicholas Groth put it, reinforcing the fears of such victims, "we've seen these guys forcibly assaulted by women, but they get in front of the police or courts, and who's going to believe them?"[4]

Most women who are charged with rape are likely not the primary aggressor but are acting in cooperation with or assisting a male partner. This is well illustrated in a recent case in California in which Susanne Perin aided her husband, who regularly raped and abused her, in hunting down other potential victims.[5]

Lesbian rape of women also occurs, though it is rarely documented or researched. Sociologist Stuart Miller asserted that the reality of rape is that "young rape old, blacks rape whites, whites rape women and girls, juveniles rape juveniles, and women rape women and girls."[6] Supporting this contention is Diana Russell's survey in which five of the respondents reported being raped by another female.[7] Rape as defined in the survey involved either the victim being forced to be engaged in oral or anal sex, or sex with lack of consent because the victim was unconscious, drugged, or otherwise physically helpless.

Women in prison seem to be particularly prone to sexual assault from other female prisoners. In a personal narrative a female prisoner noted that during the course of being attacked and burned by eight women inmates, she was raped, although she gave no details of the rape.[8] However, such admissions among female inmates are rare, and thus there is little evidence to substantiate that this is as widespread a problem in women's institutions as it is in men's prisons.

Nevertheless, female rapists are not a male fantasy but actually exist. This aspect of female criminality needs to be studied, probed, and treated as seriously as male rape.

THE FEMALE TERRORIST

Another crime of violence not generally associated with women is terrorism. This is particularly true on a global basis; many of the terrorist activities occurring today seem to be almost exclusively male perpetrated. However, women are well represented among terrorist groups, and some indications are that they are becoming more violent as well.

Defining terrorism can be difficult; not only does it comprise many forms, motivations, and issues, but often the terrorists themselves regard taking action "for a cause" rather than for terrorism per se. In general, terrorism can be politically motivated, national, international, transnational, or criminal in intent. From the view of the public at large, however, terrorism often means hijacking of airplanes, ships, or other forms of public transportation; kidnapping; bombing; murder-suicide missions; and other militant activities. The actions and escapades of the women in such organizations as the Japanese Red Army, the Irish Republic Army, the West Germany Baader-Meinhof Gang, and the U.S. group the Symbionese Liberation Army are regarded as terrorist activities.

In this country women make up the majority of terrorist group members, although men can usually be seen in the forefront. The typical female political terrorist in the United States is young, white, well educated, and from an upper-middle-class or upper-class family. Diana Oughton, Jane Alpert, and the more bizarre case of Patty Hearst are but a few notable examples.[9] Although a small percentage of black men are involved in terrorist activities, there are virtually no black female terrorists today. The blacks who are involved in the predominantly white terrorist groups are nearly always from the lower class, with criminal backgrounds, and were "drawn into the groups because white radicals regard them as symbols of the oppression they are fighting against."[10]

Traditionally female terrorists have functioned in subservient roles. They have been members of the supportive system that performs duties such as "fetcher and carrier, giver of aid and comfort to the masculine mastermind behind the scenes, and stout helpmeet—but nothing more—to the male operative in the field."[11] Some see this supportive assignment of terrorist women as utilizing them most effectively, not as male chauvinism.

Recent writers have noted a dramatic shift in the terrorist activities of women, from supportive duties to full-fledged terrorism.[12] Risks International data on 204 active female terrorists show that throughout the world women's participation in terrorist activities jumped from 12 percent of all terrorists in 1970 to as much as 30 percent in some areas by 1978. Comparatively, the breakdown of female terrorist actions between 1970 and 1978 was from noninvolvement in assassinations to 22.5 percent, and from 6 percent in kidnappings to over 17 percent of the perpetrators of facility attacks and 42 percent of maimings.[13]

Many believe that in fact female terrorists surpass their male counterparts in viciousness and cruelty:

The female terrorist has not been content just to praise the Lord and pass the ammunition; hers has been as often as not, the finger on the trigger of some of the most powerful weaponry in the arsenal of the modern-day terrorist. This new woman revolutionary is no Madame Defarge patiently, if ghoulishly, knitting beside the guillotine while waiting for heads to roll. The new breed of female terrorist not only must have its hands firmly on the lever but must be instrumental in the capture of the victim and in the process of judgment, as well as in dragging the unfortunate to the death instrument. Women terrorists have consistently proved themselves more ferocious and more intractable in these acts than their male counterparts. There is a cold rage about some of them that even the most alienated of men seem quite incapable of emulating.[14]

Female terrorists have not yet been adequately studied. However, with the recent wave of terrorism around the world and the clear association of women's involvement, this is a subject that should be of grave concern to all.

WOMEN IN GANGS

Most studies of female gang involvement (the few of them that exist) have centered on girls in juvenile gangs.[15] Somewhat ignored is the woman as a member of a criminal or delinquent gang. It is important that the words "criminal" and "delinquent" be stressed because, contrary to popular belief, gangs are not necessarily synonymous with acts of criminality or antisocial behavior.

According to law enforcement officials, hundreds of women interact with predominantly male street gangs.[16] An example of a typical female gang member is described below:

The 24-year-old woman wore a black leather jacket, tight jeans, black leather boots and a motorcycle chain around her thick waist as she walked through Central Park, talking about how and why she mugs people.
  "First I hide," she said. "Then I jump the person and pull out my switchblade. Sometimes I feel bad because I think they could be my mother. But then I think of my two kids. I have to buy food and clothes for them."[17]

A fellow female gang member probably best summed up the view of many women (and men) involved in gangs when she said, "We're one big family pulling together to survive in this world."

Sociologists, police, and gang members alike suggest that women in male-run gangs live in two contradictory worlds, one in which they may "fight, steal, and spy with the same gusto as some of the roughest men on the streets," and another that is motivated by "women's traditional desires to find a husband and build a family."[18]

Sergeant John Galea of the New York City Police Department notes that women have been in gangs in the city for more than a century. They generally have divorced parents, are members of a minority, and live under impoverished conditions. Galea contends that although street gangs in New York tend to rise and fall in decade-long cycles and seem to be in a transition period in the 1980s, women's presence in them has remained constant. "During periods of high gang activity, such as the 50's, women form their own gangs. At other times, they can be found only as members of male gangs."[19]

Researchers postulate that women join gangs for the same reasons men do: the gang offers them a sense of familial belonging they lack. Other women join gangs to increase their chances of finding a boyfriend or husband. "Gangs are the singles bars of the street set, reservoirs of some of the brightest, toughest and most sociable youths from urban ghettos."[20]

Once a female joins a gang, she can assume a broad range of roles, depending upon her own character and that of the group. Sociology professor and author of *Girls in the Gang*, Anne Campbell, claims that the role is more often that of a fighter:

A cardinal gang rule is that men fight men and women fight women. Many of the same things that trigger brawls among men—invasion of turf or harm to a fellow gang member, for instance—do so among women, gang members say. But, they add, when women are involved, the violence tends to erupt faster and end more quickly. The weapons used are more likely to be fingernails, teeth and knives rather than crowbars and guns.[21]

No comprehensive national studies exist on the scope of female memberships in adult criminal gangs or juvenile gangs, middle-class women in gangs, or the prevalence and nature of strictly women's gangs. However, on the last point some research has been done regarding girls' participation in gangs that might be useful in applying to women as gang members. Unfortunately, recent studies have been contradictory.

A national study by Walter Miller of gang activity in the fifteen largest cities in the country concluded that independent female gangs are few, their patterns of criminality were considerably less serious than male gangs' crimes, and little evidence exists to the notion that female gang activity is more violent now than in the past.[22] Freda Adler's findings on female delinquency were just the opposite. She contended that by the 1970s, "girls had become more highly integrated in male gang activity and were moving closer to parallel but independent, violence-oriented, exclusively female gangs."[23]

Obviously more effective research is needed in this field of study, particularly where it concerns women in gangs. Peter Buffum's study of homosexuality in female institutions speaks of the formation of female "families" in prison as a measure of stabilizing and legitimizing roles.[24] However, in general most of our information on female gangs, especially outside prison walls, is incomplete or tied to studies of male gangs.

WOMEN AS CON ARTISTS

The number of women arrested for fraud or confidence games has risen steadily from 1960 to the mid–1980s. Although men continue to account for the majority of fraud-related arrests, women are well represented as con artists; and if official statistics are any indication, women are slowly gaining. Nationwide, tens of thousands of people are victimized annually by frauds and most remain silent because of their shattered pride, embarrassment, and humiliation at being taken. Police estimate that only one in three con games is ever reported.

Most female confidence games are perpetrated upon other women—a reasonable assumption considering con women "can approach other women without arousing suspicion the way a strange man might."[25] However, when men and women pair up, the victims can be men, women, or children depending upon the players involved and the nature of the con.

The most prevalent of the three types of women-conning-women offenses is the pocketbook drop, also known as "the pigeon (slang for 'victim', also termed mom, lane, chump, vic) drop, dropping the leather, drag playing (from playing the main drag in town)."[26] Generally this con involves at least two people—the roper (the one who ropes the pigeon into the game) and the capper (she caps the game by producing found money or some other form of deception). The operatives are usually adept in the art of deceit, obfuscation, and disguise as they seek a likely pigeon.

The typical con victim is elderly, lonely and thus easy to befriend, lives alone, has enough money to make the game worthwhile, and talks freely about herself. The con woman's conversation is "glib, fast, mesmerizing," designed to keep the victim off guard and prevent her thinking clearly and logically. At the end of a successful con, the victim is usually bilked out of anywhere from hundreds to thousands of dollars before she realizes what has happened.

Most drag teams are recruited from ex-prostitutes. They tend to work for or with a pimp, with whom the women normally split their take. He also "takes care of them" in terms of clothes, shelter, and bail if they are arrested. Many of the women who are apprehended and convicted of defrauding a victim ultimately plea bargain for lighter sentences, something the proponents of paternalism like to point out. A leading authority in the field of con women explains it logically: "Con games look pretty mild to a criminal court judge compared to the murderers and rapists who pass before his bench, so he tends to impose lighter sentences on the players."[27]

The second most frequent con game perpetrated by women upon women is referred to as the "boujoo," a Romany term meaning "big lie." Just as with the pocketbook drop, the boujoo is calculated to fleece victims of their life savings, and often leaves them emotionally distraught as well. "An age-old swindle involving magic and the supernatural, the boujoo begins in the standard fortune telling parlor and typically ends with its pigeons in penury and shame."[28]

The third classic female flimflam is the handkerchief switch. Generally both the victim and perpetrator are black or Hispanic. The success of this game is dependent upon the player's ability to arouse in her victim the desire to assist a fellow countryman in dire straits far from home. The con essentially involves a sad tale involving money as told by the con artist, the victim producing money as an act of good faith to match the duper's money roll, which is put in a handkerchief or similar wrap, and switching the victim's handkerchief for one filled with paper.

It is difficult to imagine anyone being duped by such confidence games, but even the most intelligent are susceptible if they rely more on trust, benevolence, and the better side of human nature than caution and common sense.

Some observers question why con women, with their nerve and demonstrable intelligence, do not channel their abilities into legitimate enterprises. The same question, of course, could be asked of every skilled professional criminal or deviant from the norms of society. Psychiatrist William Frosch suggests that the same explanations apply:

Among numerous possible reasons . . . the con woman may be the product of a criminal subculture—that is to say, the child of criminal parents. . . . On another level, playing con games may be a conscious occupational choice that represents some abrasive relationship within the family. Again, we often see this motivation behind all sorts of deviant behavior.[29]

Finally, Frosch speculates that the con woman finds excitement in the game. "One imagines her asking, 'Will I make it again this time?' She is a risk taker."

Frosch left out the most significant reason many women practice fraud. The majority of con women are poor and enter the confidence game to survive, although they may remain in it longer depending upon their success and other factors, such as force exerted by a male partner and the thrill of the game.

THE FEMALE WHITE-COLLAR CRIMINAL

Undoubtedly women's crime has seen its greatest collective rise over the past decades in white-collar offenses. (See chapter 6.) FBI figures show that between 1976 and 1985 arrests of women increased 14.3 percent for larceny-theft, 35.9 percent for forgery and counterfeiting, 84.4 percent for fraud, and 55.3 percent for embezzlement. In all but larceny-theft, the rate of increase was greater than that of men arrested.[30]

A study prepared for the Center for Crime and Delinquency of the National Institute for Mental Health echoed the contention that white-collar crime is on the rise among women and at a faster rate than men: "It is larceny, embezzlement, fraud, and forgery that are proving attractive to women and not homicide, assault and armed robbery."[31]

The women committing white-collar crimes vary in their occupational status, from top executives to secretaries; they occupy jobs in large corporations, small businesses, and government offices. Several recent examples illustrate this range.

• Frances Cox pleaded guilty to embezzling $48,000 from the Fairfax, Virginia, government while serving as treasurer.
• Barbara Bowman was sentenced to three years' probation and 100 hours of community service for embezzling more than $12,000 from the Senate post office, where she was chief clerk.
• Lillian Markson, bookkeeper for the Spartacus spa, was sentenced to three years' probation and 100 hours of community service for aiding and abetting the filing of a false tax return.
• Mary Treadwell was convicted of defrauding tenants of thousands of dollars in rent money at a Washington, D.C., housing project she managed.
• Sandra Brown, feminist and author, was convicted of stealing federal and other funds that had been provided to launch women's businesses.[32]

Hence it becomes clear that women are diversifying and are opportunistic in their participation in white-collar offenses. Experts contend that "this trend was to be expected as more women moved into high level jobs that have always tempted males and females alike to cheat employers or consumers."[33] Or, as Sandra Brown notes, "Since you now have more women in business, more women are naturally going to be accused."[34] Conversely, considering the high rate of unreported or unknown crime, more women in the workplace also means that many more criminally inclined women will commit crimes unsuspectingly, unaccused, and therefore unreported.

White-collar crime is not merely a phenomenon of salaried or professional women. Often poor women resort to these crimes to help support themselves or their families. Phyllis Bannach of the U.S. Bureau of Justice Statistics reports that "many use stolen credit cards or forge checks to support the kids or buy drugs."[35]

Then there is shoplifting, an offense associated primarily with women, in which millions of dollars worth of merchandise is pilfered annually from stores. Housewives account for the largest share of arrests, but other women (and men) are also well represented, including employees.

Explanations for the reason for the boom in white-collar crime among women continue to stimulate debate. The most prominent views are usually associated with increased opportunity, the women's movement, economic distress, the "femininity factor" (women are nonviolent, so their crimes are nonviolent); and the increased pressure of women to provide, either as the head of a single-parent family or to assist the household with a second income. It is likely that each of these factors has contributed more or less to women's participation in white-collar offenses as well as other crimes. However, none of these theories have been proved to be causative factors in women's crime.

Despite the increase in female white-collar criminals, their numbers are still well behind those of their male counterparts. Nevertheless, there can be little argument that as we move into the next century and as men's and women's roles continue to expand and diversify, women as significant contributors to white-collar offenses are here to stay.

WOMEN AND DRUG ABUSE

The female narcotics abuser is not a new American phenomenon. Historically, female addicts outnumbered male addicts in the United States until the early part of the twentieth century.[36] During the last half of the nineteenth century the female-male ratio of addicts was two to one.[37]

Although today males arrested for drug abuse violations outnumber female arrestees by more than five to one, there can be no doubt that drug use is a serious problem for women in this country. In 1985, 84,959 females aged 18 and over were arrested for drug abuse violations.[38] However, most women who obtain and abuse "legal" drugs rarely come into contact with the criminal justice system. Because of this hidden or "closet" legal prescription incidence, the full extent of female drug addiction is nearly impossible to measure with any degree of accuracy.

Authorities believe that female drug addiction is somehow tied to male addiction, which is viewed, particularly in the illicit opiate racket, as the most important factor of susceptibility. Additionally, women are thought to try narcotics out of curiosity, at which point many find they like it while others get hooked, or both.

Recent surveys have shown a significantly higher incidence of psychotherapeutic drug use (a combination of medical and nonmedical drug use) among females. These drugs, also known as "prescription" or "psychotropic," include tranquilizers, sedatives and barbiturates, and stimulants, mostly amphetamines. Research has shown that women are much more likely to receive hospital emergency room treatment for psychotherapeutic drug abuse than males; the number doubles in drug overdose situations. Women who die as a result of drug use are twice as likely as their male counterparts to be over age 36, a figure attributed to women's greater use of psychotherapeutic drugs during these years.[39] Females who enter treatment programs are more inclined to be abusing psychotherapeutic drugs rather than heroin, cocaine, methadone, or alcohol. The typical woman who chronically abuses legal or prescription drugs is the middle- or upper-class housewife.[40]

Cocaine is believed to be the drug (illicit or legal) currently most abused among women after Valium, which had been the number one prescription drug during the mid–1970s, was drastically curtailed in both manufacturing and prescribing. Sixty million prescriptions for Valium were written in 1975, compared with 25 million in 1983.[41] Notes the senior vice president of a drug treatment center: "Since two out of three Valium prescriptions are written for women, presumably many females who cannot get Valium have switched to coke."[42]

A number of other reasons are ascribed to the increase in women's use of cocaine. One is that women find the image of the drug attractive. "Heroin is a grubby street product, and PCP, an animal tranquilizer known as angel dust, is the 'unemployment drug' because it relieves depression. . . . Cocaine is thought of as the champagne of drugs."[43]

Second, many women consider cocaine an aphrodisiac. Ronald Siegel, a psychopharmacologist, comments: "Women respond more euphorically and ecstatically than males to sex with coke and rate their sexual experiences with cocaine much higher than males do."[44] A third factor in the increasing cocaine use among women is thought to be simply a follow-the-leader syndrome: "Whatever substance men abuse is often later taken up by women."[45]

Finally, the increase in the number of women abusing cocaine can also be attributed to the recent emergence of a new, simpler refining process that produces inexpensive, smokable cocaine called "crack." Some experts state that crack cocaine is "rapidly taking over and increasing the number of cocaine addicts exposed to the more potent form."[46]

A common notion is that most female addicts turn to prostitution in order to supply their habit. However, this seems to be a fallacy given research showing than only 4 percent of prostitutes are drug addicts.[47] On the other hand, data reveal that although most female addicts are not normally criminal offenders (other than their drug abuse), they do get involved in a range of serious and nonserious criminal activities to pay for their drugs, including property crimes, prostitution, and drug sales.[48]

Demographic information on female drug abusers is sketchy because of both limited studies and the variety of women who take drugs. However, available data indicate some of the general characteristics of female addicts:

- Black and other minority female addicts are younger than white female addicts.
- Female addicts are older than male addicts, usually beginning drug careers in their mid-twenties.
- Female addicts are more likely to be divorced, separated, or widowed and have children than are male addicts.
- Female addicts have experienced more economic insecurity, disorganization, and family background problems (such as incestuous assaults) than male addicts.
- Female drug addicts often are high school dropouts and have unsuccessful work histories.
- Female drug use is indicative of more pathology than is male drug use.
- Female drug addicts tend to have lower self-esteem and self-image than both male addicts and female nonaddicts.[49]

In exploring some of the multifaceted roles of the female offender it becomes obvious that women's criminality, while perhaps not as extensive as men's criminality, is certainly as diverse. The changes women have experienced in the past few decades in terms of more equal access to areas of society previously dominated by men, role reversal, competition in the marketplace, more single-parent mothers, liberation, and knowledge have no doubt contributed to this diversity. However, the most crucial element in women's criminality today may well be women's adaptive capability in seizing the moment when a criminal avenue to a desired goal becomes more accessible than a noncriminal avenue.

NOTES

1. U.S. Federal Bureau of Investigation, *Crime in the United States: Uniform Crime Reports, 1985* (Washington, D.C.: Government Printing Office, 1986), p. 178.

2. "The Men Raped by Women," *San Francisco Chronicle* (March 15, 1982), p. 5.

3. Kay M. Porterfield, "Are Women as Violent as Men?" *Cosmopolitan* 197 (September 1984):276.

4. "The Men Raped by Women."

5. Diana E. H. Russell, *Rape in Marriage* (New York: Macmillan, 1982), pp. 280–282.

6. Stuart J. Miller, "Foreword," in Anthony M. Scacco, Jr., ed., *Male Rape: A Casebook of Sexual Aggressions* (New York: AMS Press, 1982), p. ix.

7. Diana E. H. Russell, *Sexual Exploitation: Rape, Child Sexual Abuse, and Workplace Harassment* (Beverly Hills: Sage Publications, 1984), p. 67.

8. Dorothy West, "I Was Afraid to Shut My Eyes," in Anthony M. Scacco, Jr., ed., *Male Rape: A Casebook of Sexual Aggressions* (New York: AMS Press, 1982), p. 171.

9. Richard Deming, *Women: The New Criminals* (Nashville, Tenn.: Thomas Nelson, Inc., 1977), pp. 125–144.

10. Ibid., pp. 127–128.

11. H. H. A. Cooper, "Woman as Terrorist," in Freda Adler and Rita J. Simon, eds., *The Criminology of Deviant Women* (Boston: Houghton Mifflin, 1979), p. 151.

12. Richard W. Kobetz and H. H. A. Cooper, "Target Terrorism: Providing Protective Services," *Risks International* (1970); Charles A. Russell and Bowman H. Miller, "Profile of a Terrorist," in John D. Elliot and Leslie K. Gibson, eds., *Contemporary Terrorism* (Gaithersburg, Md.: International Association of Chiefs of Police, 1978).

13. Risks International, Executive Risks Assessment 1 (January 1979).

14. Cooper, "Woman as Terrorist," p. 151.

15. Walter B. Miller, *Violence by Youth Gangs and Youth Groups as a Crime Problem in Major American Cities* (Washington, D.C.: Government Printing Office, 1975); Frederic M. Thrasher, *The Gang* (Chicago: University of Chicago Press, 1927); Freda Adler, *Sisters in Crime: The Rise of the New Female Criminal* (New York: McGraw-Hill, 1975).

16. "On the Wild Side: Women in Gangs," *New York Times* (January 2, 1986), p. C8.

17. Ibid.

18. Ibid.

19. Ibid.

20. Ibid.

21. Ibid.

22. Miller, *Violence by Youth Gangs*.

23. Adler, *Sisters in Crime*, p. 99.

24. Peter C. Buffum, "Homosexuality in Female Institutions," in Anthony M. Scacco, Jr., ed., *Male Rape: A Casebook of Sexual Aggressions* (New York: AMS Press, 1982), pp. 165–167.

25. John Kobler, "Con Women of the World," *Cosmopolitan* 196 (April 1984):247–249, 288–289.

26. Ibid., p. 248.

27. Ibid.

28. Ibid., p. 249.

29. Ibid., p. 289.

30. *Uniform Crime Reports, 1985* p. 169.

31. Larry Miller, "The Lady Is a White-Collar Criminal," *Cosmopolitan* 195 (July 1983):227.

32. Ibid.; "Women Expand Their Roles in Crime, Too," *U.S. News & World Report* (November 12, 1984), p. 62.

33. "Women Expand Their Roles in Crime."

34. Miller, "The Lady Is a White-Collar Criminal."

35. "Women Expand Their Roles in Crime."

36. Ronald L. Akers, *Deviant Behavior: A Social Learning Approach*, 2nd ed. (Belmont, Calif.: Wadsworth Publishing Co., 1977), p. 86.

37. Walter R. Cuskey, T. Premkumar, and Lois Siegel, "Survey of Opiate Addiction among Females in the U.S. between 1850 and 1970," in Freda Adler and Rita J. Simon, eds., *The Criminology of Deviant Women* (Boston: Houghton Mifflin, 1979).

38. *Uniform Crime Reports, 1985*, p. 178.

39. Mann, *Female Crime and Delinquency*, p. 37–38.

40. Marvin R. Burt, Thomas J. Glynn, and Barbara J. Sowder, *Psychosocial Characteristics of Drug-Abusing Women* (Rockville, Md.: U.S. Department of Health, Education and Welfare, 1979).

41. "Turning Increasingly to Cocaine." *Time* (April 2, 1984), p. 87.

42. Ibid.

43. Ibid.

44. Ibid.

45. Ibid.

46. "Cocaine Deaths Are Accelerating," *Sacramento Bee* (July 11, 1986), p. A22.

47. Alex Thio, *Deviant Behavior* (Boston: Houghton Mifflin, 1978).

48. James A. Inciardi, "Women, Heroin and Property Crime," in Susan K. Datesman and Frank R. Scarpitti, eds., *Women, Crime, and Justice* (New York: Oxford University Press, 1980).

49. Mann, *Female Crime and Delinquency*, pp. 39–40; Denise F. Polit, Ronald L. Nuttall, and Joan B. Hunter, "Women and Drugs: A Look at Some of the Issues," *Urban and Social Change Review* 9 (1976):9–16.

11

Incarcerated Women: A Correctional System Paradox

Ideally, jailing or imprisoning women is meant to exact retribution for their crimes and rehabilitation of their character; the majority of these women eventually return to society. In practice, however, the problems prevalent to most women's correctional facilities negate any real effectiveness in their stated goals. On the contrary, the one thing incarcerated women can look forward to once the door closes behind them is being transformed from an offender into a victim. Although some degree of chivalry toward women appears to exist throughout the criminal justice system, there can be no denying that for those who do find their way behind bars, the problems they encounter are more severe than those of their male counterparts. It is this paradox of incarcerated women as criminals and victims on which we shall focus in this chapter.

THE HISTORY OF CORRECTIONAL INSTITUTIONS FOR WOMEN

Prior to the penal reform movement of the late nineteenth century, all people deemed criminal offenders or degenerates (men, women, and children) were often placed in the same correctional facilities. It mattered not one's age, type of offense, or the circumstances that may have been involved. However, men and women were separated by the different emphasis on reform given to them. With women's crimes consisting primarily of sex offenses or drunkenness, they were usually regarded as disgraced, dishonorable, and pathetic women; whereas male offenders were often looked upon by society as dangerous men. Hence reformation took on a different meaning for women than for men. "Treatment" for women meant promoting sexual conformity, sobriety, obedience, and sex-role stereotyping, typically that of mother and housewife.[1]

In response to the reformatory movement, which focused on this rehabilitative goal for women and the separation of the sexes in corrections as asserted at the 1870 National Congress on Penitentiary and Reformatory Discipline, the first separate female institution evolved in Indiana. Three years later the Indiana Women's Prison opened as a model prison for females aged 16 and over and for older women.[2] By 1913, four more reformatories for women had opened.[3] In 1917, fourteen states had women's reformatories or "industrial homes."[4] Unlike men's facilities, which were intended for felons still young enough to rehabilitate, the early women's reformatories were established with young women "sex delinquents" and "inebriates" in mind, who were believed to constitute the group of women for which prison reform was most needed.

The first federal correctional institution for women opened in 1927 in Alderson, West Virginia, allowing for the transfer of female federal prisoners who had been housed in local jails, state prisons, and the District of Columbia Women's Reformatory.[5]

Despite the reformers' intentions, although perhaps some old problems were solved, others were carried over, and yet new ones arose for female inmates:

Because of their smaller numbers and the requirement of separate facilities, the per capita allotment of funds could not be utilized as efficiently as it was for males. In consequence their quarters were more cramped, women of all ages and crime types were thrown together, there was little provision for work or exercise, understaffing was thought to necessitate more rigid rules, visiting privileges were restricted, and job training was inadequate. There was little they could do besides sleep, talk, play table games, or sew.[6]

The philosophy of the reformers in viewing women's needs as separate from men's could be seen in the architecture of women's prisons. Whereas men's prisons were massive fortress-like institutions with high concrete walls, gun towers, and armed personnel, women's penal facilities took on a "domestic" quality which provided each woman her own room in the "home."

These homes, usually arranged in a quadrangle and amid trees and shrubbery, were built like cottages, housing twenty to thirty women and providing "cottage" kitchens in which they could prepare their own food, living and dining areas, and reading rooms. The object was to offer a domestic setting that would enhance the sex-role stereotypical functions of homemaker, wife, and mother.[7]

Following the cottage reformatories for women, three other types of women's penal facilities came into existence. The "campus" plan is patterned after a college campus; grass and trees surround many buildings, each with individual functions and separated by grassy court areas. In the "complex" model, a number of buildings that may function singularly or in combination as living areas, dining halls, classrooms, or vocational training facilities are clustered around the central administration building. The "single-building" type consists of one primary facility that houses all of the prison activities.[8]

In contemporary prison reform the coed prison is a recent innovation and is defined as "an adult institution, the major purpose of which is the custody of sentenced felons, under a single institutional administration, having one or more programs or areas in which male and female inmates are present and in interaction."[9] The first coed prison was created in 1971 in Fort Worth, Texas, by the Federal Bureau of Prisons.[10] Ironically, this represents somewhat of a reversal of the earlier philosophy that resulted in separating the sexes, even though this alternative to women's correctional institutions was hoped to improve the lot of both female and male inmates by

creating a more normal atmosphere through the reduction of homosexual systems and activity, permitting of heterosexual relationships, protection of inmates who would have problems in predominantly same-sex institutions, and aiding in the reduction of adjustments to be made at release time.[11]

The results of this union have varied, depending upon the institution. However, Claudine SchWeber points out two basic disadvantages of women in coed corrections: the social-sexual environment and the availability of programs in relation to their use.[12] Regarding the social/sexual environment, SchWeber contends that because female prisoners are so few and diverse in any prison system (for instance, all women's facilities house a full range of female prisoners) as opposed to the larger number of male inmates limiting their coed program participation to minimum security prisoners, it becomes virtually impossible to establish a homogeneous group of women for coed institutions.

SchWeber notes that despite the availability of more educational and vocational programs in sexually integrated institutions, many women fail to capitalize on these programs. This lack of women's participation appears to be related to the administrative emphasis on education as opposed to other activities, institutional anxiety regarding the presence of female inmates, and the proportion of women in coed institutions.

WOMEN'S PRISONS AND IMPRISONED WOMEN TODAY

As of this writing there are four federal prisons that incarcerate women. In addition to Alderson, there is a male facility in Pleasanton,

California, with a women's section, and co-correctional institutions in Fort Worth and Lexington.[13] There are forty-six state prisons for women; separate institutions for women exist in thirty-four states, the District of Columbia, and Puerto Rico; while sixteen other states house women separately in men's corrections.[14] States that have only a few women offenders place them in city or county jails; whereas eight states contract with other states for the correctional care of their female prisoners.[15]

Although earlier studies reported that few inmate populations in women's penal facilities exceeded their institutional capacity, more recent findings reveal that "existing facilities have been jammed to the rafters, or women have been forced to serve all or part of their terms in county jails."[16] This trend is a result of the increase in the number of sentenced female prisoners.

Women, who make up approximately only one of every twenty-four persons imprisoned, have continued to account for roughly 4 percent of the total prison population for a number of years. Table 11.1 provides a breakdown of state and federal prisoners by region of the country, race, and sex as of December 31, 1982. In addition to illustrating the considerable difference in the male and female prison population, the data are also useful in assessing certain distributions within the female prisoner population. For instance, we see that the largest concentration of incarcerated women per 100,000 resident population is in the South, followed by the West, North Central, and Northeast. This trend may be more a reflection of differential law enforcement and outright racism than actual crime participation among women in the various regions.

Women in Prison by Race

The racial distribution of women as shown in table 11.1 should come as no surprise. Minority women, particularly blacks, are overrepresented in proportion to their total population as compared to white women. Overall, the rate of imprisoned black women at the end of 1982 was 63 per 100,000 population, compared to 30 per 100,000 for Native Americans and only 9 per 100,000 for white women. A recent study by the U.S. General Accounting Office (GAO) of female offenders in the criminal justice system reached the same conclusion. That analysis of the distribution of incarcerated women by race in comparison to the racial distribution of women in our society produced the following results:

- Whites constitute 82 percent of the general population compared to only 36 percent of the inmate population.
- Blacks make up 11 percent of the national population but 50 percent of incarcerated women.

Table 11.1
Prisoners under the Jurisdiction of State and Federal Correctional
Authorities, by Race, Sex, Region, and Jurisdiction on December 31, 1982

(Rate per 100,000 resident population)

Region and Jurisdiction	All Races			White			Black			American Indian or Alaskan Native		
	Total	Male	Female	Total	Male	Female	Total	Male	Female	Total	Male	Female
United States, total	183	360	15	114	225	9	716	1445	63	265	504	30
Federal institutions, total	13	25	1	10	20	1	38	74	5	35	683	3
State institutions, total	170	335	14	104	205	8	678	1370	58	230	436	28
Northeast	123	248	8	69	140	4	621	1299	42	114	220	(a)
North Central	133	262	12	76	151	6	675	1359	64	313	591	41
South	240	473	20	141	277	11	689	1391	59	219	416	23
West	151	290	13	125	243	10	739	1416	70	219	417	27

aRates are not computed because of a resident population base of less than 25,000 or fewer than 10 inmates.

Source: U.S. Department of Justice, Bureau of Justice Statistics, Prisoners in State and Federal Institutions on December 31, 1982, NCJ-93311 (Washington, D.C.: U.S. Government Printing Office, 1984), p. 23.

- Hispanics account for 5 percent of the U.S. population but 9 percent of institutionalized women.
- Native Americans represent only 0.4 percent of the women nationally but constitute 3 percent of all women imprisoned.[17]

Socioeconomic and Age Characteristics of Incarcerated Women

A number of studies have found that women in prison typically share these general socioeconomic characteristics:

- Women in correctional facilities are predominantly nonwhite.
- Most female prisoners are single.
- The majority of the women are mothers.
- Imprisoned women have lower IQs and less education than nonimprisoned women.
- Women in prison tend to have few work skills and prior work histories in lower-echelon, mostly service-related occupations.
- Most come from unstable or broken homes where substance abuse, child abuse, and mental illness are common factors.
- The majority are under 30 years of age.
- Most incarcerated women are tagged "losers."

Nearly 65 percent of the women in penal institutions are under the age of 30, compared to 40 percent of this age group within the total national female population. For felons, the median age is 27 years old; for unsentenced and misdemeanants it is 24 years.

Offenses Committed by Women in Prison

The most comprehensive study of women's correctional programs in recent decades was undertaken by Ruth Glick and Virginia Neto.[18] Their national sampling consisted of states that account for about 52 percent of the female population in the United States aged 18 and over, and approximately 66 percent of all women in prisons and U.S. jails. Thus their study is believed to be fairly representative of the total female prison population in the nation.

Glick and Neto categorized offenses in which women were incarcerated by unsentenced, misdemeanants, and felons. The informative breakdowns for imprisonment are as follows:

Unsentenced Women

Property Crimes—30.6 percent
Crimes against the Person—30 percent

Drug Offenses—22 percent

Prostitution—3 percent

"Other" or "Unknown" Offenses—14.3 percent

Misdemeanants

Property Crimes—41.1 percent

Drug Offenses—20.2 percent

Violent Crimes—11.4 percent

Prostitution—7.2 percent

"Other" and "Unknown" Offenses—20 percent

Felons

Crimes against the Person—43.3 percent

Property Crimes—29.3 percent

Drug Offenses—22 percent

"Other" and "Unknown" Offenses—5.4 percent

The offense for which women were imprisoned in the Glick and Neto study tended to vary by ethnic group (table 11.2). Black and Hispanic women were incarcerated most frequently for drug offenses. However, the Hispanic percentage of 40.3 was nearly double the black rate of 20.2 percent and the 22.1 percent of the total incarcerated female population. Nationally, in 1979 only 4.7 percent of all women arrested were charged with drug offense violations.

The second most frequent offense for which black women were imprisoned was murder (18.6 percent), which accounted for only 0.2 percent of all female arrests nationally. Larceny was third at 14.1 percent, which, although higher than the total female imprisonment rate for this offense (11.2 percent), was considerably lower than the 22.2 percent national arrest rate of women for larceny in 1979.

Hispanics' second and third most frequent offense leading to imprisonment were burglary (12.7 percent) and robbery (8.7 percent). Both rates were well above the total percentage of 1979 arrests of women in these categories; whereas burglary was committed by a smaller percentage of the sample female prisoner group (5.7 percent), and all women imprisoned accounted for a higher percentage of robbery offenses (11.3 percent).

White and Native American female prisoners had the same top four offense rankings (forgery/fraud, drugs, other nonviolent, murder) that resulted in their incarceration, although Native American women were slightly more likely to be in prison for three of the four, and their third and fourth offenses were in reverse order. For three of the four offenses (forgery/fraud, drugs, and murder), both ethnic groups' percentages

Table 11.2
Partial Offense Data on U.S. Incarcerated Women Compared to 1979 Arrest Data, by Ethnic Group

OFFENSE	Ethnic Group in Rank Order (Including Percentages)				TOTAL PERCENT IN PRISON	TOTAL PERCENT 1979 ARRESTS
	WHITE	BLACK	HISPANIC	NATIVE AMERICAN		
Murder	4 (12.9%)	2 (18.6%)	4 (8.6%)	3 (13.4%)	3 (15.3%)	8 (0.2%)
Other violent	9 (2.2%)	10 (2.3%)	9 (0.9%)	9 (3.0%)	10 (2.1%)	N/A[a]
Robbery	5 (3.2%)	4 (13.8%)	3 (8.7%)	6 (6.6%)	4 (11.3%)	7 (0.6%)
Assault	8 (3.2%)	6 (7.5%)	8 (1.6%)	8 (5.8%)	8 (5.5%)	5 (2.1%)
Burglary	7 (6.2%)	8 (4.2%)	2 (12.7%)	7 (6.0%)	7 (5.7%)	6 (2.0%)
Forgery/fraud	1 (22.3%)	5 (11.3%)	5 (8.2%)	1 (23.8%)	2 (15.6%)	2 (8.1%)[b]
Larceny	6 (8.1%)	3 (14.1%)	4 (8.6%)	5 (7.2%)	5 (11.2%)	1 (22.2%)
Drugs	2 (20.4%)	1 (20.2%)	1 (40.3%)	2 (21.0%)	1 (22.1%)	3 (4.7%)
Prostitution	10 (1.3%)	9 (3.1%)	7 (2.4%)	10 (0.7%)	9 (2.4%)	4 (3.8%)
Other nonviolent	3 (14.1%)	7 (5.0%)	6 (8.0%)	4 (12.5%)	6 (8.7%)	N/A[a]

[a]Not available as categorized.
[b]Forgery and counterfeiting added to fraud.

Source: Coramae R. Mann, Female Crime and Delinquency (University, Ala.: University of Alabama Press, 1984), p. 199. See also Ruth M. Glick and Virginia V. Neto, National Study of Women's Correctional Programs (Washington, D.C.: Government Printing Office, 1977), Tables 4, 10, 14.

were much higher than the national arrest rates for women in 1979 for these offenses. However, for murder and drug offenses, their percentages were lower than the total incarcerated female prisoners for these offenses.

The comparative rank order of the Glick and Neto study should prove provocative as well for other offenses in relation to ethnic groups, prison population, and arrest figures for women.

ONCE THE WOMAN ENTERS PRISON

The objectives of the correctional system and the crimes of female offenders notwithstanding, once women enter the institution they often go from being a victim of justice to a victim of injustice. Cruel and unusual punishment is not supposed to exist today; however, one would never know it by observing life in the women's penal facility.

After arriving at her assigned correctional home, the new female prisoner must go through a series of orientation or "get-acquainted" procedures. She may come in handcuffed and be refingerprinted and photographed for institutional records. Referred to as a "fish," she soon loses all remaining dignity when she is stripped and searched for contraband, showered, and issued prison attire and bedding. Over the next two to six weeks the incarcerated woman, who is segregated during this period, goes through medical and psychiatric examinations for everything from venereal disease to mental illness.

By the time she joins the general prison population, she has been instilled with the extensive rules and regulations of her confinement, including her new status of "institutional dependency." Although women's prisons are usually not the maximum security fortresses that men's prisons are, some suggest that the rules women must abide by are stricter.[19] These rules and regulations, as well as disciplinary actions for infractions, vary from one institution to another.

In general, major infractions include escapes, fighting, property damage, possession of contraband, arson, violence, and using weapons. Glick and Neto reported that homosexuality is considered a major infraction in eight of ten women's institutions.[20] Other studies suggest that homosexual acts are commonplace among women in prisons and, if not condoned, are accepted as part of prison reality.[21]

Minor infractions include using foul language, yelling, walking on the grass, and having torn sheets; disciplinary actions range from being reprimanded to losing up to sixty days' "gain time," or having that interval deducted from the inmate's sentence for good behavior.[22] Penalties for major infractions commonly include loss of privileges and isolation for up to ninety days and, in some cases, court prosecution.

In reality, prisoners can be placed in solitary confinement, or the "hole," at any time for major or minor infractions of rules. This particular negative sanction for women goes beyond punishment and crosses over into inhumane treatment. Investigative reporter Kathryn Burkhart makes this clear in the following observation:

These cells are drearily the same in every jail I've visited—windowless and bare. Some have one thin, dirty and bloodstained mattress on the floor. Some have no mattress. Some jails provide blankets for the women confined, some do not. In some quarters, women locked in solitary are allowed to wear prison shifts— in others they are allowed to wear only their underwear or are stripped naked. Toilets are most often flushed from the outside, and women complain that on occasion sadistic matrons play games with flushing the toilets—either flushing them repeatedly until they overflow or not flushing them at all for a day or more at a time. ("If the toilet backs up, there's nothing you can do about it but live with the stench.") Food is passed into the room two or three times a day between the bottom of the dusty door and the unwashed floor, as are sanitary napkins if the woman is menstruating.[23]

Many female inmates view the rules and regulations of prisons as willful efforts to "diminish their maturity" by "treating them like children and fostering dependency."[24] An example of such a rule is at the Pennsylvania State Correctional Institution for Women, where inmates are required to "recite the Lord's Prayer in unison at bedtime."[25]

Health Care of Female Prisoners

Women often enter prison with or develop some form of medical or psychiatric problem. The most typical problems are gynecological, nervousness/anxiety, dental, headaches, diabetes, epilepsy, hypertension, and substance addiction. All institutions are staffed with at least the minimal amount of medical personnel; however, medical care can differ dramatically from institution to institution depending upon size, staff, budget, and the priority given treatment.

In some prisons women can be close to death and still not receive proper care even under the best circumstances. For example, medication may be withheld from an epileptic prisoner until she verifies her condition with a "couple of seizures." In other cases inmates may be doped or tranquilized as a means of social control rather than medical treatment. Burkhart comments on this practice:

More often, it seems, at Riker's and at other prisons, women inmates walk the halls in what seems to be a dazed, zombie-like state. Their words are slurred, their eyes are glazed, their clothes disheveled. Some women I have seen on one day having to be supported by other inmates even to walk, look like totally different people a day or two later when they said they "got off the medication." Some women complain that they are given Thorazine and Millaril against their will when they are upset about something; others complain they are unable to get tranquilizing medication when they want it.[26]

The Diet of Incarcerated Women

Frequent complaints among institutionalized women concern the food. Apart from common considerations about preparation, quality, and quantity of food, a serious dietary concern is the starch in much of the prison food and concomitant weight gain it can cause. One study reports that on the average, women at the state prison in Connecticut gained fifteen pounds during their first three months behind bars, attributing this in part to the starchy food and mandatory meal attendance.[27] When combined with limited exercise that is often the rule in women's institutions, such food and weight problems can be especially hazardous to the female inmate's health.

Recreational Facilities in Women's Institutions

Incarcerated women are at a disadvantage compared to male prisoners when it comes to recreational opportunities. Not only can recreation help keep female inmates physically fit (or at least active as a neutralizer to their diet of starchy foods), sports and other activities such as music and painting often function to release tension and frustrations and can break the monotony of incarceration. In women's correctional facilities television and board games make up the primary recreational activities.

Usually lacking in these institutions is space, equipment, and other special facilities necessary for adequate recreation programs. For instance, few women's prisons have playing fields, which are common in most men's institutions. When such areas are present, there is often lack of sufficient staff to supervise activities, and thus female prisoners in such institutions often cannot take full advantage of them.

Vocational Training and Rehabilitation Programs

Vocational education and training programs for women in many women's institutions or women's divisions of men's prisons are very limited. Female inmates who already have advanced education have little use for the educational programs that may be offered, and there is no avenue for them to make use of their academic skills (for example, as a teacher). Conversely, no special programs or incentives are available for female prisoners who are educationally handicapped, mentally retarded, or simply uninterested, assuming such women could be identified.

Vocational training programs that do exist usually are in traditional female areas such as sewing, clerical skills, food services, and cosmetology. A recent federal report found that three vocational programs existed on average in women's prisons compared to ten at men's prisons.[28] Even in the larger women's institutions, no more than two or three programs are offered, and these are virtually always geared toward preparing women in a domestic or otherwise "women's" capacity.

The scarcity of vocational and rehabilitation programs for female prisoners can usually be attributed to one of the following:

- Such programs not cost-effective, as female prisoners number so few.
- Financial expenditures are unwarranted for female inmates, who pose less of a threat to society than their male counterparts.
- There is a low rate of women's participation in such programs.
- Many female correctional facilities are inaccessible.
- Women are still regarded foremost in the traditional roles of housewife and mother.

Consequently legislators and corrections officials continue to give full priority to men's vocational programs "while teaching women merely to cook, sew, and clean."[29] Unfortunately, especially for those serving long sentences, this gives women few or no opportunities to learn new skills or earn enough money to aid their families on the outside.

Other Problems with Being an Incarcerated Woman

Several other areas of prison living victimize female inmates and make their stay that much more taxing. A major problem in women's prisons is idleness. Because recreation often means performing menial chores or walking around in one's cell, many inmates usually find themselves with a great deal of "wasted" time. This only serves to increase their introspection about the world they are now forced to live in possibly for years—a frightening prospect.

A further problem of incarceration is the psychological harm the institution inflicts upon the inmate. Unquestionably all prisons are psychologically harmful; however, the typical women's institution is particularly subject to this effect, despite its more pleasing appearance. The superficial attractiveness of a prison for women, in addition to confusing the prisoners, tends to "deaden any impetus for change."[30]

Writer Helen Gibson describes effectively the reality of the women's correctional institution for its inmates:

While convention requires women's prisons to look like minimum security institutions, economic reality decrees that they cannot be minimum security. A minimum security institution can choose the best risks, and send its failures somewhere else; a women's institution must accept every woman offender in the state. Because all women sentenced to prison must be housed in one institution, all must live by rules which are established for the control of a very few. . . . The result is an atmosphere that in spite of attractive facilities and peaceful surroundings, is really very tense and oppressive. . . . The reduction of women to a weak, dependent, and helpless status is brought about by more subtle means than by the gun or the high wall.[31]

Another area of victimization faced by female prisoners concerns institutional maintenance. In most women's prisons inmates are required to spend at least a portion of their day performing institutional maintenance labor. Rarely are they paid for this; and when they are, it is very low and usually less than that received by their male counterparts.

This unskilled labor is often camouflaged and referred to as vocational training even though few legitimate job skills can be gained through such work. Even more frustrating is the routine practice of using housework as punishment. However, the custom is the exploitation of women inmates by prison administrators and other state officials who use them as personal servants.

Glick and Neto found that some women in North Carolina and Georgia prisons worked in the governor's mansion as maids.[32] In North Carolina, for instance, eight women inmates were sent to the governor's home where their duties included cooking, cleaning, washing, and serving.[33] One writer notes distressfully of this practice: "It's usually humiliating enough to be a house servant when you're being paid meager wages [and] see no alternatives—but to have it be involuntary servitude gives me the plantation shudders."[34]

IMPRISONED MOTHERS

In addition to the various forms of victimization the woman experiences once she becomes an institutionalized prisoner, incarcerated mothers face difficulties unique to their status. The majority of female prisoners are mothers; some enter prison as expectant mothers. On rare occasions a woman becomes pregnant after she enters a correctional facility. In each of these situations, she experiences much frustration and distress.

Leaving Children Behind

Research has shown that enforced separation from their children is the greatest hardship incarcerated mothers face.[35] One inmate mother put this feeling in perspective when she stated tersely, "By taking away our rights to see our children, they're killing us." In many prisons children under the age of 16 are not allowed to visit. Even when visitation is permitted, it is usually very restricted. This situation is compounded by the inaccessibility of women's prisons that typically are located in isolated areas that are difficult to reach without an automobile.

Prison mothers often find themselves wondering if their children (many of whom are very young) will know, love, trust, or respect them once they are released; who is going to look after their children's best interests, health, education, welfare; what effect foster care will have on their relationship with their children; and how their children will come out of all this. Additionally, evidence suggests that an imprisoned mother separated from her child(ren) psychologically exhibits behavior similar to that of people who suffer loss because of death, divorce, and other mother-children separations; it is characterized by symptoms such as "remoteness, emptiness, helplessness, anger, guilt, fears of loss of attachment, and rejection."[36]

The uncertainty and anguish the inmate mother must deal with is intrinsic to her incarceration. The same holds true for the apprehension she carries as her release date nears. She will have to readjust and relate to her children, particularly concerning discipline, and conquer her own insecurities about her abilities as a parent.

Furthermore, the imprisoned mother must deal with a host of legal problems (apart from those regarding her case) relating to her status as a mother, such as parental rights issues, child placement determination, foster care, adoption battles, and visitation rights. Considering that most incarcerated mothers have little, if any, access to legal counsel, it is easy to see what an uphill battle she faces.

Pregnant Inmates

Women who enter the prison system pregnant suffer perhaps the worst kind of cruel and unusual punishment. Evidence exists that an incarcerated pregnant woman may be treated more harshly than other inmates because of her pregnancy. Correctional staffs have been shown to be especially abusive toward pregnant women because of hostility and prejudice toward those they regard as not "worthy enough to have children."[37] Often these women are either coerced into having an abortion or forced to do so through brutal and/or uncaring treatment, in order to prevent them from becoming "unworthy" mothers. Conversely, it has been reported that in some women's prisons pregnant inmates who want an abortion are being denied that right.[38] Pregnant inmates in jails are even more vulnerable to inhumane treatment at the hands of jail authorities.

Female inmates who do carry their pregnancies to term often face medical problems in correctional institutions that frequently are ignored. Most institutions do not have adequate medical facilities for either mother or baby. Pregnant inmates complain about the inability to obtain milk, vitamins, or other special foods vital to the maintenance of their optimal health and that of their unborn infant. Additionally, pregnant prisoners are more seriously affected by improper diets such as the starchy food in penal institutions and the lack of prenatal gynecological care precisely because of their pregnancy.

Finally, many pregnant inmates enter prison as drug addicts and are frequently forced to withdraw "cold turkey" or are denied the use of methadone if they are heroin addicts. Despite the many dangers to the mother and child this cruel treatment presents, and occasional challenges in the courts,[39] pregnant inmates throughout the country continue to suffer at the hands of the correctional system and its employees, in addition to suffering the normal hardships as incarcerated women.

Pregnancy after Entering Prison

Women who become pregnant while imprisoned face the same added burdens as those experienced by pregnant women entering prison. However, in some rare cases these women are victimized even more because they have been the victims of rape or consensual sex by a prison guard or other official, resulting in the pregnancy. This, of course, is a blatant example of sexual exploitation. Even when the sex is consensual, the inmate is being taken advantage of by a prison worker who has everything to gain and little to lose. Few male prison staff who engage in sexual relations with female prisoners ever face legal action. The pregnancy itself presents a new set of problems for the mother. In a recent example in which a Florida inmate became pregnant after sexual relations with a prison guard, she went to court and was successful in keeping her baby.[40] Although this issue is important in itself, the real concern in this particular case is that the sexual relations were allowed to occur at all.

JAILED WOMEN

As of June 30, 1983, women made up approximately 7 percent of our nation's total adult inmate population.[41] Regionally, most jailed women reside in southern jails, followed by jails in the West, North Central, and the Northeast. The majority of women in jails are ethnic minorities, poor, with few employable skills and limited education; yet they are often also parents with a need to support their children and themselves. Their crimes are predominantly misdemeanors; most are "victimless" type crimes such as drug abuse and prostitution. Yet their fate behind bars is anything but victimless and is perhaps the greatest criminal justice system paradox.

If women's prisons are bad (and they are), local jails around the country that house female inmates are even worse. Often in overcrowded, filthy, dangerous jails a woman suffers a range of victimizing experiences that gives new meaning to the word "dehumanizing." It starts the moment she is brought to jail in handcuffs or waist chains. After paperwork and a "pat search," she is made to strip and is thoroughly searched for narcotics, including vagina, buttocks, and under the breasts. Following a shower or bath and stinging spray for body lice, the prisoner is fingerprinted and photographed.

It gets worse. Sexual and physical abuse and harassment of female prisoners is "a common practice" in many small jails, especially in the South. Investigative journalist Patsy Sims traveled throughout the South visiting jails in an effort to determine if the case of Joan Little, a black female inmate in a North Carolina county jail who killed her white jailer after he tried to abuse her sexually, was atypical. She found it was all too common:

In my interviews with more than 50 women serving time in southern jails or work-release programs, inmate after inmate repeated virtually the same stories of what happened to them, or to the woman in the next cell: the oral sex through bars; the constant intrusion of male trustees who slither in and out of the women's cells as unrestricted as the rats and roaches; the threats of "you do, or else:" the promises of "Girl, you got thirty days, we'll knock off ten if you take care of my friend here."[42]

Although there are no statistics to fully document the magnitude of sexual abuse in jails, Sims contends that these stories are substantiated by numerous attorneys, corrections officers, and law enforcement personnel. Many cases go unreported "partly because of fear, partly because the jailer is considered more believable than a woman already accused of another crime. . . . Much of the abuse—sexual and otherwise—is due to an attitude that women prisoners, especially black ones, are little better than animals."[43]

Rarely is there any separation of men and women in rural jails; when it does occur it usually results in the woman being put into solitary confinement. The lack of housing for female offenders often means the minor crime offenders, dangerous, and mentally ill are all thrown in together. In some metropolitan jails ten or fifteen women can often be found packed like sardines in cells with no air conditioning that were meant to hold half the number, sleeping two to a bed or on the floor.

The dirty and unsanitary conditions common to many jails make the time spent there a nightmare and force some women to do anything they can to maintain their sanity. Comments Sims sympathetically:

I heard and saw a lot that made me understand why . . . the sex [among consenting female prisoners] is more a matter of self-survival than immorality. I heard about filth, about going weeks—even 10 months—without a bath or shower, without towels or sheets, or even hot water. I heard about these conditions and then I saw them.[44]

Adequate health care is also lacking in jails, particularly when it concerns women's gynecological and obstetrical problems. Further problematic in women's jails is the paucity of exercise and sports activities and educational programs of value.

In sum, jailed women suffer from any number of indignities; however, their low numbers and often minority status make them an almost invisible group without a voice.

No one can argue with the necessity of prisons and jails for people who commit crimes, even women. However, although incarceration is not a picnic for anyone (nor, some argue, should it be), clearly on a collective basis female inmates are a great deal worse off than male inmates. For one thing, it is arguable that many of these women should be in prison at all. Often their biggest crime seems to be trying to feed their families or having the misfortune to be pregnant or nonwhite. Outdated rules and regulations, poor diet, neglectful health care, degradation, lack of vocational training and recreational facilities, exploitation, abuse, and unsanitary conditions typify the conditions in many prisons and jails that house women. Reform is needed both within the correctional system and in a society that condones inhumane treatment of women prisoners.

NOTES

1. Edna Walker Chandler, *Women in Prison* (Indianapolis: Bobbs Merrill, 1973), p. 7.

2. Richard Deming, *Women: The New Criminals* (Nashville, Tenn.: Thomas Nelson, Inc., 1977), p. 157.

3. Coramae R. Mann, *Female Crime and Delinquency* (University: University of Alabama Press, 1984), p. 191.

4. Kathryn Burkhart, *Women in Prison* (Garden City, N.Y.: Doubleday, 1973), pp. 252–253.

5. Louis P. Carney, *Introduction to Correctional Science* (New York: McGraw-Hill, 1974), p. 210.

6. Freda Adler, *Sisters in Crime: The Rise of the New Female Criminal* (New York: McGraw-Hill, 1975), p. 175.

7. Burkhart, *Women in Prison*, p. 367.

8. Ruth M. Glick and Virginia V. Neto, *National Study of Women's Correctional Programs* (Washington, D.C.: Government Printing Office, 1977), p. 20.

9. James G. Ross and Esther Hefferman, "Women in a Coed Joint," *Quarterly Journal of Corrections* 1 (1977):24.

10. Mann, *Female Crime and Delinquency*, p. 193.

11. Ibid.

12. Claudine SchWeber, "The Implications and Complications of Coed Prisons." Paper presented at the annual meeting of the American Society of Criminology, 1979.

13. Mann, *Female Crime and Delinquency*, p. 194.

14. Joan Potter, "In Prison, Women Are Different," *Corrections Magazine* 4 (1978):15.

15. Mann, *Female Crime and Delinquency*, p. 195.

16. Potter, "In Prison, Women Are Different," p. 14.

17. U.S. General Accounting Office (GAO), *Female Offenders: Who Are They and What Are the Problems Confronting Them?* (Washington, D.C.: Government Printing Office, 1979), p. 8.

18. Glick and Neto, *National Study*, p. 219.

19. Linda Singer, "Women and the Correctional Process," *American Criminal Law Review* 11 (1973):301.

20. Glick and Neto, *National Study*, pp. 41–42.

21. Tom Goldstein, "Behind Prison Walls," *Cosmopolitan* 198 (November 1984):261.

22. Glick and Neto, *National Study*, p. 39.

23. Burkhart, *Women in Prison*, p. 148.

24. Mann, *Female Crime and Delinquency*, p. 210.

25. Deming, *Women: The New Criminals*, p. 159.

26. Burkhart, *Women in Prison*, p. 333.

27. Goldstein, "Behind Prison Walls," p. 261.

28. GAO, *Female Offenders*.

29. Marilyn G. Haft, "Women in Prison—Discriminatory Practices and Some Legal Solutions," *Clearinghouse Review* 8 (1974):1–2.

30. Helen E. Gibson, "Women's Prisons: Laboratories for Penal Reform," in Laura Crites, ed., *The Female Offender* (Lexington, Mass.: Lexington Books, 1976), p. 99.

31. Ibid.

32. Glick and Neto, *National Study*, p. 79.

33. Potter, "In Prison, Women Are Different," p. 20.

34. Burkhart, *Women in Prison*, p. 303.

35. Brenda G. McGowan and Karen L. Blumenthal, "Children of Women Prisoners: A Forgotten Minority," in Laura Crites, ed., *The Female Offender* (Lexington, Mass.: Lexington Books, 1976), p. 128.

36. Velma LaPoint, "The Impact of Incarceration on Families: Research and Policy Issues." Paper presented to the Research Forum on Family Issues, National Advisory Committee of the White House Conference on Families, 1980, p. 6.

37. Gerald A. McHugh, "Protection of the Rights of Pregnant Women in Prisons and Detention Facilities," *New England Journal on Prison Law* 6 (1980):235–237.

38. Mann, *Female Crime and Delinquency*, p. 213.

39. McHugh, "Protection of Rights." See also *Garnes* v. *Taylor* (1973): *Morales* v. *Turman* (1974).

40. Mann, *Female Crime and Delinquency*, pp. 230–231.

41. U.S. Department of Justice, Bureau of Justice Statistics, *The 1983 Jail Census* (Washington, D.C.: Government Printing Office, 1984), p. 5.

42. Patsy Sims, "Women in Southern Jails," in Laura Crites, ed., *The Female Offender* (Lexington, Mass.: Lexington Books, 1976), p. 137.

43. Ibid., p. 140.

44. Ibid., p. 141.

III

WOMEN IN THE CRIMINAL JUSTICE PROFESSIONS

Professional Women in the Criminal Justice System

In addition to the difficulties women face as victims and offenders of criminality and their subsequent involvement with the criminal justice system, they also struggle as practitioners of criminal justice. Sex-role stereotyping and chivalry toward women have historically minimized their employment in the criminal justice system. Despite advances in recent years sparked by the women's movement and a number of legal decisions, women continue to be underrepresented as police officers, lawyers, judges, correctional officers, and probation and parole officials. As part of our tripartite study of women and criminality, we will examine how women assert themselves as professionals in the field of criminal justice.

CONFLICT THEORY AND FEMALE PRACTITIONERS IN THE CRIMINAL JUSTICE SYSTEM

Conflict theory, which addresses conflicting interests between groups in society, has traditionally focused on explaining the inequitable treatment of poor minorities by the criminal justice system. The theory proposes that street crimes, committed most likely by lower-class minority members, have been arbitrarily defined as criminality, whereas crimes most likely perpetrated by those with political and economic clout—white-collar and professional crimes—"are legally protected from inclusion in criminal law."[1] Thus according to conflict theory, "both the substantive and procedural content of the law represent the interests of the segments of society that have the authority to shape public policy. The formulation of law allows some segments of society to protect and perpetuate their own interests."[2]

Conflict theorists have recently applied the theory to the differential treatment of female professionals in the criminal justice system and the neglect of research on women professionals by criminologists and officials within criminal justice agencies.[3] These theorists postulate that women have experienced much difficulty both entering official positions in the criminal justice system and being neglected once they obtain jobs because of sex-role stereotyping and because men dominate the system by outnumbering women and obtaining the positions of authority.

The criminal justice system has been dominated by white, middle-class males. White men are the powerful class in our society who are able to enforce their will on women who are members of the dominated class. The legal system provides the mechanism for men to control women and prevent women from becoming powerful.[4]

As both men and women have been socialized to perceive women in their traditional domestic and nurturant roles, the resistance has been strong against women moving into previously male-dominated areas. Historically women have gained entrance into law enforcement and corrections by taking clerical positions or supervising women and juveniles during their confinement. These duties have not provided women the necessary experience and training for advancement through promotion to positions of power and authority. Aside from family and juvenile law positions in women's penal institutions, women have been all but excluded from employment in jails, courts, and prisons and administrative roles throughout the criminal justice system.

Because female criminal justice professionals have consisted of a small number of women in very specialized positions, women have been virtually powerless to change the chivalrous criminal justice system. They have had to pay a heavy price for the "protection and special treatment accorded to them by the attitudes of chivalry and the paternalistic social structure."[5] Researchers have suggested that this chivalrous attitude has drawn attention away from research on women professionals.[6]

These women have not had the power to influence the direction of research. The significance of this can be seen in the conflict theorists' argument that there is a correlation between the concepts of scholars and the interests of political authorities. That is,

government agencies support scholarly research that supports the preservation of the established order. Scholars have taken as their own the perspective and interests of the ruling class. Social scientists have accepted the official reality of important research problems. This official reality does not include research on women. As a result, researchers are involved in only a half study of the field of criminology.[7]

Lack of research on women in the criminal justice system results not only from the fact that men have held the positions of authority to dictate research projects, but because too few women are employed in the criminal justice professions to make such research feasible. This in turn is the result of sex-role stereotyping of their skills.

The traditional concept of women's roles in both society and the criminal justice system has slowly but progressively changed as some women have gained entry into criminal justice positions previously attainable only by men. These strides have been made largely through legal decisions (principally the 1972 amendment to Title VII of the 1964 Civil Rights Act prohibiting employment discrimination on the basis of sex) that have resulted in policy changes regarding the employment of women in criminal justice agencies.[8] In addition, new research has emerged that focuses on female criminal justice professionals and the conflict between male and female officials in the criminal justice system. However, the fact remains that women are still a very small minority as criminal justice professionals and research subjects, and are not being welcomed with open arms by male co-workers.

WOMEN IN LAW ENFORCEMENT

The area of criminal justice in which female professionals have been given the most attention in the literature is law enforcement. Unfortunately, much of the research has focused on perceptions of these women by their male peers and the public at large, rather than their capabilities and performance.

Women have had some involvement with police work in the United States since 1845, when the first women served as prison matrons supervising women and children held in custody in institutions such as jails, prisons, and hospitals for the insane.[9] In 1905, during the Lewis and Clark Exposition in Portland, Oregon, Lola Baldwin became the first woman to do police duty on the streets.[10] She was conferred with police powers as a "safety woman" in order to deal more effectively with problems involving adolescents and young women (such as molestation and prostitution) at the Exposition. However, it was not until 1910 that the first "regularly rated and identifiable" policewoman was appointed to a U.S. police department.[11] Alice Wells, a social worker and graduate of a theological seminary, was hired by the Los Angeles Police Department. Her duties were traditional ones typically assigned to women: clerical and working with female and juvenile prisoners. Primarily her duties consisted of "supervision and enforcement of laws concerning juveniles and women at dance halls, skating rinks, movie theaters, and other similar places of public recreation."[12]

This general course of female police work endured for nearly sixty years, until 1968, when Indianapolis became the first city to hire women for patrol duty when officials assigned two women to Car 47 as regular uniformed officers.[13] As of October 31, 1985 women made up only 6.8 percent of the sworn city and county police officers in the nation and just over 3 percent of full-time state police officers.[14] Unfortunately, the majority of the women in law enforcement continue to perform those specialized bureau duties involving clerical work, female offenders, and juveniles.[15]

Hindering the movement of women into the police profession are the traditional police attitudes that law enforcement is dangerous work, that women are too weak and/or unable to perform it satisfactorily; and the general sex-role stereotype that women need to be "protected" and thus should be assigned to "safe" duties as police officers. Both police recruits and officers have steadily resisted accepting women as their equals.[16]

Yet such reasoning has not been supported by research. On the contrary, several studies have demonstrated that women are not only as effective as men in law enforcement duties but actually handle themselves better than their male counterparts in some duties and situations.[17] For instance, female officers, who generally are less aggressive and better able to communicate with the family in domestic situations than male officers, can often settle family disputes more effectively.

Despite the lack of women assigned to patrol duty, they are apparently better off than women aspiring to other police duties. *Women in Policing* author Catherine Milton discussed the virtual nonexistence in this country of women in detective work and technical (such as administering polygraph tests) and administrative positions.[18] She notes a number of reasons to account for the differential in roles of female as opposed to male police officers:

- Quotas in hiring practices
- Special entrance requirements for women (for example, higher educational requirements)
- Separate training practices in preparation for the more traditional, specialized female police roles
- Different promotional procedures and practices
- Segregated bureaus (particularly in large cities)
- Unequal pay for female officers for comparable work

Opposition from within the Female Ranks

Ironically in some instances women themselves have proved to be their own worst enemy in both a law enforcement career and advancement. One roadblock they face is reflected in the attitudes and apprehensions of the spouses of policemen. Many policemen's wives are opposed to pairing male and female officers for fear of extramarital affairs. Of course, these reactions are unfounded in nine cases out of ten and are likely a reflection of the influence of literature, film and television, and the news media, which commonly exaggerate such occurrences. Nevertheless, as a result of such objections in some departments, policemen's wives "have been an obstacle to the expansion of the role of women in policing."[19]

Researcher Susan Martin offers an important perspective on the role dilemmas policewomen face. Through her eight-month study of female patrol officers, to whom she referred as "token" officers, Martin identified two types of occupational role behavior women officers adopted as a consequence of the conflict between their sex and occupational roles in relation to the adversity they faced from male as opposed to female officers on patrol.[20]

*Police*women react to their role dilemmas through defeminization in their effort to gain acceptance of their male peers. With this desire in mind, they follow a strong law enforcement orientation, which consists of the male policing view and male actions, such as keeping high arrest rates and taking physical action while on duty. In accordance with the police subculture, *police*women are loyal to the police code by staunchly defending the department and its policies in the face of outsiders' criticisms, including charges of sex discrimination, and concurring in the men's negative evaluations of police*women*.[21]

The second group Martin identifies are police*women*, which she described as deprofessionalized, as they accept the male terms of subordination and hence are treated as "ladies." Police*women* are "polar opposites" to *police*women. They maintain a traditional feminine perspective and regard police work primarily as a source of income rather than an occupation of interest; or they engage in police work but battle with sex discrimination, lack of assertiveness, and the need to remain "ladies on the job" as well as off it. Police*women* generally are viewed as employees who take little initiative, are not highly motivated, make few arrests, and are "underachievers" as police officers.

Martin surmises that the result of these contrasting roles is a lack of unity among female police officers that limits their political power and could contribute to inadequate police performance when one considers the inherent pressures and obstacles that would likely affect their functioning as officers, albeit "token" officers. And considering the difficulty of police work itself and the conflict women are immersed in with men in the system of law enforcement, it is regrettable that occupational dilemmas and antagonism between female patrol officers exist that can only make their path more difficult.

WOMEN IN THE CRIMINAL COURTS

Very little research has been done on women as criminal lawyers and judges in the criminal court. It is known, however, that through women's changing roles and legal decisions, more and more women are entering law school and the professions of law and the judiciary. Nevertheless, law schools and court systems continue to be dominated by men. Michelle Patterson and Laurie Engelberg contend that men have maintained "control of the legal system by devising and promoting models of the legal profession. The major attributes of the legal practitioner in this model is that he is male."[22] Consistent with other branches of the criminal justice system, men control the most important positions of authority and research projects.

Women in Criminal Law

From 1920 to the present opportunities for women as lawyers have risen steadily. Today women comprise about one-third of the total number of law students in this country and approximately 14 percent of the more than 600,000 lawyers—an increase of more than 200 percent since 1970.[23] Although women have made gains across the board in the legal profession, they are most heavily represented in the traditional women's specialties of criminal, estate, and family law, research, or briefs preparation. In a recent study of career patterns among law school graduates, it was found that 12 percent of the female lawyers entered and practiced criminal law compared to only 6 percent of the men.[24]

Historically women have faced few obstacles in seeking a career in the specialty of criminal law. Thus in this area a number of female lawyers have made their mark.[25] However, this career path has not been a concession by men to women as their equals; rather, it is a specialty that men have declined in favor of more lucrative law specialties. Near the turn of the century Clarence Darrow's speech to female lawyers put this in perspective:

There is another field (after divorce) you can have solely for your own. You won't make a living at it, but it's worthwhile and you'll have no competition, that is the free defense of criminals.[26]

Darrow's message to female lawyers to concentrate on defending criminals was in recognition that law specialties such as corporate and tax law yield power, status, and high income and that women would face an uphill battle in these areas of legal practice designed to prevent them from reaping these benefits. Because most criminals are poor, defending them provides little income and almost no power or status. Very few criminal attorneys earn a large income or gain a wide reputation. Hence it becomes clear that women are still far from achieving equal status, income, and opportunities as lawyers and continue to be discriminated against in the most desired, high-stakes specialties of the legal profession.

Female Criminal Court Judges

Prior to 1920, female judges were a rarity, mainly because they were ineligible to vote or hold office before the passage of the Nineteenth Amendment. However, a few women did hold judgeships in federal, state, and county judiciaries where there were no legal prohibitions. The first female judge, Marilla Richer, had earned her reputation as a criminal lawyer. Known as the "prisoner's friend," Richer received her appointment in 1884 as United States Commissioner by the District of Columbia trial court judges. However, neither she nor those first few female judges that followed presided over a criminal court.[27]

Female judges have traditionally presided primarily over family and municipal courts, specialties considered appropriate for women—yet another example of sex-role stereotyping. This remains true today despite the steady increase over the years in the number of women becoming judges.[28] As of this writing, women comprised more than 17 percent of the judges in the nation—three times the number of female judges in 1970.[29] A Fund for Modern Courts survey reported that women fared best in states that appoint rather than elect judges, a clear indication that the sexism that exists within the legal profession is a reflection of community attitudes at large.[30]

Several women since 1920 have managed to become appointed to nontraditional judgeships, mainly in the appellate courts. Sandra Day O'Connor, a U.S. Supreme Court Associate Justice, is the most notable example. Yet it was the 1978 appointment of Joan B. Carey to preside over a New York City Criminal Court that set a precedent for women in criminal law courts.[31]

Recently an interesting comparison study of the convicting and sentencing patterns of male and female judges in the criminal court was undertaken by John Gruhl, Cassia Spohn, and Susan Welch.[32] The researchers theorized that female judges would likely be more lenient than their male counterparts; however, their findings indicated that only limited differences existed in the convictions and sentences made by male and female judges. Female judges were more likely to treat both sexes equally, whereas male judges tended to display paternalistic attitudes toward the female defendants.

Despite the emergence and capabilities of female judges in the criminal court and other nontraditional judgeships, overall judicial appointments of women have maintained traditional patterns. In the criminal courts today it is nearly a certainty that although one might see more female victims, offenders, and lawyers, the person behind the bench will likely be a reflection of men's traditional dominance in the criminal court judiciary.

WOMEN AS CORRECTIONAL OFFICERS

Women have been employed as prison administrators and correctional officers in women's prisons for many decades, which is not surprising considering these were believed to be positions compatible with the female sex role and women's capabilities. However, only in recent years have women gained the right to work in similar capacities in prisons for men.

Women were first employed in men's prisons in clerical, counselor, and teaching positions.[33] In fact, a recent survey of the American Correctional Association revealed that although 18 percent of correctional staffs are composed of women, these women are predominantly assigned to traditional women's duties such as social worker, teacher, clerk, and counselor, suggesting that women's sex roles in corrections have been slow to change.[34] Change is coming nevertheless as women seek positions in the full range of security jobs where opportunities for advancement and higher pay exist.

Women today are employed as correctional guards by nearly every state prison system and the Federal Bureau of Prisons. Although the number of female guards in men's prisons varies from state to state, women account for approximately 6 percent of the correctional guard force nationwide.[35] Their progress in this field, as in other criminal justice occupations, has been less than enthusiastically received by their male counterparts and prison administrators; issues regarding female guards' safety, their ability to perform duties, prison discipline, and male inmates' right to privacy continue to hinder the female correctional officer working in the all-male prison.

Legal Maneuvers

The sexual integration of men's prisons came about primarily as a result of the 1964 Civil Rights Act as amended in 1972, when Title VII was expanded to prohibit sex discrimination. Although this paved the way for women to obtain jobs in many traditionally "male" occupations, it was particularly significant in the field of corrections, considering that 90 percent of the state correctional systems "did not initiate the hiring of women in their adult male institutions . . . until after this mandate."[36] Furthermore, prison administrators responding to a survey overwhelmingly admitted that the legal requirements were their primary reason for discontinuing male-only hiring practices.[37]

The 1972 amendments also increased the Equal Employment Opportunity Commission's (EEOC) enforcement power to prosecute violators of Title VII in the federal courts. Despite the rise in EEOC employer sex discrimination cases, some prison administrators hesitated to hire women as guards in men's prisons, hoping to make use of Title VII's mandate of allowing some discriminatory practices to exist if there is a "bona fide occupational qualification [BFOQ] reasonably necessary to the normal operation of that particular business or enterprise."[38]

Although women managed to win a number of cases heard in the lower federal courts, where prison officials used as an affirmative defense Title VII's BFOQ, their push toward equality in corrections was, if not stymied, sidetracked somewhat by the ruling in two court cases. In *Dothard* v. *Rawlinson*, the Supreme Court ruled that in certain situations correctional jobs in men's prisons qualified for a BFOQ exemption. The court "banned the use of female correctional officers in a prison where conditions were very poor and where a woman, by virtue of her sex could undermine the security of the institution if unable to provide adequate control of the population."[39] The court also recognized other potential problems, such as invasions of privacy.[40]

In *Gunther* v. *Iowa*, the privacy issue was raised again and left unresolved, as it was in *Dothard*. The district court ruled that "privacy shall not take precedence over a female correctional officer's right to promotion and that institutional administration *will* make the necessary scheduling adjustments for women within institutions without placing them in direct confrontation with an inmate's privacy."[41]

In effect, these two cases determined that although women will still be able to move up the promotional ladder based on seniority and capability, they have yet to achieve full equality with men in the prison system. Instead, Title VII's sexual integration provisions has mandated a system of legally permitted "near equality" among male and female correctional officers. This has proved detrimental to women's momentum in corrections as well as their relationship with male guards with whom they have to compete and work at something less than full status while receiving full benefits. Equally affected are the prison administrators, whose job it is to implement and design integration policies effectively.

The full ramifications of Title VII's applicability to corrections versus sex discrimination and inmate privacy issues have yet to be fully realized. What is clear is that as of 1986 no precise guidelines for these issues have been established, leaving the problem of unequal employment in the prison system still unresolved, adding to the conflict between men and women in corrections.

Steady Resistance and Conflict

Women who enter the male prison system as guards experience the same opposition and conflict as would women entering any other male-

dominated profession. In a recent study of four male correctional institutions employing women as guards, Cheryl Peterson found that although female officers were generally well received by the inmates, the
male officers responded to them with hostility. She further contends
that "women were severely resented by male officers even before their
first day on the job."[42]

The impetus for male guards' strong resistance to women as equal co-
workers can be seen in at least three beliefs:

- There are natural, immutable differences between the sexes.
- The effectiveness of the job requires having masculine traits.
- Female guards receive preferential treatment in their duties.

Sally Simpson and Mervin White mention five sources of organization
conflicts contributing to male opposition to women:

- The nature of guard work
- Danger and trust in fellow officers
- Isolation of the correctional officers
- Alienation and cynicism
- Job stress[43]

There can be no denying that male and female correctional officers
have distinct gender-related characteristics and attitudes that influence
their occupational behavior and perceptions as well as their interpersonal
association. This will continue to be accentuated as long as women are
allowed to work as guards in a legally sanctioned system of unequal yet
equal workers.

Women's success as correctional officers in men's prisons under these
conditions has been the subject of much controversy among criminal
justice officials. However, very few scientific studies have been conducted on this subject. Hence this is where we need to proceed in hopes
of better understanding and possibly resolving existing conflicts related
to the gender and occupational variables common to men's and women's
roles in the prison system.

WOMEN AS JAIL OFFICERS

The paucity of research on female professionals in the criminal justice
system is most conspicuous where it concerns women employed in local
jails. The studies of female jail guards that exist are usually localized,
in conjunction with men guards, or concern women in corrections. No
national studies can be found on the female jail officer. What little in-

formation that is available suggests that women working in jails face the same problems and progress as do women in prisons. That is, there is considerable resistance among men to women's equal status as jail guards, yet the court decisions, the women's movement, and a slight shift in public attitudes have increased women's opportunities in this field.

There is a higher percentage of female jail officers than female correctional officers.[44] This, however, can be misleading, as the overwhelming majority of American jails house both sexes on a pretrial and sentenced basis. Considering that female prisoners make up a higher percentage of the total jail population than the prison population, it is not surprising that more female jail officers would be employed since guarding jailed prisoners still tends to follow, either officially or unofficially, traditional same-sex patterns. Also, because of the presence of male and female prisoners, the need for female guards is imperative in most jails with the constant threat of sexual abuse of female prisoners by male guards or prisoners.

Another factor accounting for women's increased numbers in jail employment can be seen in the less lucrative and professional status of many local jails; women gain the opportunities that men have passed up. For instance, Kenneth Kerle cites Kentucky and several other states where women work as jailers for no pay.[45] "According to the Kentucky Local Detention Study . . . twenty-one county jails had unsalaried employees, of which all but three were female."[46] In a number of other county jails female officers were paid salaries lower than their male counterparts for the same type of work.[47]

Kerle also notes, from his survey of 554 jails, the roadblocks to promotion female jailers face. Only seven of the jails had female administrators. Women's chances for promotion were impeded by their working only with female prisoners. Many of the local government officials gave sex-role stereotypical explanations for this, such as women's lack of experience and inability to supervise male prisoners. Certainly experience cannot be gained if women are not given a chance. Furthermore, when given the opportunity, women have shown that age-old discriminations against them for the most part are based more on prejudice than on sound rationale.

One of the few scientific studies of the effect of women guarding male jail inmates was conducted in 1975 at the county jail in Boulder, Colorado.[48] Ten women were hired by the Boulder County Sheriff's Department to work at the jail under the same conditions as male guards, excluding strip searches, which were to be conducted by guards of the same sex as the inmates. Few inmates reported "that their privacy was threatened . . . resentment at taking orders from women or sexual frustration at having women in living quarters."[49]

Many of the inmates, however, did believe male officers were better equipped to handle problems of violence. But this was mitigated somewhat by the fact that a large percentage of the inmates believed that the presence of women jailers made their jailing more livable—or, as the researchers explained it, female jail officers "could be said to exert a 'softening' influence on inmate behavior which could avert some potential crisis situations before they grow into physical confrontations."[50]

Over two-thirds of the male guards favored employing women in the jail, although most still felt the need at times to protect female officers.

Regrettably, the gains women have made in jail employment are dampened somewhat by the perceived differences between the sexes, exploitation, and continuing sexism among jail officials. More research on women's employment and opportunities in jails is needed, along with perhaps more legal action to effect positive change toward full equality within the jails and from those who run them.

A WORD ABOUT FEMALE PRIVATE EYES

Although many criminal justice officials frown at the mention of private investigators or detectives in the same breath as police detectives, on some occasions private investigation crosses over to criminal investigation, and more and more women are joining the ranks of what traditionally has been one of the most male-dominated professions. There are no reliable national statistics—nor has there been adequate research—on female private investigators. However, in New York City alone it has been estimated that currently about 30 percent of the licensed and unlicensed private investigators are women, whereas a decade earlier the number was closer to 1 percent.[51]

As with other nontraditional professions women are now entering, the move into private detecting is attributed in part to the women's movement, legal decisions, the greater number of women looking for jobs, and the perceived money-making potential. In addition, the glamorous image of women as detectives on TV has created a new surge of interest in this field.

In truth, most detective work for men or women is boring, routine, nonadventurous, and certainly not glamorous. The pay varies, but at times it can be quite generous. Take the example of one New York woman who runs her own detective agency—she claims it grosses $2 million a year. Even if this is atypical among women detectives, the fact remains that in relation to other criminal justice-related occupations, women are beginning to make their presence felt in the world of private investigation, as well as feeling the heat from their male counterparts.

Women as professionals in the criminal justice system continue to make their way into a nontraditional field against opposition by men who have steadfastly resisted accepting women as their equals. The women's movement and legal decisions have aided women in their cause. However, their numbers are still quite low, especially pertaining to administrative and other management-level positions. Men, by virtue of establishing positions of authority, still dominate the criminal justice agencies and control the structure of the system. Additionally, men control the research projects that have traditionally neglected women employed by the criminal justice system. At least in part this neglect can be attributed to the relatively few women involved. Obviously the need is great to recruit more women into the field and create greater awareness of the female criminal justice professional. Both goals can only be accomplished with an emphasis on research, funding, and planning for the utilization of women as practitioners in the system of criminal justice.

NOTES

1. Imogene L. Moyer, "Crime, Conflict Theory, and the Patriarchal Society," in Imogene Moyer, ed., *The Changing Roles of Women in the Criminal Justice System: Offenders, Victims, and Professionals* (Prospect Heights, Ill.: Waveland Press, 1985), p. 9.

2. Ibid., p. 8.

3. Elizabeth Moulds, "Chivalry and Paternalism: Disparities of Treatment in the Criminal Justice System," *Western Political Quarterly* 31 (1978):416–430; Nicole Rafter and Elena Natalizia, "Marxist Feminism: Implications for Criminal Justice," *Crime and Delinquency* 27 (1981):81–98.

4. Moyer, "Crime, Conflict Theory," p. 10.

5. Ibid.

6. Jane R. Chapman, *Economic Realities and the Female Offender* (Lexington, Mass.: Lexington Books, 1980); Ruth M. Glick and Virginia V. Neto, *National Study of Women's Correctional Programs* (Washington, D.C.: Government Printing Office, 1977).

7. Moyer, "Crime, Conflict Theory," p. 15.

8. Several of these court cases are cited in Roi Townsey, "Women in Municipal Policing." Paper presented at the annual meeting of the American Society of Criminology, 1980.

9. Peter Horne, *Women in Law Enforcement*, 2nd ed. (Springfield, Ill.: Charles C. Thomas, 1980), p. 26.

10. Ibid., p. 27.

11. Lewis J. Sherman, "Policewomen around the World," *International Review of Criminal Policy* 33 (1977):25–33.

12. Horne, *Women in Law Enforcement*, p. 28.

13. Catherine Milton, *Women in Policing* (Washington, D.C.: Police Foundation, 1972).

14. U.S. Federal Bureau of Investigation, *Crime in the United States: Uniform*

Crime Reports, 1985 (Washington, D.C.: Government Printing Office, 1986), pp. 248–249.

15. Carl Glassman, "How Lady Cops Are Doing," *Tallahassee Democrat* (July 27, 1980).

16. Townsey, "Women in Municipal Policing"; Constance Breece and Gerald Garrett, "The Emerging Role of Women in Law Enforcement," in Jack Kinton, ed., *Police Roles in the Seventies* (Ann Arbor: Edwards Brothers, 1975).

17. Ibid., p. 113; Kenneth W. Kerber, Steven M. Andes, and Michele B. Mittler, "Citizen Attitudes Regarding the Competence of Female Police Officers," *Journal of Police Science and Administration* 5 (1977):333–347.

18. Milton, *Women in Policing*.

19. Ibid., p. 25.

20. Susan E. Martin, "*Police*women and Police*women*: Occupational Role Dilemmas and Choices of Female Officers," *Journal of Police Science and Administration* 7 (1979):314–323.

21. Ibid., p. 318.

22. Moyer, *The Changing Roles of Women*, p. 243; Michelle Patterson and Laurie Engelberg, "Women in a Male-Dominated Profession: The Women Lawyers," in Barbara Price and Natalie Sokoloff, eds., *The Criminal Justice System and Women* (New York: Clark Boardman, 1982), p. 387.

23. Emily Couric, *Women Lawyers: Perspectives on Success* (New York: Law & Business, Inc., 1984), p. 5; "Women to Watch," *Ladies' Home Journal* 101 (November 1984):214.

24. Rita Simon and Kathryn Gardner, "Career Patterns among University of Illinois Women Law Graduates," *Women Lawyers Journal* 67 (1981:19–27.

25. Clarice Feinman, *Women in the Criminal Justice System* (New York: Praeger, 1980), p. 99.

26. Quoted in D. Kelly Weisberg, "Barred from the Bar: Women and Legal Education in the United States 1870–1890," *Journal of Legal Education* 28 (1977):497.

27. Feinman, *Women in the Criminal Justice System*, p. 100.

28. Cynthia F. Epstein, *Women in Law* (New York: Basic Books, 1981), p. 243.

29. "Women to Watch."

30. "Minority and Women Judges," *U.S. News & World Report* (January 20, 1986), p. 11.

31. Clarice Feinman, "Women Lawyers and Judges in the Criminal Courts," in Imogene L. Moyer, ed., *The Changing Roles of Women in the Criminal Justice System* (Prospect Heights, Ill.: Waveland Press, 1985), p. 274.

32. John Gruhl, Cassia Spohn, and Susan Welch, "Women as Policymakers: The Case of Trial Judges," *American Journal of Political Science* 25 (1981):308–322.

33. Joan Potter, "Should Women Guards Work in Prisons for Men?" *Corrections Magazine* 6, no. 5 (1980):30–38.

34. Osa D. Coffey, "ACA Women—Who and Where Are They!" *Corrections Today* 42 (1979):36–37.

35. Lynn E. Zimmer, *Women Guarding Men* (Chicago: University of Chicago Press, 1986), p. 1.

36. Sandra Nicolai, "The Upward Mobility of Women in Corrections," in Robert R. Ross, ed., *Prison Guard/Correctional Officer: The Use and Abuse of the Human Resources of Prisons* (Toronto: Butterworth, 1981), p. 223.

37. Joann B. Morton, "Women in Correctional Employment: Where Are They Now and Where Are They Headed?" Proceedings of the 109th Annual Congress of Correction of the American Correctional Association, Philadelphia, August 1979.

38. 42 U.S.C. 2000e–2 (1976), 703(e).

39. Nicolai, "The Upward Mobility of Women," p. 224; *Dothard* v. *Rawlinson*, 433 U.S. 321 (1977).

40. Eric P. Matusewitch, "Equal Opportunity for Female Correctional Officers: A Brief Overview," *Corrections Today* 42 (1980):36–37.

41. Nicolai, "The Upward Mobility of Women," p. 224; *Gunther* v. *Iowa*, 462 F. Supp. 952 (1979).

42. Cheryl Peterson, "Doing Time with the Boys: An Analysis of Women Correctional Officers in All-Male Facilities," in Barbara Price and Natalie Sokoloff, eds., *The Criminal Justice System and Women* (New York: Clark Boardman, 1982).

43. Sally Simpson and Mervin F. White, "The Female Guard in the All-Male Prison," in Imogene L. Moyer, *The Changing Roles of Women in the Criminal Justice System* (Prospect Heights, Ill.: Waveland Press, 1985), pp. 280–283.

44. Kenneth E. Kerle, "The American Woman County Jail Officer," in Imogene L. Moyer, *The Changing Roles of Women in the Criminal Justice System* (Prospect Heights, Ill.: Waveland Press, 1985), p. 301.

45. Ibid., pp. 309–310.

46. Ibid.; *Kentucky Local Detention Study* (Kentucky Department of Justice: Bureau of Corrections, 1978).

47. Kerle, "The American Woman," pp. 311–312.

48. Potter, "Should Women Guards Work?" pp. 34–35.

49. Ibid., p. 35.

50. Ibid.

51. "Look Out Sam Spade, Susan's on the Case," *New York Times* (September 16, 1985), p. B7.

IV

IMPLICATIONS FOR FUTURE LEGAL AND SOCIAL ACTION

Responding to Women as Victims, Offenders, and Professionals

The response of the criminal justice system and social and community services to the plight of female victims, offenders, and criminal justice practitioners has been less than adequate on the whole. A major reason for this is the traditional stereotypes assigned women and men that have influenced perceptions of women involved in crime or the system of criminal justice. In this chapter we will address present practices in responding to the female crime victim and legislative reform and implications for women and female criminality.

CRIMINAL JUSTICE SYSTEM RESPONSE

In general, the criminal justice system's response to female victims of crime has tended to favor the criminal, who is often an adult male. That is, fewer offenders are arrested, convicted, or incarcerated for crimes against women than for crimes against men. Conversely, female victims are often ignored, disbelieved, or discredited by those they need most. This is a reflection of both a double standard in the male-dominated criminal justice system and the types of crimes women are most often victimized by. The two most frequent are undoubtedly wife battering and rape.

Battered Women

Wife battering, like any other offense that constitutes bodily harm or assault, is currently classified as a criminal offense in every legal jurisdiction in the nation; therefore in theory is subject to the appropriate criminal justice response and criminal penalties. In practice, however, the law is somewhat ambiguous in its enforcement when the parties concerned are husband and wife. More often than not wife battering is treated not as a crime but as a civil issue. The failure of the legal system to protect the victim from this violence is a reflection of the societal norms that stress the sanctity of the family and that support the belief that a man's home is his castle. The perspective that the family is generally off-limits for intervention by the criminal justice system can be seen in the "covert toleration of wife beating, as indicated in the policy and personal attitudes of the police, prosecutors, and judges."[1]

This usually begins with the police, who represent the first line of legal system contact for most victims. Although a high percentage of the calls police receive are for domestic disturbances, they do not differentiate between family "squabbles" and violent situations. More likely the police fail to respond in either case, and when they do, they are usually more supportive of the batterer, while discouraging the victim from exercising or realizing her rights. Arrests are seldom made, in any event.

This nonintervention by the police is often associated with three factors: (1) they view intervention as a waste of their time and energy, as women frequently drop assault charges once the immediacy of the situation has passed; (2) a genuine belief that wife beating is not really criminal behavior; and (3) a similar strategy of inaction at the prosecutorial level. "Prosecutors treat police investigation as though it had not happened. The battered wives are treated as though there were no corroboration of injury by responding officers, and no basis for arrest. . . . Nonprosecution shows police officers that it does not pay to be diligent."[2] In part prosecutors' response is predicated by their heavy caseloads. With their time at a premium in encouraging cooperation from reluctant victims, prosecutors "may focus on the likelihood of conviction rather than on seriousness of offense or likelihood of its repetition."[3] Hence the battered woman often becomes an issue of low priority.

Judges share in this nonintervention position of the criminal justice system. They often shrug off wife beating as a "private matter" between spouses, the result being only minimal sentences or fines and the quick release of an abusive husband. Marital counseling or divorce is frequently recommended, the implication being that the victim shares equally in the guilt with the batterer. Sex discrimination within the legal system can be seen further in its extreme reluctance to compensate the wife.

Recent Trends. Policy shifts in the criminal justice system concerning battered wives have been slow in coming. Nevertheless, recent trends suggest that reforms are being brought about. The International Association of Chiefs of Police (IACP) training material reflects this change in attitude. Once regarding domestic disputes as a family matter in which arrest should come only as a last resort, the IACP now maintains that a policy of arrest, when the elements of the offense are present, promotes the well-being of the victim. . . . The officer who starts legal action may give the wife the courage she needs to realistically face and correct her situation.[4]

When there is no probable cause for arrest, the IACP encourages police to assist women in seeking other support services. The idea behind these trends is that increased arrests and attention to abuse cases will be beneficial in the long run to both the public and the system of law enforcement.

Legislative action has also demonstrated increased awareness and involvement of the judicial system in wife abuse cases. In the last few years nearly every state has enacted new legislation addressing this problem. Included among these are

- Laws prohibiting rape by husband
- Laws authorizing the court to direct a batterer to change his behavior, to evict the wife beater from the premises shared with his spouse, to require the batterer to compensate the victim monetarily, to impose a jail term for violating a protective order
- Laws authorizing enforcement officials to make arrests in cases of domestic violence, to make arrests without a warrant when probable cause is present that there was violation of a protective order, to transport the battered to a hospital, to inform the victim of legal options
- Laws that require organizations offering assistance to violent families to maintain records

Raped Women

Female victims of rape equally find their involvement with the criminal justice system to be trying. The job of the police in rape cases is to investigate reported rape, collect and preserve evidence, apprehend and arrest suspects, and prepare cases for possible prosecution. Although rape statutes vary from state to state, in order for a prosecution to be successful, three elements must generally be proved beyond a reasonable doubt: the sexual assault did take place (either through penetration or other contact), the sexual assault was forcible or without the victim's consent, and the sexual assault was perpetrated by the defendant. |

Law enforcement agencies and personnel have been widely criticized concerning their procedures in handling the initial investigation and succeeding steps in the process. They have been attacked by women's groups and victim advocates as being unsensitive and callous; by medical professionals who have resented police interference in their treatment of the victims and gathering of medical evidence; and by prosecuting agencies that fault police for not being thorough enough in their investigation or jeopardizing cases by violating the rights of defendants.

Undoubtedly all of these criticisms have some basis in fact. However, this generally negative response to rape victims exists throughout the criminal justice system as well as within other professions and social services. Rape victims are constantly being put on trial by most agencies they contact as the sexism, bias, victim culpability, and other stereotypes that pervade society regarding this sex crime exist in the actions and inactions of the system of criminal justice. Consequently, it is conservatively estimated that at least half of all sexual assaults are never reported.

Yet this should not detract from the difficulty of proving a reported case of rape. Evidentiary requirements, departmental practices, victim cooperation and credibility, noncooperation and coordination among the involved agencies, and inconsistent rape statutes all contribute to a criminal justice system that favors the rapist instead of the victim. As a result, historically only a small percentage of reported rapes have resulted in convictions or been aggressively prosecuted.

It is not surprising under these circumstances that many cooperative victims ultimately drop their charges. Lengthy criminal justice proceedings, confusion about the system that is supposed to help them, the emotional impact of remembering their victimization, and across-the-board insensitive treatment often are perceived by the victims as an even worse crime against their person than the rape itself.

Recent Trends. Although the criminal justice system's response to rape victims is still far from adequate, advances have been made in recent years across the country in dealing more aggressively with the crime of rape. Innovations within criminal justice agencies include improved forensic techniques, specialized training for trial deputies, an emphasis on providing services to the victims as well as traditional enforcement of the law, and pursuing further involvement of female criminal justice professionals in the investigation and prosecution stages of forcible rape.

Rape law reform has taken place in most states in recent years as public interest in this crime has grown. The act of forcible rape "and the subsequent treatment of the victim by criminal justice authorities have come to symbolize the most extreme example of the abuse of a woman's body and her integrity."[5] Most of the legislative changes have been in two areas: adopting new and broader definitions of rape and relaxing the proof requirements.

In some instances rape has been redefined "in terms of sex-neutral assault or battery, with several degrees based on the dangerousness of the circumstances of the assault or the kind of assault."[6] In a number of states, corroboration requirements have been abandoned or limited. Additionally, some states now prohibit inquiry into a rape victim's prior sexual conduct, and others have taken steps to "eliminate both the cautionary instruction to the jury that the testimony of the victim is suspect and the chastity instruction that permits the jury to infer that a woman who has once consented to sexual intercourse is more likely to consent again than one who has not."[7]

Good examples of changes in the law can be seen in Michigan and California. Michigan has replaced the traditional rape law with a new legal terminology defining an array of sexual crimes. In 1986 the California Supreme Court reinstated a rape conviction after ruling that rape without resistance is possible. The ruling was based on a 1980 amendment to the California rape statute that deleted most references to resistance and is defined as sexual intercourse accomplished against the will of a person by means of force or fear of immediate and unlawful bodily injury, or by the threat of retaliation against the victim or another person.[8] This definition is now also applicable to marital rape.

Further legislative reform can be found in mandates to provide specialized training for law enforcement and special medical procedures for the examination of rape victims.

Other Crimes against Women

Criminal justice practices regarding women victimized by other crimes have been just as frustrating on the whole. Crimes such as incest, when discovered at all, rarely result in apprehension of the abuser. This is another crime that many in the criminal justice system shrug off as a family matter, victim perpetrated, civil in nature, or less important than other crimes. Additionally, although incest laws exist in most states, they are generally nonuniform in definition, even within a state. Many times prosecutors are left to use their own discretion in handling a case and choosing the right statute. Too often they make a decision that favors anyone but the victim.

Other crimes against women such as pornography and, in many instances, prostitution are labeled as either "victimless" or basically unenforceable. For instance, despite laws in almost every state prohibiting the distribution of obscene materials, differences exist both in laws and how often they can be or should be enforced. Hence although much evidence has associated pornography (hard- and soft-core) with crime against women, the availability of pornography in this country has never been greater. It seems that few producers and distributors fear prosecution under existing laws.

Fortunately there are those who continue to fight for a responsible reaction among criminal justice agencies toward female crime victims. For example, the Attorney General's Commission on Pornography has recommended ninety-two changes in federal law and law enforcement policies to curb pornography. Within most states legislation is being proposed or drafted better to assist women victimized by crime, heighten penalties against those who commit these crimes, improve reporting procedures, and coordinate efforts.

In the criminal justice system greater emphasis is being placed on better educating and informing women about the problems they may encounter in their involvement with the system. Conversely, criminal justice personnel, particularly judges, are being educated to better handle and understand cases of female victimization that commonly come before them, such as rape and wife beating.

Despite the positive reform currently being seen throughout the criminal justice system, the need is great for still better treatment of female victims of crime and stiffer penalties for those who commit these crimes.

TRENDS IN SOCIAL SERVICES

Since the early 1970s a variety of support groups have surfaced throughout the country for female victims of crime. Two of the most useful are the battered women's shelters and rape crisis centers.

Battered Women's Shelters

The shelter or safe home concept has proved to be an effective means for providing relief to battered women and their children. Begun in England in 1972 when the first refuge was opened by Erin Pizzey, battered women's shelters quickly caught on in the United States as a way to protect women and children from the immediate threat or aftermath of domestic attack, usually at the hands of the man of the household.[9] Today women's shelters come in all shapes and sizes, with trained volunteers and paid staff whose duties include counseling, advocacy, medical care, and referral services.

Despite the great need for these shelters, there are questions concerning their overall effectiveness in an abusive situation as well as their basic philosophy, which can vary from shelter to shelter. Because of severe cutbacks in funding, many shelters are not adequately equipped to handle the women or children who come to them; often there is nowhere else for them to go except back to a violent home. In other instances, because of the rules and regulations of a shelter or overcrowding, a battered woman may get only a minimal amount of relief from the immediate danger without being given the time to recover, let alone weigh her future options. These and other problems notwithstanding, community shelters continue to be important to female victims, providing at least a temporary answer to a long-term problem.

Rape Crisis Centers

Since the first rape crisis centers opened during the early 1970s, more than one hundred have been organized throughout the nation. Their philosophy has remained basically the same: to offer the support and comfort to rape victims that is unavailable from other sources. Rape crisis centers have had a major impact on drawing attention to sexual assault and its dynamics. However, their most prominent contributions have been in helping the thousands of rape victims cope with what happened to them, educating members of their communities about rape and how to fight it, and improving other services for victims (such as criminal prosecution).

Rape crisis centers are staffed by trained volunteers and offer an array of services to victims including telephone counseling, information regarding medical and legal procedures, and support during trials. Many of the staff are members of the community or have had personal experiences with rape. As with battered women's shelters, controversy about rape crisis centers exists concerning philosophical issues, professionalism, and exploitation of volunteers. Lack of sufficient funding is another major problem these centers face. All of these issues are important to the future of the centers and those they serve. Until the problems can be resolved satisfactorily, rape crisis centers will not be able to operate at their full potential, which can only hurt the people who will need them in the future.

Other Social Services Trends

A number of other social services, most publicly funded, are available to the female victim. These include 24-hour hot lines, welfare agencies, legal aid, public health departments, church-supported programs, civil and fraternal organizations, and political groups (for example, the National Organization for Women). Many of these support services have established a working relationship with other fields such as law enforcement, medical, and mental health. On the other hand, there are times when staff offering these services appear insensitive, unhelpful, or patronizing, which only adds to the woes of a victim seeking assistance. Additionally, limited funding and differential concepts can affect the type and quality of services offered. Overall, considering the relatively few useful social services available to the crime victim, these and other support groups remain vital as a resource for women in need.

THE FUTURE FOR WOMEN AND CRIMINALITY

Although female victims, offenders, and criminal justice practitioners have made some gains in terms of their treatment by the criminal justice system and society at large, it is apparent that they are still fighting traditional sex-role stereotyping. Hence as women's roles in society continue to change, so must the attitudes and practices of those who seek to dominate or control them. What follows are recommendations for positive reform within the criminal justice system and society as it pertains to the woman's relationship with crime and criminal justice.

Research on Women

The dearth of research on women involved in victimization and criminal justice is a major drawback in understanding the nature, dynamics, and causal factors of this relationship, as well as treatment, prevention, planning, utilization, and related factors that can effect positive change. It is imperative that the research policies in this field be revised, expanded, and funded by criminal justice and other agencies that have a stake in the issues of criminality and criminal justice so that we may broaden our knowledge of women in this field and seek improvements in their treatment both in and outside the criminal justice system.

The Female Victim

1. The criminal justice system must change its posture regarding female victims of crime: that is, sexist attitudes that ultimately hinder the performance of personnel throughout the system.

2. Law enforcement must develop new strategies and procedures to improve (a) response time to all crimes against women, but especially woman battering and rape; (b) investigative techniques; (c) arrest policies; and (d) understanding of the victim's point of view.

3. More education and greater awareness are needed among police officers, prosecutors, and judges in more effectively working with female victims and better meeting their needs within the system of justice.

4. Improved coordination and communication among criminal justice and other agencies and groups working with and for female victims is urgently called for.

5. A greater emphasis on the rights of the victim is needed among those who deal with victims and offenders.

6. Victimization surveys need to be more explicit in details concerning adult victims, better methodology procedures must be developed, and sample groups must be expanded to be more indicative of population trends.

7. Legislation must be revised or implemented to broaden the definition of what constitutes crimes against women, such as sexual assault and to increase arrest, conviction, and incarceration rates of offenders

of women, compensation for women victims, and funding for improved support services.

8. Greater response in the community is needed in reporting suspected or known crimes against women, supporting its members, improving police-community relations, and keeping abreast of changes in the law and law enforcement programs.

The Female Offender

1. The correlation between women as victims and criminals must be better studied, recognized, and understood throughout the criminal justice system and society at large so that treatment of women as offenders might be made more effective.

2. Differential enforcement of the law, chivalry, and paternalism need further study to determine their significance in women's criminality and the treatment of women in the criminal justice system.

3. Laws and law enforcement practices pertaining to prostitution, pornography, and other crimes in which women (mostly minorities) are overrepresented insofar as criminal justice system intervention are clearly sexist and prejudicial and need to be changed.

4. The increase in certain crimes among women in the last quarter of a century indicate that more study is needed in assessing these patterns and how they relate to society at large and the treatment of women.

5. A greater emphasis in the criminal justice system and other organizations is needed on crime prevention and societal conditions that create criminal opportunities and the need to commit crimes.

6. Official statistics of women's crime need to be improved by developing more effective, detailed information on arrests, offenses, offender characteristics and by gaining more uniformity and participation among law enforcement agencies and their measurement of crime.

7. Better vocational, educational, rehabilitation, parenting, and exercise programs are needed in women's jails and prisons to occupy female prisoners and improve their opportunities once they get out.

8. There is a strong need to improve conditions within jails and prisons for women and to investigate sexual and physical abuse of female prisoners by male personnel and prisoners, and misuse of female prisoners by jail or prison staff.

9. More alternative programs for female offenders are needed.

The Female Criminal Justice Professional

1. Better hiring practices are needed in all areas of criminal justice, but especially for administrative positions, specialized, and nontraditional posts.

2. New or revised legislation is needed to clarify the applicability of the female professional's right against sexual discrimination in the criminal justice system and positions such as in corrections where legal inequality still exists.

3. More sex discrimination court cases by women may be necessary to break the barriers still present in criminal justice employment.

4. Criminal justice agency administrators must devise procedures and programs to lessen tensions between the sexes, create job harmony, and improve working conditions and results for female and male professionals.

5. More women need to become aware of the opportunities available to them today in the criminal justice system. This can only be accomplished through education, availability of information, and greater interest on the part of women.

6. Universities and colleges need to revise existing programs and create new ones designed to encourage women's interest in pursuing a career in criminal justice.

7. More female criminal justice professionals are needed in positions in which female arrestees or prisoners might be prone to victimization, exploitation, and/or violation of their rights.

8. Acceptance of women by men as their equals in the profession of criminal justice is essential to the overall effectiveness of the system and its components.

Perhaps what is needed most in the future study of women and criminality is to recognize that research is only as effective as its parts. As female victims, criminals, and criminal justice professionals are intrinsically linked by their common traditional sex roles and consequent perceptions by their male counterparts, fragmented studies of them (for example, the female offender) provide us with only a limited view of the woman, crime, and criminal justice in a changing society. Fortunately, in this book we have set a standard for others to follow in examining the multifaceted woman and criminality. Let us hope we never have to look back.

NOTES

1. Maria Roy, "Some Thoughts Regarding the Criminal Justice System and Wifebeating," in Maria Roy, ed., *Battered Women: A Psychosociological Study of Domestic Violence* (New York: Van Nostrand Reinhold, 1977), p. 138.

2. Marjory D. Fields, "Wife Beating: Government Intervention Policies and Practices." Transcript of verbal remarks, in *Battered Women: Issues of Public Policy* (Washington, D.C: U.S. Commission on Civil Rights, 1978), p. 24.

3. Anna Kuhl and Linda E. Saltzman, "Battered Women and the Criminal

Justice System," in Imogene L. Moyer, ed., *The Changing Roles of Women in the Criminal Justice System: Offenders, Victims, and Professionals* (Prospect Heights, Ill.: Waveland Press, 1985), p. 188.

4. Ibid., p. 189; International Association of Chiefs of Police, *Wife Beating: Training Key, No. 245*, 1976.

5. Donna D. Schram, "Rape," in Jane Roberts Chapman and Margaret Gates, eds., *The Victimization of Women* (Beverly Hills: Sage Publications, 1978), p. 54.

6. Ibid., p. 73.

7. Ibid., pp. 73–74.

8. Claire Cooper, "Rape without Resistance Is Possible, Justices Rule," *Sacramento Bee* (August 1, 1986), p. A15.

9. Erin Pizzey, *Scream Quietly or the Neighbors Will Hear* (London: Penguin, 1974).

Selected Bibliography

THE CRIMINAL VICTIMIZATION OF WOMEN

Amir, Menachem. *Patterns in Forcible Rape*. Chicago: University of Chicago Press, 1971.

Barry, Kathleen. *Female Sexual Slavery*. Englewood Cliffs, N.J.: Prentice-Hall, 1979.

Bart, Pauline B. *Stopping Rape: Successful Survival Strategies*. New York: Pergamon Press, 1985.

Brownmiller, Susan. *Against Our Will: Men, Women and Rape*. New York: Simon & Schuster, 1975.

Chapman, Jane Roberts, and Margaret Gates, eds. *The Victimization of Women*. Beverly Hills: Sage Publications, 1978.

Clark, Lorenne M. G., and Debra J. Lewis. *Rape: The Price of Coercive Sexuality*. Toronto: Canadian Women's Educational Press, 1977.

Davidson, Terry. *Conjugal Crime: Understanding and Changing the Wife-Beating Pattern*. New York: Hawthorne Books, 1979.

Dobash, Rebecca Emerson, and Russell Dobash. *Violence against Wives*. New York: Free Press, 1979.

"Female Victims: The Crime Goes On." *Science News* 126 (1984):153.

Flowers, Ronald B. *Children and Criminality: The Child as Victim and Perpetrator*. Westport, Conn.: Greenwood Press, 1986.

Hofeller, Kathleen H. *Social, Psychological and Situational Factors in Wife Abuse*. Palo Alto, Calif.: R & E Publishers, 1982.

Horos, Carol V. *Rape*. New Canaan, Conn.: Tobey Publishing Co., 1974.

James, Jennifer. "The Prostitute as Victim." In Jane R. Chapman and Margaret Gates, eds. *The Victimization of Women*. Beverly Hills: Sage Publications, 1978.

Johnson, Hilary. "Violence against Women—Is Pornography to Blame?" *Vogue* 175 (September 1985):678–680.

Katz, Sedelle, and Mary Ann Mazur. *Understanding the Rape Victim: A Synthesis of Research Findings*. New York: John Wiley & Sons, 1979.

Levine, Judith. "Crimes against Women Are Growing. So Are Our Fears." *Glamour* 84 (February 1986):210–213.

Longino, Helen E. "Pornography, Oppression, and Freedom: A Closer Look." In Laura Lederer, ed. *Take Back the Night: Women on Pornography*. New York: William Morrow, 1980.

Malamuth, Neil M., and Edward Donnerstein. *Pornography and Sexual Aggression*. Orlando, Fla.: Academic Press, 1984.

Martin, Del. *Battered Wives*. San Francisco: Glide Publications, 1976.

Patai, Frances. "Pornography and Woman Battering: Dynamic Similarities." In Maria Roy, ed. *The Abusive Partner: An Analysis of Domestic Battering*. New York: Van Nostrand Reinhold, 1982.

Rodabaugh, Barbara J., and Melanie Austin. *Sexual Assault: A Guide for Community Action*. New York: Garland STPM Press, 1981.

Roy, Maria, ed. *The Abusive Partner: An Analysis of Domestic Battering*. New York: Van Nostrand Reinhold, 1982.

Russell, Diana E. H. *Sexual Exploitation: Rape, Child Sexual Abuse, and Workplace Harassment*. Beverly Hills: Sage Publications, 1984.

Schwendinger, Julia R., and Herman Schwendinger. *Rape and Equality*. Beverly Hills: Sage Publications, 1983.

Stanko, Elizabeth A. *Intimate Intrusions: Women's Experience of Male Violence*. London: Routledge & Kegan Paul, 1985.

Stanmeyer, William A. *The Seduction of Society: Pornography and Its Impact on American Life*. Ann Arbor: Servant Books, 1984.

Steinmetz, Suzanne, *The Cycle of Violence: Assertive, Aggressive, and Abusive Family Interaction*. New York: Praeger Publishers, 1977.

U.S. Department of Justice. *Attorney General's Commission on Pornography: Final Report*. Vol. 1. Washington, D.C.: Government Printing Office, 1986.

U.S. Department of Justice. *Criminal Victimization in the United States, 1973–1983*. National Crime Survey Reports. Washington, D.C.: Government Printing Office.

U.S. Merit Systems Protection Board. *Sexual Harassment in the Federal Workplace: Is It a Problem?* Office of Merit Systems Review and Studies. Washington, D.C.: Government Printing Office, 1981.

"U.S. Report on Rape Cases Cites Victims' Frustrations with Law." *New York Times* (March 25, 1985), p. A17.

Walker, Lenore E. *The Battered Woman Syndrome*. New York: Springer Publishing Co., 1984.

Walker, Marcia J., and Stanley L. Brodsky, eds. *Sexual Assault: The Victim and the Rapist*. Lexington, Mass.: Lexington Books, 1976.

West, Lois A., William M. Turner, and Ellen Dunwoody. *Wife Abuse in the Armed Forces*. Washington, D.C.: Center for Women Policy Studies, 1981.

X, Laura. *Clearinghouse on Marital Rape*. Berkeley: Women's History Research Center, 1981.

THE CRIMINALITY OF WOMEN

Adler, Freda. *Sisters in Crime: The Rise of the New Female Criminal*. New York: McGraw-Hill, 1975.

Benedek, Elissa A. "Women and Homicide." In Bruce L. Danto, John Bruhns, and Austin H. Kutscher, eds. *The Human Side of Homicide*. New York: Columbia University Press, 1982.

Benjamin, Harry, and R. E. L. Masters. *Prostitution and Morality*. New York: Julian Press, 1964.

Bowker, Lee H. *Women, Crime, and the Criminal Justice System*. Lexington, Mass.: Lexington Books, 1978.

Burkhart, Kathryn. *Women in Prison*. Garden City, N.Y.: Doubleday, 1973.

Chapman, Jane Roberts. *Economic Realities and the Female Offender*. Lexington, Mass.: Lexington Books, 1980.

Crites, Laura, ed. *The Female Offender*. Lexington, Mass.: Lexington Books, 1976.

Deming, Richard. *Women: The New Criminals*. Nashville, Tenn.: Thomas Nelson Inc., 1977.

Freud, Sigmund. *New Introductory Lectures in Psychoanalysis*. New York: W. W. Norton, 1933.

Glick, Ruth M., and Virginia V. Neto. *National Study of Women's Correctional Programs*. Washington, D.C.: Government Printing Office, 1977.

Goldstein, Paul J. *Prostitution and Drugs*. Lexington, Mass.: Lexington Books, 1979.

Greenwald, Harold. *The Elegant Prostitute: A Social and Psychoanalytic Study*. New York: Walker and Co., 1970.

Haft, Marilyn G. "Women in Prison—Discriminatory Practices and Some Legal Solutions." *Clearinghouse Review* 8 (1974):1–2.

Heidensohn, Frances M. *Women and Crime: The Life of the Female Offender*. New York: New York University Press, 1985.

James, Jennifer. "Motivations for Entrance into Prostitution." In Laura Crites, ed. *The Female Offender*. Lexington, Mass.: Lexington Books, 1976.

Kobler, John. "Con Women of the World." *Cosmopolitan* 196 (April 1984):247.

Leonard, Eileen B. *Women, Crime, and Society: A Critique of Theoretical Criminology*. New York: Longman, Inc., 1982.

Lombroso, Cesare, and William Ferrero. *The Female Offender*. New York: Appleton, 1900.

Mann, Coramae Richey. *Female Crime and Delinquency*. University: University of Alabama Press, 1984.

"The Men Raped by Women." *San Francisco Chronicle* (March 15, 1982), p. 5.

Miller, Larry. "The Lady Is a (White-Collar) Criminal." *Cosmopolitan* 195 (July 1983):227–230.

"On the Wild Side: Women in Gangs." *New York Times* (January 2, 1986), p. C8.

Piers, Maria W. *Infanticide*. New York: W. W. Norton, 1978.

Polit, Denise F., Ronald L. Nuttall, and Joan B. Hunter. "Women and Drugs: A Look at Some of the Issues." *Urban and Social Change Review* 9 (1976):9–16.

Pollak, Otto. *The Criminality of Women*. Philadelphia: University of Philadelphia Press, 1950.

Pollock, Joy. "Early Theories of Female Criminality." In Lee H. Bowker, ed., *Women, Crime, and the Criminal Justice System*. Lexington, Mass.: Lexington Books, 1978.

Porterfield, Kay Marie. "Are Women as Violent as Men?" *Cosmopolitan* 197 (September 1984):276–279.

Russell, Alene B., and Cynthia M. Trainor. *Trends in Child Abuse and Neglect: A National Perspective*. Denver: American Humane Association, 1984.

Simon, Rita James. *Women and Crime*. Lexington, Mass.: D. C. Heath, 1975.

Singer, Linda. "Women and the Correctional Process." *American Criminal Law Review* 11 (1973):301.

Smart, Carol. "The New Female Criminal: Reality or Myth." *British Journal of Criminology* 19 (1979):50–59.

Thomas, William I. *The Unadjusted Girl: With Cases and Standpoint for Behavior Analysis*. New York: Harper & Row, 1923.

"Turning Increasingly to Cocaine." *Time* (April 2, 1984):87.

U.S. Federal Bureau of Investigation, *Crime in the United States: Uniform Crime Reports, 1960–1985*. Washington, D.C.: Government Printing Office.

Vetter, Harold J., and Ira J. Silverman. *The Nature of Crime*. Philadelphia: W. B. Saunders, 1978.

Warren, Marguerite Q., ed. *Comparing Female and Male Offenders*. Beverly Hills: Sage Publications, 1981.

Winick, Charles and Kinsie, Paul M. *The Lively Commerce*. Chicago: Quadrangle Books, 1971.

WOMEN AS CRIMINAL JUSTICE PRACTITIONERS

Breece, Constance, and Gerald Garrett. "The Emerging Role of Women in Law Enforcement." In Jack Kinton, ed., *Police Roles in the Seventies*. Ann Arbor: Edwards Brothers, 1975.

Chester, Ronald. *Unequal Access: Women Lawyers in a Changing America*. South Hadley, Mass.: Bergin & Garvey Publishers, 1985.

Coffeey, Osa D. "ACA Women—Who and Where Are They!" *Corrections Today* 42 (1979):36–37.

Couric, Emily, ed. *Women Lawyers: Perspectives on Success*. New York: Law & Business, Inc., 1984.

Epstein, Cynthia Fuchs. *Women in Law*. New York: Basic Books, 1981.

Feinman, Clarice. "Women Lawyers and Judges in the Criminal Courts." In Imogene L. Moyer, ed. *The Changing Roles of Women in the Criminal Justice System*. Prospect Heights, Ill.: Waveland Press, 1985.

Horne, Peter. *Women in Law Enforcement*. 2nd ed. Springfield, Ill.: Charles C. Thomas, 1980.

Kerle, Kenneth E. "The American Woman County Jail Officer." In Imogene L. Moyer, ed., *The Changing Roles of Women in the Criminal Justice System*. Prospect Heights, Ill.: Waveland Press, 1985.

Martin, Susan Ehrlich. *Breaking and Entering: Policemen on Patrol*. Berkeley: University of California Press, 1980.

Matusewitch, Eric P. "Equal Opportunity for Female Correctional Officers: A Brief Overview." *Corrections Today* 42 (1980):36–37.

Moulds, Elizabeth. "Chivalry and Paternalism: Disparities of Treatment in the Criminal Justice System." *Western Political Quarterly* 31 (1978):416–430.

Moyer, Imogene, ed. *The Changing Roles of Women in the Criminal Justice System:*

Offenders, Victims, and Professionals. Prospect Heights, Ill.: Waveland Press, 1985.

Nicolai, Sandra. "The Upward Mobility of Women in Corrections." In Robert R. Ross, ed. *Prison Guard/Correctional Officer: The Use and Abuse of the Human Resources of Prisons*. Toronto: Butterworth & Co., 1981.

Potter, Joan. "Should Women Guards Work in Prisons for Men?" *Corrections Magazine* 6, no. 5 (1980):30–38.

Price, Barbara, and Natalie Sokoloff, eds. *The Criminal Justice System and Women*. New York: Clark Boardman, 1982.

Sherman, Lewis J. "A Psychological View of Women in Policing." In James T. Curran and Richard H. Ward, eds., *Police and Law Enforcement*. Vol. 2. New York: AMS Press, 1975.

Simpson, Sally, and Mervin F. White. "The Female Guard in the All-Male Prison." In Imogene L. Moyer, ed. *The Changing Roles of Women in the Criminal Justice System*. Prospect Heights, Ill.: Waveland Press, 1985.

"Women to Watch." *Ladies' Home Journal* 101 (November 1984):214.

Zimmer, Lynn E. *Women Guarding Men*. Chicago: University of Chicago Press, 1986.

Bibliographical Essay

Women and Criminality: The Woman as Victim, Offender, and Practitioner is unique in its contribution to women's studies, criminology, victimology, and criminal justice as it presents a tripartite exploration of the woman's involvement in crime and the profession of criminal justice. However, a number of outstanding works have devoted their analysis to specific segments of the woman's role in criminality and criminal justice.

Literature that is especially informative in the study of women as victims of criminality include Menachem Amir, *Patterns in Forcible Rape* (Chicago: University of Chicago Press, 1971); Pauline B. Bart, *Stopping Rape: Successful Survival Strategies* (New York: Pergamon Press, 1985); Susan Brownmiller, *Against Our Will: Men, Women and Rape* (New York: Simon & Schuster, 1975); Jane Roberts Chapman and Margaret Gates, eds., *The Victimization of Women* (Beverly Hills: Sage Publications, 1981); Terry Davidson, *Conjugal Crime: Understanding and Changing the Wife-Beating Pattern* (New York: Hawthorne, 1979); Rebecca Emerson Dobash and Russell Dobash, *Violence against Wives* (New York: Free Press, 1979); Nancy Gager and Cathleen Schurr, *Sexual Assault: Confronting Rape in America* (New York: Grosset and Dunlap, 1976); Sedelle Katz and Mary Ann Mazur, *Understanding the Rape Victim: A Synthesis of Research Findings* (New York: John Wiley & Sons, 1979); Laura Lederer, ed., *Take Back the Night: Women on Pornography* (New York: William Morrow, 1980); Neil M. Malamuth and Edward Donnerstein, eds., *Pornography and Sexual Aggression* (Orlando, Fla.: Academic Press, 1984); Del Martin, *Battered Wives* (San Francisco: Glide, 1976); Barbara J. Rodaburgh and Melanie Austin, *Sexual Assault: A Guide for Community Action* (New York: Garland STPM Press, 1981); Maria Roy, ed., *Battered Women: A Psychosociological Study of Domestic Violence* (New York: Van Nostrand Reinhold, 1977); Diana E. H. Russell, *Rape in Marriage* (New York: Macmillan, 1982); Julia R. Schwendinger and Herman Schwendinger, *Rape and Inequality* (Beverly Hills: Sage Publications, 1983); Elizabeth A. Stanko, *Intimate Intrusions: Women's Experience of Male Violence* (London: Routledge & Kegan Paul, 1985); Lenore E. Walker, *The Battered Woman* (New York: Harper & Row, 1979); Marcia J. Walker and Stanley L. Brodsky, eds., *Sexual Assault: The Victim and the Rapist* (Lexington, Mass.: Lexington Books, 1976); Lois A. West, William M. Turner, and Ellen Dunwoody, *Wife Abuse in the Armed Forces* (Washington, D.C.: Center for Women Policy Studies, 1981).

Two government publications that are notable for their study on the victimization of women are U.S. Department of Justice, *Attorney General's Commission on Pornography: Final Report*, Vols. 1 and 2 (Washington, D.C.: Government Printing Office, 1986); and U.S. Department of Justice, *Criminal Victimization in the United States, National Crime Survey Reports* (Washington, D.C.: Government Printing Office, annual).

A number of articles reflect the growing interest in the woman as a crime victim. Among the most provocative publications are Irene Frieze, "Investigating the Causes and Consequences of Marital Rape," *Signs: Journal of Women in Culture and Society* 8, no. 3 (1983); Joel Greenberg, "Incest Out of Hiding," *Science News* 117, no. 14 (1980):218–220; Jennifer James, "The Prostitute as a Victim," in Jane Roberts Chapman and Margaret Gates, eds., *The Victimization of Women* (Beverly Hills: Sage Publications, 1978); Hilary Johnson, "Violence against Women—Is Pornography to Blame?" *Vogue* 175 (September 1985):678; Judith Levine, "Crimes against Women Are Growing. So Are Our Fears," *Glamour* 84 (February 1986):210–213; William H. Masters and Virginia E. Johnson, "The Aftermath of Rape," *Redbook* 147 (November 1976); Murray A. Straus, "Sexual Inequality, Cultural Norms, and Wife-Beating," *Victimology* 1 (1976):62–66.

In the study of female offenders of crime, the following works stand out: Freda Adler, *Sisters in Crime: The Rise of the New Female Criminal* (New York: McGraw-Hill, 1975); Sheila Balkan, Ronald Berger, and Janet Schmidt, *Crime and Deviance in America: A Critical Approach* (Belmont, Calif.: Wadsworth Publishing Co., 1980); Lee H. Bowker, *Women, Crime, and the Criminal Justice System* (Lexington, Mass.: Lexington Books, 1978); Kathryn Burkhart, *Women in Prison* (Garden City, N.Y.: Doubleday, 1973); Jane Roberts Chapman, *Economic Realities and the Female Offender* (Lexington, Mass.: Lexington Books, 1980); Laura Crites, ed., *The Female Offender* (Lexington, Mass.: Lexington Books, 1976); Ruth M. Glick and Virginia V. Neto, *National Study of Women's Correctional Programs* (Washington, D.C.: Government Printing Office, 1977); Sheldon Glueck and Eleanor Glueck, *Five Hundred Delinquent Women* (New York: Alfred A. Knopf, 1934); Paul J. Goldstein, *Prostitution and Drugs* (Lexington, Mass.: Lexington Books, 1979); Harold Greenwald, *The Elegant Prostitute: A Social and Psychoanalytic Study* (New York: Walker and Co., 1970); Eileen B. Leonard, *Women, Crime, and Society: A Critique of Theoretical Criminology* (New York: Longman, Inc., 1982); Cesare Lombroso and William Ferrero, *The Female Offender* (New York: Appleton, 1900); Coramae Richey Mann, *Female Crime and Delinquency* (University: University of Alabama Press, 1984); Otto Pollak, *The Criminality of Women* (Philadelphia: University of Philadelphia Press, 1950); Rita James Simon, *The Contemporary Woman and Crime* (Rockville, Md.: National Institute of Mental Health, 1975); Carol Smart, *Women, Crime and Criminology—A Feminist Critique* (London: Routledge & Kegan Paul, 1977); William I. Thomas, *The Unadjusted Girl: With Cases and Standpoint for Behavior Analysis* (New York: Harper & Row, 1923).

Further addressing issues in the criminality of women are several exceptional articles: Elissa A. Benedek, "Women and Homicide," in Bruce L. Danto, John Bruhns, and Austin H. Kutscher, eds., *The Human Side of Homicide* (New York:

Bibliographical Essay

Columbia University, 1982); Marilyn Haft, "Hustling for
Review 1 (1974):8–26; Jennifer James, "Motivations for En
tion," in Laura Crites, ed., The Female Offender (Lexington
Books, 1976); Dorie Klein, "The Etiology of Female Crime:
Literature," Issues in Criminology 8 (1973):3–30; Denise F. Polit, P
and Joan B. Hunter, "Women and Drugs: A Look at Some of the
and Social Change Review 9 (1976):9–16; Kay Marie Porterfield, "A
Violent as Men?" Cosmopolitan 197 (September 1984):276–279.

Although literature is particularly scarce regarding women practiti
criminal justice system, the following readings merit attention for t
bution to this field of study: Peter Bloch and Deborah Anderson, Poli
on Patrol (Washington, D.C.: Police Foundation, 1973); Ronald Chester,
Access: Women Lawyers in a Changing America (South Hadley, Mass.: Be
Garvey Publishers, 1985); Emily Couric, ed., Women Lawyers: Perspectives o
cess (New York: Law & Business, Inc., 1984); Cynthia Fuchs Epstein, Wom
Law (New York: Basic Books, 1981); Clarice Feinman, Women in the Criminal Jus
System (New York: Praeger, 1980); Peter Horne, Women in Law Enforcement, 2n
ed. (Springfield, Ill.: Charles C. Thomas, 1980); Susan Ehrlich Martin, Breaking
and Entering: Policemen on Patrol (Berkeley: University of California Press, 1980);
Catherine Milton, Women in Policing (Washington, D.C.: Police Foundation,
1972); Imogene Moyer, ed., The Changing Roles of Women in the Criminal Justice
System: Offenders, Victims, and Professionals (Prospect Heights, Ill.: Waveland
Press, 1985); Barbara Price and Natalie Sokoloff, eds., The Criminal Justice System
and Women (New York: Clark Boardman, 1982); Lynn E. Zimmer, Women Guarding
Men (Chicago: University of Chicago Press, 1986).

Additional prominent research on female criminal justice professionals can be
found in the following articles: Constance Breece and Gerald Garrett, "The
Emerging Role of Women in Law Enforcement," in Jack Kinton, ed., Police Roles
in the Seventies (Ann Arbor: Edwards Brothers, 1975); Eric P. Matusewitch, "Equal
Opportunity for Female Correctional Officers: A Brief Overview," Corrections
Today 42 (1980):36–37; Sandra Nicolai, "The Upward Mobility of Women in
Corrections," in Robert R. Ross, ed., Prison Guard/Correctional Officer: The Use
and Abuse of the Human Resources of Prisons (Toronto: Butterworth & Co., 1981);
Joan Potter, "Should Women Guards Work in Prisons for Men?" Corrections
Magazine 6, no. 5 (1980):30–38; Lewis J. Sherman, "Policewomen around the
World," International Review of Criminal Policy 33 (1977):25–33.

All of the cited studies have been significant in adding to the exploration of
female victims, criminals, and criminal justice practitioners. Nevertheless, wom-
en's studies continue to be woefully weak on the whole as compared to men's
studies. In order that we may learn more about the dynamics of the woman's
role in the fields of crime and criminal justice, it is imperative that we continue
to address these issues in the form of increasing research projects.

Rights," Civil Liberties
trance into Prostitu-
Mass.: Lexington
A Review of the
onald L. Nuttall,
Issues," Urban
re Women as

oners in the
eir contri-
re Women
Unequal
rgin &
Suc-
n in
tice
d

Index

About the Author

RONALD BARRI FLOWERS, criminologist, scholar, professional writer, and research analyst in the study of crime and criminal justice and human and social issues, is the author of *Criminal Jurisdiction Allocation in Indian Country* and *Children and Criminality: The Child as Victim and Perpetrator* (Greenwood Press, 1986), the first in a series of four criminological studies.